Topology via Logic

Cambridge Tracts in Theoretical Computer Science

Titles in the series

TOPOLOGY VIA LOGIC

STEVEN VICKERS

Department of Computing, Imperial College of Science and Technology,
University of London

Published by the Press Syndicate of the University of Cambridge
The Pitt Building, Trumpington Street, Cambridge CB2 1RP
40 West 20th Street, New York, NY 10011–4211, USA
10 Stamford Road, Oakleigh, Melbourne 3166, Australia

First published 1989
Reprinted 1990
First paperback edition 1996

British Library Cataloguing in Publication Data available

Library of Congress Cataloguing in Publication Data available

ISBN 0 521 36062 5 hardback
ISBN 0 521 57651 2 paperback

Transferred to digital printing 2003

CONTENTS

PREFACE

There are already many introductions to topology available, and any newcomer must justify its existence. This one is based on a postgraduate course given in the Department of Computing at Imperial College, and both its subject matter and its approach derive from a particular view of topology that has arisen in theoretical computer science. It is therefore primarily intended for computer scientists, at whatever level, who require an introduction to topology. However, mathematicians will also find it of interest for the different light that it sheds on the subject.

On the computer science side, the story starts with the theory of *domains,* as founded by Scott and Strachey [71] to provide a mathematical foundation for the semantics of programming languages.

As well as defining domains, Scott also showed that they could be put into a topological setting, and Mike Smyth [83] has developed the idea that this is not merely a technical trick. The topology captures an essential computational notion, under the slogan *"open sets are semidecidable properties"*. This emphasis gives the open sets a life independent of the points of the topological space, and this led Smyth to make connections with an unexpected strand of mathematics, *locale* theory.

Modern applications of topology, many of them in algebraic geometry, have given point to two ideas.

First, interesting topological spaces need not satisfy the Hausdorff separation axiom. This is well born out in domains, whose rich specialization ordering is entirely alien to Hausdorff separation.

Second, it is often worth thinking of the open sets as forming an algebraic structure – a *frame* – in its own right. To a large extent one can then ignore the points, and do *pointless* or *localic* topology. Locale theory is well described in Johnstone's excellent book [82].

The link between the two is via *sobriety,* a generalization of Hausdorff separation whose significance only becomes really clear in terms of locales. It seems that when – as in domain theory – one is dealing with sober, non-Hausdorff spaces, the localic view is at least as fundamental as the spatial one, and the present work attempts in introducing topology to give equal weight to the two viewpoints.

The traditional – spatial – motivation for general topology and its axioms relies on abstracting first from Euclidean space to metric spaces, and then abstracting out, for no obvious reason, certain properties of their open sets. I believe that the localic view helps to clarify these axioms, by interpreting them not as set theory (finite intersections and arbitrary unions), but as logic (finite conjunctions and arbitrary disjunctions: hence the title). Smyth's slogan implies that topology represents the logic of semidecidable properties. A modification of this, *"geometric logic [topology] is the logic of finite observations,"* appeared in Abramsky [87], and I have tried to argue directly from these logical intuitions to the topological axioms, and to frames as the algebraic embodiment of them.

I then introduce the notion of *topological system.* This subsumes both ordinary topological spaces and locales, and allows us to switch our attention freely between the spatial and localic viewpoints. This device is partly for pedagogical reasons, but it also has the advantage in the domain theoretic applications that it is convenient to forget whether the domain was originally a space or a locale.

I use the excuse of seeking logic on the model side ("point logic") to introduce the specialization order, the Scott topology and compactness.

The high point of these ideas to date is Abramsky's applications to domain theory (to Scott domains in [87], and SFP domains in [88]), where he defined a syntactical language, logic and proof theory for their open sets. (I should also mention the group at Cambridge, and in particular Martin Hyland [81] and Edmund Robinson [86, 87], who have been doing parallel work.) Chapters 10 and 11 present part of this work, albeit in a more algebraic form, together with Smyth's topological description of power domains. For the sake of interested mathematicians, there is also a chapter on spectra of rings, an early example of non-Hausdorff topology.

Most of the Computer Science here is not new, even though much of it has not previously appeared in book form. In particular, the standard reference for the technicalities of domain theory is Plotkin's excellent and comprehensive lecture notes [81], of which good, complete copies are highly prized. My own original contributions are confined largely to – first, the general exposition; second, the particular choice of topological systems and spectral algebraic locales (without bottom or second countability) as expository arenas; and, third, the adaptation of established work to these arenas.

Prerequisites

The book is intended to be self-contained for a course at MSc level in a computing department. It assumes an understanding of logical notation and of set theory on the level of – say – Halmos [60]. Familiarity with the construction of Lindenbaum algebras would be useful experience.

The methods rely heavily on ideas of universal algebra, but this is not intended to be a prerequisite.

Acknowledgements

My greatest debt is to Samson Abramsky and Mike Smyth. As colleagues at Imperial College, they have taught me most of the domain theory I know and have offered detailed and helpful criticisms of the book in all its stages. Axel Poigné and Paul Taylor (at Imperial) and Harry Simmons (at Aberdeen) have also shown consistent interest and I have greatly benefited from their helpful comments.

I must also mention Peter Johnstone. His book "Stone Spaces" [82] is a most lucid account of the mathematical theory on which the computer science described here is based, and without it our work would have been much harder.

I wrote this book while a Research Assistant on the *Formal Methods for Declarative Languages* project in the Department of Computing at Imperial College, London University, and I should therefore like to acknowledge the financial support of the Alvey Programme, which funded the project.

Finally, I must thank my daughter Harriet for the philosophical speculations provoked by the changing colour of her eyes.

Notes on second impression

The opportunity has been taken to make some corrections. In particular, Theorem 8.2.5 (previously the "Scott Open Filter Theorem") has been renamed the "Hofmann-Mislove Theorem" in recognition of its appearance in Hofmann and Mislove [81].

Definition 12.2.4 (of prime elements of a quantale) was wrong, and so was the statement of Theorem 12.2.7 (though not its applications): although part (iii) is valid for general coherent quantales, the lemma part (i), though useful, works only in special cases.

NOTATION

Some attempt has been made to arrange these entries in alphabetical order of the functional parts of the notation, rather than that of typical parameters.

S^c Complement of S, in some understood superset. In particular, if a is an open set then a^c is the corresponding closed set.
Also, if a is an element of a distributive lattice, then a^c is its complement, if it exists.

Cl(S)   Topological closure of S.

DL⟨ G | R ⟩   Distributive lattice generated by the elements (generators) of G subject to the elements (relations) of R.

false   Bottom with respect to ≤.

Fr⟨ G | R ⟩ Frame generated by the elements (generators) of G subject to the elements (relations) of R.

Idl(P)   Ideal completion of a poset P.

C-Idl(S)   Frame of C-ideals for a coverage C on a semilattice S.

Int(S)   Interior of S.

KP   Set of compact elements of a poset P.

lift D   Locale D with a new bottom adjoined (same as $D_\perp$).

Loc D   Localification of a topological system D.

$\mathbb{N}$ Set of natural numbers, zero or positive.

f°g   g followed by f (f, g functions or continuous maps or morphisms in any category)

P^{op} Poset opposite to P.

ω $\mathbb{N}$, again.

ω-Idl(P) ω-chain completion of a poset P.

ΩD   Frame of opens of a topological system (or space or locale) D.

Ωf   Inverse image part of a continuous map f.

$\wp$X   Power set of X.

$\wp_{fin}$X   Set of finite subsets of X.

P_H D   Hoare (lower) power locale of D, including $\emptyset$.

P_P D   Plotkin (Vietoris) power locale of D, including $\emptyset$ (isolated).

P_P^+ D   Plotkin (Vietoris) power locale of D, excluding $\emptyset$.

P_S D   Smyth (upper) power locale of D, including $\emptyset$.

patch D   A spectral space D with its patch topology.

pt D   Set of points of a topological system (or space or locale) D.

pt f   Points part of a continuous map f.

QD   Set of Scott open filters of ΩD for a locale D.

$\mathbb{R}$ Space of real numbers.

Spat D   Spatialization of a topological system D.

Spec K   Spectrum of a distributive lattice K.

starts l   Open in $2^{*\omega}$ comprising the sequences prefixed by l, a finite bit sequence.

true   Top with respect to $\leq$.

0   Topological system with no points and one open.

1   Topological system with one point and two opens.

$\mathbf{1}$ Frame with one element.

$\mathbf{2}$ Frame with two elements.

$2^{*\omega}$ Kahn domain on two letters.

2^{ω} Cantor space.

D+E   Disjoint sum of topological systems.

D×E   Product of topological systems.

[D→E]   Space of continuous maps from D to E.

A⊗B   Tensor product of frames A and B.

x ⊢ a   Point or Scott open filter x satisfies the open a.

$\sqsubseteq$ (Usually) the specialization preorder on the points of a topological system. Also (in particular for maps), approximation order, and prefix order for lists.

$\sqsubseteq_{EM}$ Egli-Milner preorder on subsets of a poset.

$\sqsubseteq_L$ Lower preorder on subsets of a poset.

$\sqsubseteq_U$	Upper preorder on subsets of a poset.
$S\equiv_{EM}T$	$S\sqsubseteq_{EM}T$ and $T\sqsubseteq_{EM}S$; similarly for $\equiv_L$ and $\equiv_U$.
$\ll$	Way below relation.
$D\cong E$	D homeomorphic, or isomorphic, to E.
$\sqcap, \bigsqcap$	Meets with respect to $\sqsubseteq$.
$\sqcup, \bigsqcup$	Joins with respect to $\sqsubseteq$.
$\bot$	Bottom with respect to $\sqsubseteq$.
$D_\bot$	Locale D with a new bottom adjoined (same as lift D).
$\wedge, \bigwedge$	Meets with respect to $\leq$.
$\vee, \bigvee$	Joins with respect to $\leq$.
$\uparrow x$	$\{y: y \geq x \text{ (or } y \sqsupseteq x)\}$, x an element of some poset.
	In particular, in a spectral algebraic locale –
	• if x is a compact point then $\uparrow x$ is the corresponding compact coprime open.
	• if p is a compact coprime open, then $\uparrow p$ is (the completely prime filter identified with) the corresponding compact point.
$\uparrow S$	Upper closure of S, a subset of a poset.
$\left.\begin{array}{l}\bigvee\uparrow S\\\bigsqcup\uparrow S\end{array}\right\}$	Join of S, on the understanding that S is directed.
$\downarrow x$	$\{y: y \leq x \text{ (or } y \sqsubseteq x)\}$, x an element of some poset.
$\downarrow S$	Lower closure of S, a subset of a poset.
$\left.\begin{array}{l}\bigwedge\downarrow S\\\bigsqcap\downarrow S\end{array}\right\}$	Meet of S, on the understanding that S is downward directed.
$C\text{-}\downarrow X$	The C-ideal generated by a set X.
$(q\pm\delta)$	$\{x \in \mathbb{R}: q-\delta < x < q+\delta\}$
f;g	f followed by g (f, g functions or continuous maps or morphisms in any category)
$\square a$	Every element satisfies a. (If a is a property of elements, then $\square a$ is a property of sets.)
$\Diamond a$	Some element satisfies a. (If a is a property of elements, then $\Diamond a$ is a property of sets.)
Widgets	The category of widgets (as objects; morphisms usually defined separately).
$\mathbb{T}\langle G \mid R \rangle$	The $\mathbb{T}$-algebra generated by the elements (generators) of G subject to the elements (relations) of R.
l<>m	Concatenation of lists l and m.
$X\backslash Y$	Set difference $\{x \in X: x \notin Y\}$.

CHAPTER ONE

INTRODUCTION

A Historical Overview

The origins of topology are very different from the context we shall be working in, and it is probably as well to compare some different ideas of what it is.

I – The first idea is that of *rubber sheet geometry,* that is to say geometry in which we don't mind stretching our space. This geometry is not at all concerned with distances or angles; it wants to answer questions like, "Is there a hole in this object?" (Although stretching is allowed, tearing isn't.) Martin Gardner [66] says, "Topologists have been called mathematicians who do not know the difference between a cup of coffee and a doughnut," the reason being that each has exactly one hole through it. According to rubber sheet geometry they are equivalent, because if they are made of stretchy enough material, one can be manipulated into the other. (The hole in the cup that counts is the one where you put your finger to hold it. The place where the coffee goes is a mere hollow. Of course, we are thinking of *ring* doughnuts.)

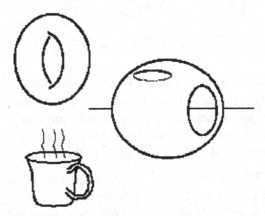

II – *The study of boundaries.* Since tearing is what makes a difference in rubber sheet topology, and since tearing creates new *boundaries* in the sheet, these would seem an important thing to look at. The characteristic of a boundary point of a set is that however closely you look at it, you can see some neighbouring points inside the set and some outside.

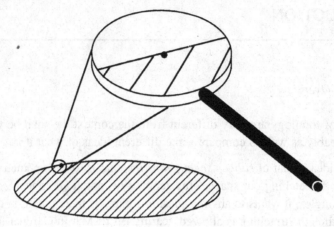

Part of this will entail studying *closed* sets, which include all their boundary points (like a circle with its circumference), and *open* sets, which include none of their boundary points (like a circle without its circumference). Of course, these are just extreme cases. There will also be sets that include some of their boundary points but not all.

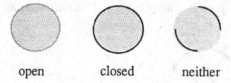

open   closed   neither

III – *The abstract study of open and closed sets.* The next step is one of abstraction. We forget all the geometry and just take an abstract set of "points", a *topological space*. We specify certain subsets as being *open* (their complements are the *closed* subsets), and we make sure that certain axioms, due to Hausdorff, are satisfied. Then we translate topological arguments from stage II into this abstract setting.

IV – *Locale theory.* The next step is to forget even about the points, and just take an abstract set of "open sets", with abstract algebraic operations to represent union and intersection. This structure is a *frame*. Sometimes, the points can be reconstructed from this frame of open sets.

This may seem like the ultimate in abstraction, but we shall see how considerations of *logic* make this an appropriate starting point from which to work backwards.

Hausdorff spaces

The topological axioms for open sets are very general and cover far more situations than just those arising from the rubber sheet ideas. Therefore in practice, topologists will apply extra axioms to restrict attention to the kind of space they're interested in. A very common one is the *Hausdorff separation axiom*, which says that any two distinct points can be "housed orf" from each other by disjoint open sets. The mainstream of topology deals with these *Hausdorff spaces*.

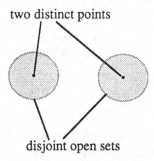

In computer science, however, topology is used to explain *approximate* states of information: the points include both approximate points and more refined points, and these relate to the topology by the property that if an open set contains an approximate point then it must also contain any refinement of it. Thus the approximate point and its refinement cannot possibly be "housed orf" by disjoint open sets and the topological space cannot possibly be Hausdorff. This means that topology as used in computer science – at least for the methods described here – runs in a different direction from the mainstream, even though it is still topology.

This book approaches topology in an unusual way, starting from frames and an explanation in terms of logic, and ends up with unusual applications – the non-Hausdorff topologies used in computer science. For computer scientists it is designed to provide a self-contained introduction, but as a route to the more traditional applications it is written to complement the standard introductions, of which there are many.

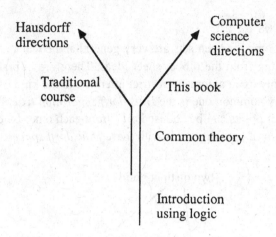

Other books to read

For rubber sheet geometry – browse through Martin Gardner's collections from his
Scientific American column "Mathematical Puzzles and Diversions". Gardner [63]
and [86] both contain relevant articles.

For a traditional approach to topology, giving greater emphasis to Hausdorff
spaces, there is a wide choice of texts. A standard one is Kelley's "General
Topology" [55].

For more on locale theory, an excellent book is Johnstone's "Stone Spaces" [82].
However, the later chapters do assume a good acquaintance with traditional
topology.

Category theory

Interspersed throughout the text are remarks such as "categorically speaking, ...".
These refer to category theory, and readers familiar with this will understand. The
rest can ignore the remarks if they want. They indicate that we are, in a hidden
way, using the methods of category theory. It is not necessary to know category
theory to be able to understand this book, and in fact it is probably useful to see the
methods in action informally before going on to the formal theory. The classic
introduction is MacLane's "Categories for the Working Mathematician" [71], but a
helpful one for computer scientists is the tutorial part of Pitt et al. [85].

Such remarks, and also those on other topics that are slightly off the main
development, are often printed in a smaller typeface.

AFFIRMATIVE AND REFUTATIVE ASSERTIONS

In which we see a Logic of Finite Observations and take this as the notion we want to study.

The final idea of what topology is is *A Theory of Information*. To motivate this, we investigate some of the properties that an assertion might have, one such as

"My baby has grey eyes."

The obvious question is, "Is this true or false?" Well, here's my baby, so let's have a look:

Readers of the luxury edition of this book will agree without hesitation that she *has* got grey eyes. Monochrome readers, while waiting until they can afford better, can usefully consider what the answers might eventually be.

First, we may agree that her eyes really are grey – we can *affirm* the assertion.

Second, we may agree that her eyes are some other colour, such as brown – we can *refute* the assertion.

Third, we may fail to agree; but perhaps if we hire a powerful enough colour analyser, that may decide us.

Fourth, the baby may be away at her grandparents' today, so that we just have to wait.

Fifth ... the diligent reader will think of many more.

Just on the basis of these ruminations, we can draw a Venn diagram in which each point is a "circumstance", or actual colour. All borderline cases are arguable, so the sets corresponding to agreement – affirmation or refutation – are *open* (no boundary points).

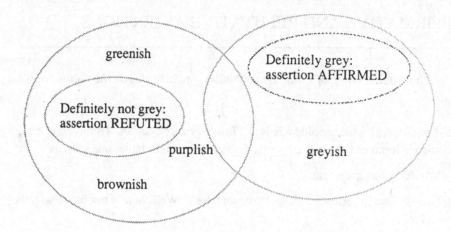

Given an assertion, we can therefore ask –

- Under what circumstances could it be affirmed?
- Under what circumstances could it be refuted?

Notice that these affirmations and refutations are supposed to be done on the basis of what we can actually observe. An observation must be made in finite time, after a finite amount of work. To be emphatic on this point, we can refer to *finite* observations. A finite observation in itself is neutral in its logical content. It can be used positively, to affirm an assertion (most concretely, the assertion "this observation can be made"), or negatively, to refute an assertion ("this observation can never be made"). However, we shall tend to give the observations an implicit logical content by taking the positive viewpoint.

Having now established in what circumstances (for what spectral analyses of the colour) the assertion can be affirmed or refuted, let us now ask when it is true or false. In the present case, it is affirmed (they really are quite unmistakably grey), and hence definitely true. However, at the time of the first draft of this book, they were quite unmistakably blue: hence the assertion was then refuted, and definitely false. What has happened since then? When did the assertion change from being true to being false?

The answer depends on how we classify all the borderline cases. There are many different ways of doing this, but we can see two extremes. If we say that for all borderline cases the assertion is false, then "true" means "affirmably true". In the Venn diagram, this means that sets corresponding to truth are open. Let us call this interpretation *affirmative:*

An assertion is affirmative *iff it is true precisely in the circumstances when it can be affirmed.*

On the other hand, we may count all the borderline cases as true, so that "true" means "irrefutable" and the sets corresponding to truth are closed. Let us call this interpretation *refutative:*

An assertion is refutative *iff it is false precisely in the circumstances when it can be refuted.*

The word *irrefutable* is commonly taken to mean "definitely true". As Popper [63] has pointed out, the more correct meaning of "can never be shown to be definitely false" is very much weaker. In his words, "Irrefutability is not a virtue of a theory (as people often think), but a vice."

More examples
• "Some babies have tartan eyes"

To affirm this, find a baby with tartan eyes. If the assertion is true, there is a baby with tartan eyes, then finding it affirms the assertion. Hence the assertion is affirmative.

To refute it, find all the babies in the world and check that their eyes are definitely not tartan. Make sure you don't miss any. To be complete, you ought also to check all past or future babies. In any practical sense, this assertion can never be refuted. On the other hand, I'm sure you will admit that the assertion is probably false (regardless of whether "having tartan eyes" is interpreted affirmatively or refutatively). Thus it is not refutative.

• "All ravens are black."

This is probably true, but cannot be affirmed. Hence it is not affirmative. It is refutative, and is like a *scientific hypothesis.* We act on the assumption that it's true, but one day the evidence may force us to revise it. (c.f. "All swans are white," before Australia was discovered.)

• "Smith [let's assume there's no argument about who Smith is] is exactly six feet tall."

This is not affirmable, because we can never measure accurately enough. It can be refuted, for instance by measuring Smith's height to be within an inch or two of five feet. In fact, it is a refutative assertion, because if Smith is not exactly six feet tall then we can imagine a measuring device accurate enough to discriminate between his actual height and six feet.

• "Jones is between five foot eleven inches and six foot one."

There are many heights of Jones for which this could be affirmed or refuted, but if, *as it happens,* Jones is exactly five foot eleven, we shall never be able to do either. This is a boundary case. We can make the assertion affirmative or refutative by excluding or including the boundary cases, in other words by specifying whether "between" means strictly or non-strictly between.

The logic of affirmative and refutative assertions

We saw for the simple assertion "my baby has grey eyes" that its truth was a matter for interpretation, and that it could be interpreted affirmatively, refutatively, or in other hybrid ways. Once the truth interpretation has been decided for the simple assertions, for the compound assertions constructed with logical connectives such as "and" and "or" it follows in the standard way of classical logic. What we do now is to investigate, informally but systematically, what happens when you use these with affirmative or refutative assertions. Is the compound assertion still affirmative or refutative?

1. *Negation (not, ¬)*

To affirm $\neg P$, we have to make some finite observation to show that P is definitely false, in other words we must refute P. It follows that $\neg P$ is affirmative iff P is refutative.

Therefore,

negation transforms affirmative assertions into refutative ones and vice versa.

As an example, take P to be the statement "Some ravens are not black." This is affirmative but not refutative. Then $\neg P$ is equivalent to "All ravens are black," which is refutative but not affirmative.

An important consequence of this is that if we just want to talk about refutative assertions, we can take their negations and talk about affirmative ones instead. On this justification we shall generally restrict our attention to affirmative assertions.

2. *Disjunction (or, ∨)*

We can affirm $P \vee Q$ (P **or** Q) either by affirming P or by affirming Q. Therefore, if P and Q and both affirmative, then so is $P \vee Q$: for $P \vee Q$ is true iff either P is true or Q is, i.e. iff either P can be affirmed or Q can, i.e. iff $P \vee Q$ can be affirmed.

By induction, the disjunction of any finite number of affirmative assertions is still affirmative. However, we can do much better than this and go beyond ordinary logic. Suppose we have a whole family of affirmative assertions P_i, possibly infinitely many. We can imagine an infinite disjunction $\bigvee_i P_i$, to affirm which we just affirm any individual P_i. Thus,

> Any *disjunction, even an infinite one, of affirmative assertions is still affirmative.*

3. Conjunction (*and*, $\wedge$)

We can affirm $P \wedge Q$ by affirming both P and Q. If P and Q are both affirmative, then so is $P \wedge Q$: for $P \wedge Q$ is true iff both P is true and Q is, i.e. iff both P can be affirmed and Q can, i.e. iff $P \wedge Q$ can be affirmed. Again, this extends to any finite conjunction. But this time, to affirm an infinite conjunction $\bigwedge_i P_i$, we must affirm every single one and this will take an infinite amount of work. Therefore for conjunctions,

> Any finite *conjunction of affirmative assertions is still affirmative.*

Of course, there may be special methods available to us in special cases. For instance, an assertion about all natural numbers could be thought of as an infinite conjunction of specialized assertions, one for each number. This can then be affirmed by an inductive proof. But this is not part of the general logic of affirmative assertions.

The argument here makes no mention of the order in which the conjuncts are affirmed, nor of the number of times each is affirmed. There is really a tacit assumption that observations do not affect what is being observed, so that order and multiplicities don't matter. In Chapter 12 we shall see the concept of *quantales,* and these can be thought of as maintaining our present idea of disjunction, but replacing finite conjunctions by finite sequences of observations giving composite, *product* observations.

4. *true and false*

These can be seen as special cases, **true** and **false** being respectively the conjunction and disjunction of no assertions (the *empty* conjunction or disjunction, $\wedge \emptyset$ or $\vee \emptyset$). These are related to the logical equivalences **true**$\wedge$P $\Leftrightarrow$ P $\Leftrightarrow$ **false**$\vee$P. They ought both therefore to be affirmative as special cases of our discussion so far, but let's just check.

To affirm **true**, you don't need to do anything. You can always affirm it without formality. Since it is thus always both true and affirmable, it is affirmative.

To affirm **false**, you must find something contradictory. You thus never can affirm it. It is never true and never affirmable, and so it is an affirmative assertion.

5. Implication (→, if ... then ...)

P→Q ("if P holds then so does Q") is again like a scientific law, and can be refuted by affirming P and refuting Q. We can deduce that if P is affirmative and Q is refutative then P→Q is refutative, and so it has a good standing in a mixed logic of affirmativity and refutativity. However, suppose P and Q are both just affirmative. Then P→Q is true iff P is false or Q is true, but the only way we can affirm P→Q is by affirming Q. Thus P→Q is not (in general) affirmative. For a particular example, take P to be any affirmative assertion and Q to be **false**. Then P→Q is logically equivalent to ¬P, which is refutative, but not in general affirmative. Therefore,

> *The logic of affirmable assertions must not include implication.*

6. Distributivity

There are two standard distributive laws. The first says that conjunction distributes over disjunctions, which is to say that $P \wedge \bigvee_i Q_i$ should be equivalent to $\bigvee_i (P \wedge Q_i)$. But informally, to affirm either of these, you must affirm P and at least one of the Q_is. Thus we expect this distributive law to hold.

The second says that disjunction distributes over conjunction, in other words that $P \vee \bigwedge_i Q_i$ should be equivalent to $\bigwedge_i (P \vee Q_i)$. In line with our previous discussion, we assume that the conjunction is finite. To affirm $P \vee \bigwedge_i Q_i$, we must affirm either P or all the Q_is. To affirm $\bigwedge_i (P \vee Q_i)$, for every i we must affirm either P or Q_i, and the only way we can do this without affirming P is to affirm all the Q_is. Again, we therefore expect this distributive law to hold.

Summary

The discussion up to here has been rather informal, but we shall use it as our motivation for studying a *logic of affirmative assertions* that has –

- arbitrary disjunctions, including both the empty disjunction **false** and infinite disjunctions.
- finite conjunctions, including the empty conjunction **true**.
- two distributive laws: conjunction distributes over arbitrary disjunction and disjunction distributes over finite conjunctions.

It does not include negation, implication or infinite conjunctions.

By looking at the negations of affirmative assertions, and using de Morgan's laws

$$\neg \bigvee_i P_i \Leftrightarrow \bigwedge_i \neg P_i$$
$$\neg \bigwedge_i P_i \Leftrightarrow \bigvee_i \neg P_i$$

we get the logic of refutative assertions. It has arbitrary conjunctions and finite disjunctions, the corresponding distributive laws, and excludes negation, implication and infinite disjunctions.

By taking a positive view of finite observations, we identify them with the affirmative assertions: an observation corresponds to the assertion "this observation can be made", and an assertion corresponds to the set (disjunction) of observations that affirm it. Thus our logic of affirmative assertions can also be seen as a logic of finite observations.

Notes

This logic of affirmative assertions/finite observations is technically known as *propositional geometric logic,* "propositional" referring to the lack of variables or quantifiers. Full geometric logic has variables, equality, the arbitrary disjunctions and finite conjunctions that we have introduced, and the existential quantifier ∃ – but not the universal quantifier ∀. It is a well-established body of mathematics, originating in algebraic geometry and its treatment by toposes, and an introduction for computer scientists can be found in Fourman and Vickers [85].

The identification of propositional geometric logic as a logic of finite observations appeared first in print in Abramsky [87], although it is, of course, related to Mike Smyth's idea [83] that open sets in a topological space are analogous to semi-decidable properties. It would be interesting to discover whether the full predicate geometric logic can be used in a similar way.

CHAPTER THREE

FRAMES

In which we set up an algebraic theory for the Logic of Finite Observations: its algebras are frames.

3.1 Algebraicizing logic

We are going to apply a fairly standard trick in logic, which is to *identify,* in other words treat as equal, formulae that are logically equivalent. The logical connectives then become *algebraic operators subject to laws,* and we can use the methods of algebra to prove equivalences. For instance,

$$y \vee (x \vee y) = y \vee (y \vee x) = (y \vee y) \vee x = y \vee x = x \vee y$$

The idea is that, for instance, $x \vee y$ and $y \vee x$ are really just different ways of saying the same thing. We want to concern ourselves with *what we can say* rather than *how we can say them.*

Readers familiar with the propositional calculus will probably have already seen this done in the construction of the *Lindenbaum algebra.* This takes a countable set of variables, representing propositions, forms all possible formulae that can be made using them and the logical connectives, and then takes equivalence classes for logical equivalence. In the Lindenbaum algebra, the logical connectives and the axioms of logic become the operators and laws of Boolean algebra. Thus given the original propositional variables as things we can say, the Lindenbaum algebra contains them and all other propositions that derive from them. It is a complete system of propositions, closed under logic.

We wish to form similar systems of propositions, but with some generalizations.

First, the Lindenbaum algebra is constructed using the connectives and axioms of classical logic. We want to use our logic of finite observations (geometric logic), so we have different connectives and axioms. In fact, different logics will correspond to different algebraic theories: classical logic has Boolean algebras, intuitionistic logic has *Heyting algebras,* and geometric logic has the *frames* which it is our purpose to develop.

Second, the Lindenbaum algebra that one sees most commonly is *free* on its countably many variables. The only equalities that hold in the algebra are those that derive purely from the logic itself. We shall want to incorporate assumptions about the real world, for instance that two particular propositions p_3 and p_{10} are inconsistent: $p_3 \wedge p_{10} = \mathbf{false}$. This means that we shall be able to tailor a frame to the circumstances that its propositions are supposed to be talking about.

To define frames, we shall need to investigate in more detail the way in which algebra will reflect logic. Building in more and more logic, we shall see in turn the concepts of *poset, lattice, distributive lattice* and, finally, *frame*.

3.2 Posets

Definition 3.2.1 A *poset* (also known as a *partially ordered set,* or a *partial order*) is a set P equipped with a binary relation ≤ (formally, a subset of P×P; it is pronounced "is less than") that satisfies the following laws:

reflexivity: $a \le a$ for all $a \in P$
transitivity: if $a \le b$ and $b \le c$ ($a, b, c \in P$) then $a \le c$
antisymmetry: if $a \le b$ and $b \le a$ ($a, b \in P$) then $a = b$

Let P and Q be posets. Then a function f: P → Q is *monotone* iff for all a, b ∈ P, if $a \le b$ then $f(a) \le f(b)$. (So f preserves order.)

We shall think of the elements of a poset as being *propositions,* and of ≤ as meaning "⇒", or "entails", or "is logically stronger than". Then it is precisely antisymmetry that says that if two propositions are logically equivalent (each entails the other) then they are equal: we identify them.

Little posets can be drawn using diagrams such as –

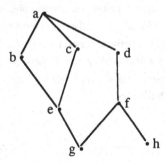

Here each line represents an inequality: for instance, $b \le a$ (because b is at the bottom end of the line), $e \le b$. We can deduce other inequalities, such as $f \le f$, $e \le a$, from the poset axioms.

We are also prepared to use notation such as $a \ge b$, $b \nleq f$ (b is not less than f), $b \ngeq f$. Two elements such as b and f, neither of which is less than the other, are called *incomparable*.

Examples 3.2.2

(i)   Let X be a set and $\wp$X its power set, i.e. the set of all subsets of X. Taking
        $\leq$ to mean "$\subseteq$", $\wp$X is a poset. Antisymmetry corresponds to the
        extensional definition of set equality, which says that equality between sets
        is to be determined entirely by what elements they have.

(ii)   Let P be any poset. The *opposite* poset, P^{op}, has the same elements as P, but
        with the reverse ordering: $a \leq b$ in P^{op} iff $b \leq a$ in P.

As we have already implied with our talk of "algebraicizing logic", the
antisymmetry law of posets, saying in effect that equivalent elements are identified,
is often not present initially, but has to be imposed. We now formalize this.

Definition 3.2.3 A *preorder* is a set P equipped with a binary relation $\leq$ that is
reflexive and transitive.

Proposition 3.2.4 Let P be a preorder. We define a binary relation $\equiv$ on P by

$a \equiv b$ iff $a \leq b$ and $b \leq a$

Then $\equiv$ is an equivalence relation, and the equivalence classes [a] form a poset P/$\equiv$,
with $[a] \leq [b]$ iff $a \leq b$.   ]

Many notions concerning posets are also appropriate to preorders. We shan't
usually go into this; our normal approach to a preorder is to turn it into a poset.

Categorically, a preorder is a category in which for any two objects a and b, there is at most one
morphism from a to b; it is a poset iff for all a and b there is at most one morphism between a and b in
either direction. The monotone functions between posets (or preorders) are precisely the functors,
and can be considered the morphisms of two categories, **Posets** and **Preorders**. The process by
which preorders are converted to posets (Proposition 3.6.4) is functorial, and left adjoint to the
forgetful functor from **Posets** to **Preorders**.

3.3 Meets and joins

Thinking of $\leq$ as meaning $\Rightarrow$, we next wish to describe what corresponds to **and**
and **or**. First, the *meets*, which correspond to **and**.

Definition 3.3.1 Let P be a poset, $X \subseteq P$ and $y \in P$. Then y is a *meet* (or *greatest
lower bound* or *glb* or *inf*) for X iff

  • y is a *lower bound* for X, i.e. if $x \in X$ then $y \leq x$, and
  • if z is any other lower bound for X then $z \leq y$

In symbols, we write $y = \bigwedge X$.

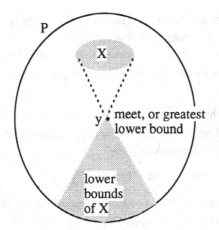

Proposition 3.3.2 Let P be a poset and X a subset. Then X can have at most one meet.

Proof Let y and y' be two meets of X. Since y is a meet and y' is a lower bound, y' ≤ y. Similarly, y ≤ y'. By antisymmetry, y = y'.]

Next, we define *joins* to correspond to **or**.

Definition 3.3.3 Let P be a poset, X ⊆ P and y ∈ P. Then y is a *join* (or *least upper bound* or *lub* or *sup*) for X iff

- y is an *upper bound* for X, i.e. if x ∈ X then y ≥ x, and
- if z is any other upper bound for X then z ≥ y

In symbols, we write y = ⋁X.

We could prove immediately an analogue to Proposition 3.3.2; but in fact we can save a lot of labour by noticing a *duality principle:*

Proposition 3.3.4 Let P be a poset, X ⊆ P and y ∈ P. Then y is a join for X iff y is a meet for X in P^{op}.

Proof The proof is immediate from the definitions.]

Despite the simplicity of this, it often cuts our work in half. Having proved a result for meets, we can immediately state without proof a *dual* result for joins. For instance, we know immediately from Propositions 3.3.2 and 3.3.4 that subsets of posets can have at most one join.

Proposition 3.3.5 Let P be a poset. Then for all x, y ∈ P,

$$x = \bigwedge\{x, y\} \Leftrightarrow x \leq y \Leftrightarrow y = \bigvee\{x, y\}$$

Proof We prove the first equivalence. The second could be proved in the same way, but in fact it follows immediately by duality.

If $x = \bigwedge\{x, y\}$, then x is a lower bound for $\{x, y\}$ and hence $x \leq y$. Conversely, if $x \leq y$ then x is a lower bound for $\{x, y\}$, and is greater than any other lower bound.]

The significance of this proposition is that if we define $\bigwedge$ or $\bigvee$ independently, as algebraic operators, then it tells us how we have to define $\leq$ to have any hope of recovering $\bigwedge$ or $\bigvee$ as actual meets or joins.

Proposition 3.3.6 Let P be a poset. Then for all $y \in P$,

(i)   y is the empty meet iff it is a top (greatest) element, and
(ii)   y is the empty join iff it is a bottom (least) element.

Proof
(i) Suppose $y = \bigwedge\varnothing$. Every $z \in P$ is a lower bound of $\varnothing$: for the condition

if $x \in \varnothing$ then $z \leq x$

is satisfied vacuously. Therefore $z \leq y$, so y is greater than every other element of P.

Conversely, if y is top then it is a lower bound for $\varnothing$ (because everything is) and it is greater than all the other lower bounds (because it's greater than everything), so $y = \bigwedge\varnothing$.
(ii)   This follows by duality.]

Empty meets and joins need not exist. We have already seen an example (the picture in 3.2) that had two *minimal* elements g and h, but no *least* element. A least element would have to be less than everything else. Thus this example does not have an empty join, although it does have an empty meet, namely a.

An empty meet (top) is often written as $\top$, and an empty join (bottom) as $\perp$.

Example 3.3.7 – In logic, meets are conjunctions and joins are disjunctions. We are, of course, thinking of $\leq$ as meaning $\Rightarrow$.

First, $P \wedge Q = \bigwedge \{P, Q\}$, a meet for the set $\{P, Q\}$. We check

$P \wedge Q \Rightarrow P$ and $P \wedge Q \Rightarrow Q$

so that $P \wedge Q$ is a lower bound for $\{P, Q\}$. These are often seen as *elimination rules* for $\wedge$, ways of deriving formulae without it.

Next, if R is another lower bound for $\{P, Q\}$, in other words $R \Rightarrow P$ and $R \Rightarrow Q$, then $R \Rightarrow P \wedge Q$. This is an *introduction rule* for $\wedge$.

true is easily seen to be a top element: it holds unconditionally, so anything implies **true**.

Now for joins. The parts of the definition correspond to the properties that

$P \Rightarrow P \lor Q$ and $Q \Rightarrow P \lor Q$ (introduction rules),

and

if $P \Rightarrow R$ and $Q \Rightarrow R$ then $P \lor Q \Rightarrow R$

(This is an elimination rule, because given $P \Rightarrow R$, $Q \Rightarrow R$ and $P \lor Q$ you can eliminate $\lor$ by deducing R.) Moreover, **false** is bottom because of the standard logical idea that if you assume a contradiction then you can prove anything: **false** $\Rightarrow P$.

Example 3.3.8 – In set theory, meets are intersections and joins are unions. We work with subsets of a "universe" U, and $\leq$ is set inclusion, $\subseteq$.

First, meets. Clearly if each X_i is a subset of U, then

$\bigcap_i X_i \subseteq X_i$ for all i.

If $Y \subseteq X_i$ for all i and $y \in Y$, then $y \in X_i$ for all i and so $y \in \bigcap_i X_i$. Therefore

$Y \subseteq \bigcap_i X_i$.

The empty meet is the top subset, U itself.

For joins, $X_i \subseteq \bigcup_i X_i$ for all i. If $X_i \subseteq Y$ for all i and $x \in \bigcup_i X_i$, then $x \in X_i$ for some i and so $x \in Y$. Therefore $\bigcup_i X_i \subseteq Y$. The empty join is the bottom subset, $\emptyset$.

To summarize,

Orders	Logic	Sets
$\leq$	$\Rightarrow$	$\subseteq$
$=$	$\Leftrightarrow$	$=$
top, $\top$, empty meet, $\bigwedge\emptyset$	**true**	universe
bottom, $\bot$, empty join, $\bigvee\emptyset$	**false**	$\emptyset$
meet, $\wedge$, greatest lower bound, glb, infimum, inf	conjunction, **and**, $\wedge$	intersection, $\cap$
join, $\vee$, least upper bound, lub, supremum, sup	disjunction, **or**, $\vee$	union, $\cup$

Definition 3.3.9 Let P and Q be posets, and $f: P \to Q$ a function. f *preserves meets* iff whenever $X \subseteq P$ has a meet y, then $f(y)$ is a meet for $\{f(x): x \in X\}$.

We can similarly describe f as preserving meets of a particular kind, e.g. finite, binary, non-empty, etc., or as preserving joins.

It is easy to see that if P has all binary meets, and f preserves them, then f is monotone.

Let's now pause to map out our route to frames. Posets aren't guaranteed to have anything except the order $\leq$; *lattices* have all finite meets and joins; *distributive lattices* obey an additional *distributive* law that brings them closer to logic; and *frames* have in addition all joins, and an infinite distributivity law.

3.4 Lattices

Definition 3.4.1 A poset P is a *lattice* iff every finite subset has both a meet and a join.

A function between two lattices is a *lattice homomorphism* iff it preserves all finite meets and joins.

Notice that this is *self-dual:* the opposite of a lattice is still a lattice.

Our definition of *lattice* includes the requirement of the empty meet and join, in other words a top and a bottom. Some authors use the term to mean a poset with all finite *non-empty* meets and joins. Johnstone calls such a "lattice without top or bottom" a *pseudolattice*.

The concept of a poset in which every finite subset has a meet (a *meet-semilattice*) is also important, together with its dual, the *join-semilattice*. We shall see more of these in Chapter 4.

Proposition 3.4.2 A poset P is a lattice iff $\emptyset$ and all two-element subsets have meets and joins.
Proof
$\Leftarrow$: Let $X = \{x_1, \ldots x_n\}$ be a finite subset of P. We show by induction on n that X has a meet.

If $n = 0$, then $X = \emptyset$ and we are told that $\emptyset$ has a meet.

If $n = 1$, it is easy to see that $\bigwedge X = \bigwedge\{x_1\} = x_1$.

Now suppose $n \geq 2$, and let $X' = \{x_1, \ldots, x_{n-1}\}$. By induction X' has a meet x'; we show that $\bigwedge X = \bigwedge\{x', x_n\} = x''$ (say). If $1 \leq i \leq n-1$ then $x'' \leq x' \leq x_i$, and also $x'' \leq x_n$, so x'' is a lower bound for X. Now suppose y is another lower bound. A fortiori, y is a lower bound for X', so that $y \leq x'$; and also $y \leq x_n$, so we deduce that $y \leq x''$ as required.

X has a join by duality.   ]

Notationally, this proposition is very important, for it means we can write finite meets and joins of more than two elements using the binary meets and joins:

$$\bigwedge\{x_1, x_2 \ldots x_n\} = x_1 \wedge x_2 \wedge \ldots \wedge x_n$$

(It doesn't matter how this expression is bracketed.) Of course, the proof by induction only works for *finite* sets X. For infinite meets and joins, when they exist, we still have to use the big symbols $\bigwedge$ and $\bigvee$.

We also take the opportunity to introduce special notation for the empty meets and joins in a lattice. Since we are thinking of lattices as systems of propositions, we write **true** for $\bigwedge\emptyset$ and **false** for $\bigvee\emptyset$.

We note some easily proved algebraic properties of $\wedge$ and $\vee$:

commutativity:	$x \wedge y = y \wedge x$	$x \vee y = y \vee x$
associativity:	$(x \wedge y) \wedge z = x \wedge (y \wedge z)$	$(x \vee y) \vee z = x \vee (y \vee z)$
unit laws:	$x \wedge \mathbf{true} = x$	$x \vee \mathbf{false} = x$
idempotence:	$x \wedge x = x$	$x \vee x = x$
absorption:	$x \wedge (x \vee y) = x$	$x \vee (x \wedge y) = x$

Also, relating the order to the algebraic operations as in Proposition 3.3.5,

$$x \leq y \Leftrightarrow x \wedge y = x \Leftrightarrow x \vee y = y$$

Definition 3.4.3 A lattice P is *distributive* iff for every x, y and z $\in$ P we have

$$x \wedge (y \vee z) = (x \wedge y) \vee (x \wedge z)$$

i.e. $\wedge$ *distributes over* $\vee$, in the same way as, for numbers, multiplication distributes over addition.

Proposition 3.4.4 In a distributive lattice P, $\vee$ also distributes over $\wedge$.
Proof

$$(x \vee y) \wedge (x \vee z) = [(x \vee y) \wedge x] \vee [(x \vee y) \wedge z] = x \vee [z \wedge (x \vee y)] = x \vee [(z \wedge x) \vee (z \wedge y)]$$
$$= [x \vee (z \wedge x)] \vee (y \wedge z) = x \vee (y \wedge z) \qquad\qquad]$$

Examples of distributive lattices

Example 3.4.5 If U is a set, then we have already seen in Example 3.3.8 that its power set $\wp U$ is a lattice (it actually has all meets and joins, not just the finite ones). It is distributive.

Example 3.4.6 A poset P is *linearly* ordered if any two elements are comparable:

if x, y $\in$ P then either x $\leq$ y or y $\leq$ x (or both, iff x = y)

Such a poset has all binary meets and joins, for instance

$$x \wedge y = \min (x, y) = \begin{cases} x & \text{if } x \leq y \\ y & \text{if } y \leq x \end{cases}$$

(Exercise – show that this actually is a meet.)

Therefore, if P has a top and a bottom then it is a lattice. In fact, it must be distributive. For take x, y and z ∈ P. It is easy to prove in any lattice that

$$x \wedge (y \vee z) \geq (x \wedge y) \vee (x \wedge z)$$

so we just need to demonstrate the reverse inequality. But y∨z must be either y or z, so x∧(y∨z) must be either x∧y or x∧z, both of which are less than (x∧y)∨(x∧z).

Example 3.4.7 If P is a distributive lattice then so is its opposite P^{op}. This is the content of Proposition 3.4.4.

Example 3.4.8 *Not quite a distributive lattice*. Let U be an infinite set, and let $\wp_{fin}U$ be the set of all *finite* subsets of U. This has binary meets and joins (intersection and union), and they each distribute over the other, and it even has the nullary join Ø. But it lacks the nullary meet U, because that is an *infinite* subset. $\wp_{fin}U \cup \{U\}$ is a distributive lattice.

Example 3.4.9 *Two Non-examples of distributive lattices*

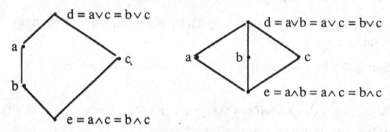

We shall study the left-hand example in more detail. First of all, it *is* a lattice. The nullary meets and joins are d and e, and we know binary meets and joins of comparable elements always exist. All that is left to check are meets and joins for the incomparable pairs {a, c} and {b, c}. These are as written in the diagram.

However, the lattice is not distributive, because

$$a \wedge (b \vee c) = a \wedge d = a \neq b = b \vee e = (a \wedge b) \vee (a \wedge c)$$

Exercise: show that the right-hand poset is also a non-distributive lattice.

Fact – Any non-distributive lattice L has five distinct elements arranged as in one of the diagrams, with meets and joins as shown there (so the diagram embeds in L as a *subpseudolattice*). See, e.g., Birkhoff [67]).

3.5 Frames

A frame is supposed to consist of the possible finite observations for some system, with equivalent observations identified, and the logic of finite observations (arbitrary disjunctions and finite conjunctions) built in as joins and meets.

Definition 3.5.1 A poset A is a *frame* iff

(i)   every subset has a join
(ii)   every finite subset has a meet
(iii)   binary meets distribute over joins:

$$x \wedge \bigvee Y = \bigvee \{x \wedge y : y \in Y\} \qquad\qquad (frame\ distributivity)$$

We write **true** for the empty meet (top) and **false** for the empty join (bottom).

A function between two frames is a *frame homomorphism* iff it preserves all joins and finite meets.

Some authors use the terms *locale* or *complete Heyting algebra* (*cHa*) for what we have called a frame, and it is important to be aware of this. We follow Johnstone's [82] careful distinction between frames and locales (see Section 5.4), and also between frames and cHa's (Section 3.10).

A frame is clearly a distributive lattice. It is also worth noting that clause (ii) of the definition is unnecessary:

Proposition 3.5.2 Let P be a poset in which every subset has a join. Then every subset has a meet.
Proof Let $S \subseteq P$, and let L be the set of its lower bounds. If a meet (greatest lower bound) of S exists, then it must be $\bigvee L$. Thus all we need to show is that $\bigvee L$ is a lower bound of S. But if $x \in S$ and $y \in L$, then $y \leq x$, so $\bigvee L \leq x$. ❵

Such a poset, with all joins and hence also all meets, is called a *complete lattice*.

This Proposition is at first sight rather curious, because it shows that even infinite meets exist in a frame. This will be discussed further in Section 3.10.

We can now redefine frames as complete lattices satisfying the frame distributivity law.

Examples 3.5.3
- Any finite distributive lattice is a frame (because all subsets are finite and hence have joins).
- If U is a set, then $\wp U$ is a frame (because we can take infinite unions, and the infinite distributivity law holds). In fact, $(\wp U)^{op}$ is also a frame, because we can take infinite intersections and the infinite distributivity holds. However ...
- In general, if A is a frame, A^{op} is not a frame. See Exercise 3.

- **1** = •, the *inconsistent frame* (**true** = **false**).
- **2** = {**false** ≤ **true**}, sometimes called the *Sierpinski* frame.

3.6 Topological spaces

Let X be a set, and A any *subframe* of $\wp$X – i.e. any family of subsets of X that forms a frame under the frame operations of $\wp$X:

- If S ⊆ A then ∪S ∈ A,
- If S ⊆ A is finite then ∩S ∈ A

This kind of frame is well-known in mathematics as a *topology* (on X).

Definition 3.6.1 A *topological space* is a set X equipped with a topology ΩX on it.

The elements of ΩX are known as the *open* subsets of the space.

Examples 3.6.2

(i)   ΩX = $\wp$X (all subsets are open). This is the *discrete* topology on X. It is the *finest* topology on X, i.e. the one with the most open sets.

(ii)   ΩX = {∅, X}. This is the *indiscrete* topology on X, its *coarsest* topology.

(iii)   Let P be a poset. A subset S ⊆ P is called *upper closed* iff for all x, y ∈ P,

$$y \geq x \in S \Rightarrow y \in S$$

Any intersection or union of upper closed subsets is still upper closed, so they form a subframe of $\wp$P. This is known as the *Alexandrov* topology on P. By duality, the *lower closed* subsets of P, i.e. the upper closed subsets of P^{op}, also form a topology.

For reference, we also introduce some definitions connected with the Alexandrov topology.

Definition 3.6.3 Let P be a poset. If x ∈ P and S ⊆ P, we write

$\uparrow$x = {y ∈ P: y ≥ x}, the *upper closure* of x
$\uparrow$S = {y ∈ P: ∃x ∈ S. y ≥ x} = ∪{$\uparrow$x: x ∈ S}, the *upper closure* of S
$\downarrow$x = {y ∈ P: y ≤ x}, the *lower closure* of x
$\downarrow$S = {y ∈ P: ∃x ∈ S. y ≤ x} = ∪{$\downarrow$x: x ∈ S}, the *lower closure* of S

At present, topologies look like just a rather concrete way in which some particular frames can arise. But later we shall see how we can often reconstruct a topological space X from a frame A so that the frames ΩX and A are essentially the same (isomorphic). This can be very helpful. For the present, we take the opportunity to introduce some standard terminology.

Definition 3.6.4 Let X be a topological space, $S \subseteq X$. S may or may not be open, but we can define its *interior* as

$$\text{Int}(S) = \bigcup \{U \in \Omega X: U \subseteq S\}$$

Int(S) is open, and in fact it is the largest open set contained in S.

A subset $F \subseteq X$ is *closed* iff its complement $F^c = X \backslash F$ is open. Closed sets are preserved under arbitrary intersections and finite unions.

A subset is *clopen* iff it is both open and closed.

The (*topological*) *closure* of a subset $S \subseteq X$ is

$$\text{Cl}(S) = (\text{Int}(S^c))^c = \bigcap \{F: S \subseteq F, F \text{ closed}\}$$

If $x \in N \subseteq X$, then N is a *neighbourhood* of x iff there is some open set U with $x \in U \subseteq N$.

The four concepts of closedness, interior, closure and neighbourhood can each be used as the basis for defining topological spaces, as any standard text will explain.

3.7 Some examples from computer science

Finite observations on bit streams

The idea of a stream is that items of data are arriving one by one at a reading device. For simplicity, we assume that each item is a *bit*, 0 or 1, but the same ideas will work for more general data (sometimes with the restriction that there are only finitely many possible values for each item). We are going to describe a frame whose elements represent finite observations on some bit stream; in fact, we are going to describe three. The differences between them correspond to different physical assumptions and show how we can tailor a frame to our particular needs.

The most elementary observations are the values of individual bits: so for each natural number $n \geq 1$ we have two *subbasic* observations

'$s_n = 0$'	– the nth bit has been read as a zero
'$s_n = 1$'	– the nth bit has been read as a one

You can think of s as meaning "the stream you're looking at", but formally it is just a notation used as part of the way we write an observation. Without doubt, we shall want never to read the same bit as both zero and one –

$$\text{‘}s_n = 0\text{’} \wedge \text{‘}s_n = 1\text{’} \quad = \quad \textbf{false} \tag{$*$}$$

You might think we also want ‘$s_n = 0$’ $\vee$ ‘$s_n = 1$’ = **true** (the nth bit must be either zero or one), but in fact we are going to be more subtle. We take ‘$s_n = 0$’ $\vee$ ‘$s_n = 1$’ to mean that the nth bit has now been read, but we're not saying what its value was. On this interpretation, we build in an important physical assumption about streams:

$$\text{‘}s_{n+1} = 0\text{’} \vee \text{‘}s_{n+1} = 1\text{’} \quad \leq \quad \text{‘}s_n = 0\text{’} \vee \text{‘}s_n = 1\text{’} \tag{$\dagger$}$$

Recalling that $\leq$ means "implies", this means that you can't read a bit until you've read the previous one – the bits come out strictly in order.

Now that we have these subbasic observations, what can we build out of them using the frame logic?

Step 1 – Finite meets of subbasics.

Step 2 – Joins of finite meets of subbasics.

Step 3 – Finite meets of joins of finite meets of subbasics. But at this point we can use frame distributivity. For instance if each C_i and D_j is a finite meet of subbasics, then

$$(\vee_i C_i) \wedge (\vee_j D_j) = \vee_{i,j} C_i \wedge D_j$$

We have thus rewritten a binary meet of joins of finite meets of subbasics (a step 3 expression) as a join of finite meets of subbasics (a step 2 expression). This can be done to all step 3 expressions, so step 3 doesn't give us anything new.

We have now presented some "subbasic" propositions ‘$s_n = 0$’ and ‘$s_n = 1$’, and some axioms ($*$) and ($\dagger$) that are supposed to hold for them. The idea is that this defines a logical theory, and that from this we can get a frame as a kind of Lindenbaum algebra. The mathematical justification for this, showing that this process does always lead to a well-defined frame, is non-trivial, and we postpone it to Chapter 4. For the present, and on the assumption that the frame does indeed exist, we shall show how we can play with the subbasics and the axioms to arrive at a more concrete definition of it.

To summarize the general argument so far, *every observation is a join of finite meets of subbasic observations*. But what the general argument doesn't tell us is when two different such expressions represent the same observation. We now investigate this in our particular case. The argument all follows from the axioms ($*$) and ($\dagger$) and the frame laws (Exercise – work out the details of this).

Take as an example the subbasic ‘$s_2 = 0$’. We can't read the second bit until we've read the first, so

$$'s_2=0' \quad = \quad 's_2=0' \wedge ('s_1=0' \vee 's_1=1')$$
$$= \quad 's_1=0' \wedge 's_2=0' \ \vee \ 's_1=1' \wedge 's_2=0'$$

We can also do this with finite meets of subbasics, as long as they're consistent (they don't read the same bit twice with different values), e.g.

$$'s_1=0' \wedge 's_2=1' \wedge 's_5=1'$$
$$= \quad ('s_1=0' \wedge 's_2=1' \wedge 's_3=0' \wedge 's_4=0' \wedge 's_5=1')$$
$$\vee ('s_1=0' \wedge 's_2=1' \wedge 's_3=0' \wedge 's_4=1' \wedge 's_5=1')$$
$$\vee ('s_1=0' \wedge 's_2=1' \wedge 's_3=1' \wedge 's_4=0' \wedge 's_5=1')$$
$$\vee ('s_1=0' \wedge 's_2=1' \wedge 's_3=1' \wedge 's_4=1' \wedge 's_5=1')$$
$$= \textbf{starts } 01001 \vee \textbf{starts } 01011 \vee \textbf{starts } 01101 \vee \textbf{starts } 01111$$

using an obvious notation. Therefore,

> *every observation is a disjunction of observations* **starts** l *where l is a finite list of bits.*

What this means is that since an assertion can only be affirmed on the evidence of a finite part of the stream, it can be fully described by saying what finite starting sequences allow us to affirm it.

Next, we address the question of when two such disjunctions are equal. Alternatively, and equivalently, we can ask when one is less than another. Our starting point is to compare predicates **starts** l and **starts** m.

Definition 3.7.1 Let l and m be two finite lists (of bits, in our case). Then l *prefixes* m, in symbols $l \sqsubseteq m$, iff for some list x, $m = l <> x$ (l concatenated with x). In other words, m starts off with the bits of l, and then possibly has some more (x).

Lemma 3.7.2 If $l \sqsubseteq m$ then **starts** $l \geq$ **starts** m.
Proof starts m is a meet of the subbasics of **starts** l and some more.]

We have proved this just from the laws of frame algebra. We could also argue the converse as follows. Suppose **starts** $l \geq$ **starts** m. Imagine a stream that starts off with the bits of m, but which we haven't read any further. We can affirm **starts** m, and hence **starts** l, and so we must already have observed the bits of l. This tells us that l is a prefix of m.

Since the converse argument uses our intuition of what streams are, and we haven't defined these with any precision, this is not very rigorous at present. However, it represents an important technique (the use of *models* or *points*) that will be developed further in the rest of the book.

Next, we look at more general joins.

Proposition 3.7.3 Let L and M be sets of finite lists of bits, and suppose for every $l \in$ L there is some $m \in$ M that prefixes it. Then

$$\bigvee_{l \in L} \textbf{starts } l \leq \bigvee_{m \in M} \textbf{starts } m$$

Proof If $l \in$ L, $l = m<>x$ with $m \in$ M, then

$$\textbf{starts } l \leq \textbf{starts } m \leq \bigvee_{m \in M} \textbf{starts } m$$

The conclusion follows from the defining property of joins.   ]

Again, we can argue the converse by imagining streams.

Now suppose L is a set of finite lists of bits. The Proposition tells us that $\bigvee_{l \in L} \textbf{starts } l$ is unchanged if we add to L lists with prefixes already in it. Adding all such lists, we obtain the upper closure of L (under $\sqsubseteq$). Thus:

Proposition 3.7.4 Every observation is a disjunction of the form $\bigvee_{l \in L} \textbf{starts } l$, where L is an upper closed set of finite lists of bits.   ]

This tells us that every observation can be represented by an upper closed set. Is this representation unique? Is it possible to deduce, from the laws of frame algebra and from our axioms (*) and (†), that

$$\bigvee_{l \in L} \textbf{starts } l = \bigvee_{m \in M} \textbf{starts } m$$

for some *distinct* upper closed sets L and M?

We can argue this using our – so far irrigorous – intuitions about streams. But in fact we can do better, because we have now arrived at a concrete definition of the frame we are looking for. From Example 3.6.2 (iii) we already know that the upper closed sets of finite lists form a frame A, the Alexandrov topology, ordered by $\subseteq$. In A, we can interpret all the observations:

'$s_n = 0$'	is	{lists l: length $l \geq n$ and $l[n] = 0$}
'$s_n = 1$'	is	{lists l: length $l \geq n$ and $l[n] = 1$}
starts l	is	$\uparrow l$
$\bigvee_{l \in L}$ **starts** l	is	$\uparrow L$, i.e. L itself if it is already upper closed

Now '$s_n = 0$' $\wedge$ '$s_n = 1$' is interpreted as

$$\{\text{lists l: length } l \geq n \text{ and } l[n] = 1 \text{ and } l[n] = 0\} = \emptyset$$

so that the axioms (*) are valid, and '$s_n = 0$' $\vee$ '$s_n = 1$' is interpreted as

$$\{\text{lists l: length } l \geq n \text{ and } l[n] = 1 \text{ or } l[n] = 0\} = \{\text{lists l: length } l \geq n\}$$

from which we deduce that the axioms (†) are valid in A.

Since A is a frame satisfying the axioms (*) and (†), and since our reasoning uses only the frame laws and these axioms, if we can deduce that if

$$\bigvee_{l \in L} \textbf{starts } l = \bigvee_{m \in M} \textbf{starts } m$$

with L and M upper closed, then this equality must also hold in A, and so L = M.

We have now shown in a particular case how to reason from a *presentation* of a frame (using subbasics and axioms) to a concrete *definition*. In Chapter 4 we shall see how to do this in full generality.

Definition 3.7.5 We write $\Omega 2^{*\omega}$ for the frame of Alexandrov opens in the set of finite lists of bits under the prefix ordering.

The reason for this notation is that we shall later define it as a topology (Ω) on a poset of all finite (*) and infinite (ω) lists of bits (2).

Different physical assumptions

Recall our assumption that you can't read one bit until you've read its predecessors. We used this when we expressed the subbasic observations '$s_n=0$' and '$s_n=1$' in terms of the conjunctions **starts** l, so it was a necessary part of Proposition 3.7.4, our description of the structure of the frame. We now explore rather briefly some different assumptions. They will all have the same subbasic observations, and so any observation will be a disjunction of finite conjunctions of these, but they will have different axioms and so different descriptions of when two such expressions are equal.

1. Different bits are read independently. This is more like an infinite read-only memory, where there is no obligation to read the data in order. Now, for instance,

$$\text{'}s_2=0\text{'} \quad \neq \quad \text{'}s_1=0\text{'} \wedge \text{'}s_2=0\text{'} \vee \text{'}s_1=1\text{'} \wedge \text{'}s_2=0\text{'}$$

The frame constructed here will have fewer equalities holding between the possible expressions than the first frame, so it has more elements.

2. Time is not important. We assume that every bit can be read sooner or later (so whatever is generating them is not allowed ever to stop). We don't distinguish between the bits that we have already read and those that we are going to read in the future, so the assumption is expressed by the formal axiom

$$\text{'}s_n = 0\text{'} \vee \text{'}s_n = 1\text{'} \quad = \quad \textbf{true} \tag{††}$$

As a corollary, the axiom (†) above holds, so, as in our main example, we can reduce every element to a join of elements **starts** l. However, there are now more equalities holding than we had in our main example, so the frame here is smaller.

Definition 3.7.6 After Chapter 4, we shall know that the subbasics '$s_n = 0$' and '$s_n = 1$' ($n \geq 1$), together with the axioms (*) and (††) above, "present" a frame. We shall call it $\Omega 2^{\omega}$.

See Exercise 11 of Chapter 6 for some collected properties.

Flat domains

We have already seen that if X is any set, then $\wp X$ is a frame. We can view the subsets as being observations on some object that has a value in X, $S \subseteq X$ being interpreted as

$$\bigvee_{x \in S} \textbf{it's } x \quad \text{(set theoretically, } S = \bigcup_{x \in S} \{x\})$$

A singleton $\{x\}$ represents an observation **it's** x that the object definitely has value x, while a larger set means that the object has been observed to be within some range, but not yet pinned down exactly.

We can also define this frame via a logical theory. It has propositions **it's** x for each $x \in X$, and satisfies axioms

$$\textbf{it's } x \wedge \textbf{it's } y = \textbf{false} \quad (x \neq y)$$

In $\wp X$ we also have

$$\bigvee_{x \in X} \textbf{it's } x = \textbf{true}$$

which says that the object must have some value. However, to be realistic, we might distinguish between the join $\bigvee_{x \in X} \textbf{it's } x$ ("we've observed the object to be in X, although we're not being any more precise than that"), and the weaker **true** ("we haven't observed the object at all yet").

The frame now has the subsets of X, as before, together with a new **true**, bigger than any subset.

This can also be described as an Alexandrov topology. We construct a poset

$$X_{\perp} = X \cup \{\perp\}$$

(X *lifted*, or the *flat domain* on X) where $\perp$ ("bottom") represents a computation that will never finish, and define a partial order $\sqsubseteq$ by

$$\perp \sqsubseteq \perp$$
$$\perp \sqsubseteq x \qquad\qquad (x \in X)$$
$$x \sqsubseteq y \text{ iff } x = y \qquad (x, y \in X)$$

The upper closed subsets are all subsets of X, and also the whole of $X_{\perp}$.

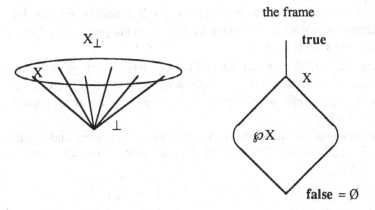

The presence of an Alexandrov topology is rather typical of our computer science applications, but it is only appropriate when the elements of its poset P – roughly speaking – represent finite pieces of information (they are *compact* in the sense of Chapter 9). If P is also to include infinite elements, then the more complicated Scott topology (Chapter 7) is called for.

Function spaces
An important topic concerns the observations that can be made on functions. The general idea is that we know how to make observations on the result, and we also know how to manufacture arguments. A subbasic observation on a function f is then [x→a], meaning "we have manufactured x, fed it to f, and observed a of the result f(x)". Let us imagine f as a black box.

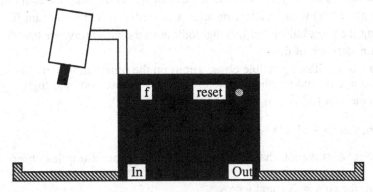

First of all, notice the reset button. Our general theory said that to make a conjunction of observations, you must observe all the individual conjuncts. However, we didn't say anything about the order in which to do these, so it is important that this shouldn't matter. It is best to make a *physical assumption,* that *the observations have no effect on what is observed.* Probably, the box does undergo change as it does its computation, but this is not permanent because we can always press the reset button.

Next, notice the video camera above the input tray. This is what f uses to examine its argument, using the observations appropriate to it. We can't tell it directly what observations to make; we must just present it with an x and let it observe that for itself.

For definiteness, consider an f for which both the argument and result have values in $X = \{t, f\}$. Naturally, we want to make observations appropriate to the flat domain $X_\perp$.

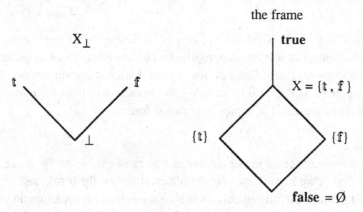

The x's that we can put in the input tray are t and f (fully computed inputs), and also $\perp$ (nothing in the tray). The point of this last one is that the function may be able to compute f(x) without knowing what x is at all – if it is a constant function. By pressing the reset button but leaving nothing in the input tray, we can discover whether it makes use of this.

We now have fifteen possible observations on the function, namely $[x \rightarrow a]$ where $x \in X_\perp$ and $a \in A$, and we should like to know how these combine logically.

First, note that for all $x \in X_\perp$ and $a, b \in A$,

$$\text{if } a \leq b, \text{ then } [x \rightarrow a] \leq [x \rightarrow b] \tag{1}$$

a is a stronger observation than b, so observing a for input x implies observing b for it.

Second, for all $x \in X_\perp$ and $a \in A$,

$$[\perp \rightarrow a] \leq [x \rightarrow a] \tag{2}$$

If the function allows us to observe a on the basis of no input at all, it is not allowed to retract that if we subsequently put in a more solid x.

Third, for all $x \in X_\perp$ and $S \subseteq A$,

$$[x \to \bigvee S] = \bigvee_{a \in S} [x \to a] \tag{3}$$

This says that to observe $\bigvee S$ for input x, we have to observe some $a \in S$. A corollary of this is that $[x \to \textbf{false}] = \textbf{false}$, so we have reduced our fifteen original observations to thirteen.

Fourth, for all $x \in X_\perp$ and finite $S \subseteq A$,

$$[x \to \bigwedge S] = \bigwedge_{a \in S} [x \to a] \tag{4}$$

This is somewhat subtle. The important part of this equality (given (1)) is that

$$[x \to \bigwedge S] \geq \bigwedge_{a \in S} [x \to a]$$

Thus for binary meets, we want to know that if we observe a for input x, and we observe b for input x, then we can observe a∧b. But the first two observations may have been made on different runs of the function, and (4) is tantamount to another physical assumption, that *different runs with equal arguments give equal results.* In other words, the function is *deterministic.*

For nullary meets, we want to say $[x \to \textbf{true}] = \textbf{true}$, in other words by putting in x and observing nothing of the result, we find out nothing new about the function. If the box told us when it had finished, this extra information would make the difference between $[x \to \textbf{true}]$ and **true**. Our axiom therefore rules out such possibilities.

At this point, we have described some subbasic observations, and formulated some physical assumptions in terms of axioms. Again, the results of Chapter 4 show that these present a frame. We could also, as before, define the frame concretely as an Alexandrov topology, this time one whose elements are partial functions. However, we shall leave the details of this to later chapters. (Exercise – read the rest of the book, and then show that the frame we have just presented has 78 elements.) The point to be stressed here is the relation between physical assumptions and axioms about the observations.

3.8 Bases and subbases

It's worth paying attention to a particular part of the argument in Section 3.7. Quite often in a frame we want to say that we start off with some simple assertions and *generate* the rest from these using the frame operations ∧ and ∨. The simple assertions are called *subbasic,* and they form a *subbasis.*

In any frame, the steps of generation can be done as –

Step 1: Finite conjunctions of subbasics;

Step 2: Disjunctions of finite conjunctions of subbasics;

Step 3: Anything more complicated can be reduced to a step 2 expression by using
the frame distributivity law.

Sometimes we can do better and say that any assertion is a disjunction of
subbasics (we don't have to bother with the finite conjunctions). Then the subbasis
is called a *basis,* and its elements are *basic.*

For example, given any subbasis, the finite conjunctions of subbasics form a
basis.

In section 3.7, in the frames $\Omega 2^{*\omega}$ and $\Omega 2^\omega$, the assertions **starts** 1 form a basis.

3.9 The real line

We now describe a frame of assertions for real numbers. It is based on the idea of
taking measurements of some real-valued quantity, all measurements giving results
that are *rational,* and *subject to error*. We write a subbasic assertion as $(q \pm \varepsilon)$
where q, a rational number, is the result, and ε, a *positive* rational number, is the
possible error.

If x is a given real number, then we write $x \vDash (q \pm \varepsilon)$ (x *satisfies* the assertion)
iff x is a possible exact value for the quantity, i.e. iff $q{-}\varepsilon < x < q{+}\varepsilon$.

Having the strict inequality < here enables us to avoid the embarrassing
possibility of pinning a value down to an exact real number. If we measure both (0
$\pm$ 1) and (2 $\pm$ 1), then we deduce not that the quantity has a value of exactly 1, but
that something is wrong with the measurements.

A finite conjunction of these subbasic measurements is either **false**
(contradiction, fault in measurements) or another such measurement. For instance,

$$(0 \pm 1/2) \wedge (1 \pm 3/4) = (3/8 \pm 1/8)$$

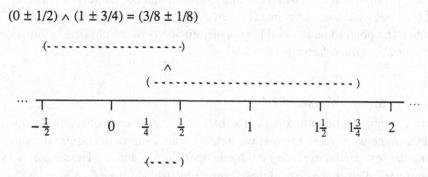

Thus the subbasics form a basis. Disjunctions give us many new assertions, e.g.

'x > 0' $= \bigvee \{(n \pm 1) : n \geq 1$ a natural number$\}$

'x ≠ 0' = 'x > 0' ∨ 'x < 0'
'x > √2' – can be expressed using a sequence of rationals tending to √2

We might therefore ask for a concrete description of all the assertions that can
be derived as disjunctions of basics, like the one we had for streams. Our idea of
the real numbers is better fixed than our idea of streams, so we aim to have an
assertion defined by the real numbers that satisfy it. Otherwise, we should have
different assertions that could never be distinguished in practice.

Therefore, we identify the derived assertions with certain sets of real numbers.
For instance,

$$(q \pm e) = \{x \in \mathbb{R} : q{-}\varepsilon < x < q{+}\varepsilon\} \qquad \text{(usually written as } (q{-}\varepsilon, q{+}\varepsilon))$$

Then,

≤	is	⊆
true	is	ℝ (the set of all reals)
false	is	∅
join, ∨	is	union, ∪
meet, ∧	is	intersection, ∩

Proposition 3.9.1 A set U is a union of basic assertions (q±ε) iff

$$\forall x \in U.\ \exists\, \delta \in \mathbb{R}.\ (\delta > 0 \wedge (x{-}\delta < y < x{+}\delta \rightarrow y \in U))$$

Proof *Intuitively,* if x ∈ U, then for some δ, x ∈ (x ± δ) ⊆ U. Therefore,

$$U = \bigcup \{(x \pm \delta) : (x \pm \delta) \subseteq U\}.$$

But x and δ might be irrational. We need to get down to the basics (q ± ε) in
terms of rationals, because we can only measure the reals in terms of rationals.
⇒:   First, suppose x ∈ U = (q ± ε), so that q–ε < x < q+ε.

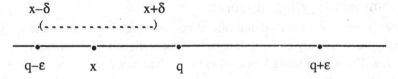

Choose δ to be min (x–(q–ε), (q+ε)–x). Then (exercise),

$$x{-}\delta < y < x{+}\delta \Rightarrow q{-}\varepsilon < y < q{+}\varepsilon \Rightarrow y \in U$$

Now if U is actually a join of basics, instead of a basic, we can still find one of
the basic disjuncts containing x and choose δ for that, and that is good enough for U.

⇐:   Given $x \in U$, we look for rationals q_x and ε_x such that $x \in (q_x \pm \varepsilon_x) \subseteq U$, and then U is the join of the $(q_x \pm \varepsilon_x)$'s and hence is affirmative. We shall use the following important

> FACT: If x and y are real numbers with $x < y$, then there is a rational q between them: $x < q < y$.

Now take $x \in U$, with its corresponding δ.

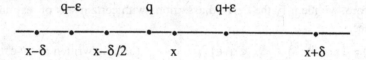

Choose –

> a rational q with $x-\delta/2 < q < x$
> a rational ε with $x-q < \varepsilon < q-(x-\delta)$

Then (exercise)

> $x \in (q \pm \varepsilon) \subseteq (x \pm \delta) \subseteq U$

which is what we wanted for our q_x and ε_x.   ]

   This now formalizes the informal notion of openness in Chapter 1. For if U is a union of basics and x is an element of it, we ask whether x can be a boundary point. But if we use a magnifying glass of power δ, then all the neighbouring points of x in our field of vision are in $(x\pm\delta)$ and hence in U. There are no points outside U, which is what we'd see if x were on the boundary. The argument is reversible: open sets are unions of basics.

3.10 Complete Heyting algebras

In Chapter 2, we carefully ruled out infinite conjunctions, implication and negation from our logic. Curiously enough, frames have operations to support these connectives. The reason for ignoring them is not that they don't exist, but that they are less well-behaved.

   We have already seen, in Proposition 3.5.2, that a frame is a complete lattice and hence has infinite meets. Apparently, this contradicts our argument in Chapter 2 that infinite conjunctions were inadmissible in the logic of finite observations. However, the correct conclusion is that the infinite meets do not represent true conjunctions. In a topology, it is easy to see that the meet can be expressed in terms of interiors, by

$$\bigwedge S = \text{Int}(\bigcap S)$$

We can reasonably think of $\bigcap S$ as the conjunction of the open sets in S; but if $\bigcap$ S is not itself open, then the meet $\bigwedge S$ is not really a conjunction.

As an example, in the real line, take

$$S = \{(0\pm\varepsilon): \varepsilon > 0\}$$

Then

$$\bigcap S = \{0\} \quad - \text{not open}$$
$$\bigwedge S = \emptyset \quad - \text{open}$$

Next, we look at implication.

Definition 3.10.1 Let A be a lattice. A is a *Heyting algebra* iff for every a, b $\in$ A there is an element a$\rightarrow$b satisfying

$$c \leq a\rightarrow b \quad \text{iff} \quad c\wedge a \leq b \tag{*}$$

A *Heyting algebra homomorphism* is a function f between Heyting algebras that preserves finite meets and joins, and also the $\rightarrow$ operation:

$$f(a\rightarrow b) = f(a)\rightarrow f(b)$$

A Heyting algebra A is a *complete Heyting algebra* (cHa) iff it is a complete lattice.

A *cHa homomorphism* is a function between cHa's that is a Heyting algebra homomorphism and moreover preserves all joins.

Proposition 3.10.2 Let A be a lattice. Then A is a frame iff it is a cHa.
Proof Note that when a$\rightarrow$b exists, then it is defined uniquely by (*).

To define $\rightarrow$ in a frame, we put

$$a\rightarrow b = \bigvee \{c: c\wedge a \leq b\}$$

Distributivity assures us that $(a\rightarrow b)\wedge a \leq b$, from which we deduce (*).

To show that a cHa is a frame, we just need to prove the frame distributivity law. Let $S \subseteq A$, $a \in A$.

$$b' \in S \Rightarrow a\wedge b' \leq \bigvee \{a\wedge b: b \in S\} \Rightarrow b' \leq a\rightarrow\bigvee \{a\wedge b: b \in S\}$$

Therefore

$$\bigvee S \leq a\rightarrow\bigvee \{a\wedge b: b \in S\}$$

so

$$a \wedge \bigvee S \leq \bigvee \{a \wedge b : b \in S\}$$

The reverse inequality is easy.

Categorically, for each a, the functor $c \mapsto c \wedge a$ is left adjoint to the functor $b \mapsto a \rightarrow b$ and hence preserves all colimits, i.e. joins.   ]

In themselves, therefore, frames and complete Heyting algebras are the same thing. However, the notions become different when we consider homomorphisms, in other words when we compare two algebras. A frame homomorphism need not preserve the $\rightarrow$ operation, and hence need not be a cHa homomorphism.

If we define negation by

$$\neg a = a \rightarrow \mathbf{false}$$

then any Heyting algebra is a model for propositional intuitionistic logic. Roughly speaking, this is the same as classical logic except that the law of excluded middle, $x \vee \neg x = \mathbf{true}$, may fail (see, e.g., Goldblatt [79] for details of the axiomatization). This means that any frame, and in particular that of open sets of a topological space, forms such a model.

Logicians have found these topological models, and in particular $\Omega \mathbb{R}$, useful for proving completeness of propositional intuitionistic logic. Suppose ϕ is a formula of propositional intuitionistic logic (note that we do not allow infinite joins here). If for each propositional variable p in ϕ we are given an element v(p) of some frame A, then we can extend this to an element $v(\phi)$ because we know how to interpret all the logical connectives in A. We say that ϕ is *valid* in A iff however the v(p)'s are chosen, $v(\phi) = \mathbf{true}$. For example, $p \rightarrow p$ is valid in any frame, because $v(p \rightarrow p) = v(p) \rightarrow v(p) = \mathbf{true}$ whatever value v(p) takes.

Theorem 3.10.3 If ϕ is valid in $\Omega \mathbb{R}$ then it is an intuitionistic theorem (hence valid in any frame). **Proof** See Rasiowa and Sikorski [63], Theorem IX.3.2. $\mathbb{R}$ is a dense-in-itself, non-empty metric space. Their "pseudo-Boolean algebras" are our Heyting algebras.   ]

Exercises

1. Prove directly that the subsets of $\mathbb{R}$ that satisfy the second condition in Proposition 3.9.1 are closed under finite intersections and arbitrary unions and hence form a frame (a subframe of $\wp \mathbb{R}$).

2. If x is real, show that $\{x\}$ is not open. Thus our assertions do not allow us to observe that a real number is exactly equal to another given one.

3. Show that in $\Omega \mathbb{R}$, $\vee$ does not distribute over $\wedge$. That is $(\Omega \mathbb{R})^{op}$ is not a frame.

4. Show that in a topological space,

$$U \rightarrow V = \text{Int}(U^c \cup V)$$
$$\neg\neg U = \text{Int}(\text{Cl } U)$$

(By comparison, in *classical* logic, $p \rightarrow q \Leftrightarrow \neg p \vee q$ and $\neg\neg p \Leftrightarrow p$.)

5. For negation $\neg x$ in a frame, show that $x \wedge \neg x = \textbf{false}$ but find an example in $\Omega\mathbb{R}$ for which $x \vee \neg x \neq \textbf{true}$.

6. *Metric spaces.* These are the prototype topological spaces in most approaches. Define the *distance* function d: $\mathbb{R} \times \mathbb{R} \rightarrow \mathbb{R}$ by $d(x, y) = |x - y|$. Then

(i) $d(x, y) \geq 0$ with equality iff $x = y$

(ii) $d(x, y) = d(y, x)$

(iii) $d(x, z) \leq d(x, y) + d(y, z)$ (the *triangle inequality*)

A *metric space* is a set X equipped with a function d: $X \times X \rightarrow \mathbb{R}$ (the *metric*) satisfying these three axioms. Show that the open balls $B_\varepsilon(x) = \{y \in X: d(x, y) < \varepsilon\}$ form a base of open sets for a topology on X. For $\mathbb{R}$ with the metric already defined, the topology thus derived is the same as the one in Section 3.9.

An *ultrametric space* is a metric space X in which d satisfies the stronger *ultrametric inequality:*

(iii') $d(x, z) \leq \max \{d(x, y), d(y, z)\}$

We shall say very little about metric spaces, despite their importance in mainstream topology (as discussed in any standard introduction) and even in some computing applications. The domains of Chapter 10 cannot possibly be metric spaces (see the remark after Definition 5.5.2), but Smyth [87] has some relevant results involving *quasi-metrics*, which drop the symmetry axiom (ii).

7. Show that in a Heyting algebra (whether complete or not), meets distribute over all joins that exist.

8. Let A be a finite, linearly ordered poset (hence a frame). Show that $\rightarrow$ in A is defined by

$$a \rightarrow b = \begin{cases} \textbf{true} & \text{if } a \leq b \\ b & \text{if } a > b \end{cases}$$

If B is another frame, show that a function f: $A \rightarrow B$ is a frame homomorphism iff it is monotone and preserves **true** and **false**. Give an example of a frame homomorphism that is not a Heyting algebra homomorphism.

CHAPTER FOUR

FRAMES AS ALGEBRAS

In which we see methods that exploit our algebraicizing of logic.

4.1 Semilattices

Logic on the whole has both conjunctions and disjunctions, and so it seems natural to think in terms of lattices. However, in the algebraic development upon which we now embark, it is convenient to consider *semilattices,* which have only one of these. As we shall see, to investigate the algebra of frames, we shall look first at the meet on its own and then at the joins when they are added in.

Definition 4.1.1 A poset S is a *semilattice* iff every finite subset has a meet.

A *semilattice homomorphism* is a function between semilattices that preserves finite meets.

More precisely, these are *meet-semilattices;* their opposites (every finite subset has a join) are *join-semilattices*. There is no special reason for focusing on one rather than the other, except that we are going to use semilattice theory to talk about the *meets* in frames. Just as for lattices, it suffices to find a top element **true** and meets x∧y for all pairs {x, y}. Note that a semilattice homomorphism f is monotone:

$$x \leq y \Rightarrow x = x{\wedge}y \Rightarrow f(x) = f(x){\wedge}f(y) \Rightarrow f(x) \leq f(y)$$

An important property of semilattices that contributes to their usefulness is that their theory is purely algebraic. Unlike the case with posets, where the inequality ≤, a non-algebraic idea, is essential, in semilattices it can be defined in terms of ∧ and equality: $x \leq y$ iff $x{\wedge}y = x$; and we can also characterize ∧ by algebraic properties.

Proposition 4.1.2

(i)   Semilattices are equivalent to algebras equipped with two *operators*, **true** (nullary) and ∧ (binary), subject to the following equational *laws:*

commutativity:	$x{\wedge}y = y{\wedge}x$
associativity:	$x{\wedge}(y{\wedge}z) = (x{\wedge}y){\wedge}z$
unit law:	$x{\wedge}\textbf{true} = x$
idempotence:	$x{\wedge}x = x$

Then $x \leq y$ iff $x{\wedge}y = x$.

(ii)   A function f: A → B between semilattices is a homomorphism iff

$$f(\textbf{true}) = \textbf{true}$$
$$f(x \land y) = f(x) \land f(y) \qquad \text{for all } x, y \in A$$

Proof

(i) We have already seen in lattices how the meets give rise to **true** and $\land$. The interesting case here is to go from an algebra S to a semilattice. By Proposition 3.3.5, we must define $\leq$ as stated. Then $\leq$ is reflexive by idempotence, transitive because if $x \leq y$ and $y \leq z$ then

$$x \land z = (x \land y) \land z = x \land (y \land z) = x \land y = x$$

so that $x \leq z$, and antisymmetric because if $x \leq y \leq x$ then $x = x \land y = y \land x = y$. Hence S is a poset under $\leq$.

The unit law says that **true** is top, and it remains to show that $x \land y$ is the meet of x and y. $(x \land y) \land y = x \land (y \land y) = x \land y$, so that $x \land y \leq y$, and $x \land y = y \land x \leq x$, so it is a lower bound. If z is any other, then

$$z \land (x \land y) = (z \land x) \land y = z \land y = z,$$

so $z \leq x \land y$.

(ii) This follows by induction on the number of conjuncts in the finite meet. ⟧

A combination like this of operators and equational laws makes up an *algebraic theory,* and puts us in the realms of universal algebra. In the rest of this chapter, we shall see this yielding powerful results.

For completeness, we note that lattices (and hence distributive lattices) and Heyting algebras can also be described algebraically in this way (see Exercise 1). In a sense, frames can too. But the join in frames, being a possibly infinitary operation (the join of infinitely many elements) falls slightly outside the scope of the usual algebraic methods, and Section 4.4 is devoted to showing that this doesn't matter.

4.2 Generators and relations

Suppose we want to describe a frame. One method, which we have already seen informally (in Section 3.7) but not yet justified, *presents* a frame in four steps.

Step 1: Specify some subbasic elements (*generators*)

Step 2: Derive from these all possible joins of meets of subbasics.

Step 3: Specify certain axiomatic *relations* to hold between expressions of Step 2. They can be of the form $e_1 \leq e_2$ (*inequations*) or $e_1 = e_2$ (*equations*). It doesn't matter which you use, because, as in Proposition 4.1.2, the two forms are interconvertible.

Step 4: Deduce, just from the relations and the frame laws, when any two given
         expressions must be equal. This, then, is an equivalence relation on the Step
         2 expressions.

The Step 4 equivalence relation is supposed to mean "equal in the frame we're
defining", so formally the frame is the set of equivalence classes. We can deduce
that it actually is a frame from the fact that all consequences of the frame laws have
been built in to Step 4.

From one point of view, this is a method of logic. The generators are the
primitive propositional symbols, the Step 2 expressions are well-formed formulae,
the Step 3 relations (written as inequations) are the axioms, and the Step 4
equivalence is mutual entailment.

However, it also represents a very general method of Universal Algebra,
enabling us in a wide class of algebraic theories to present an algebra by writing
down generators and relations for it. Unfortunately, for the theory of frames the
infinite joins give rise to obstacles to formalizing the general argument. In Section
4.4 we shall see that these can be overcome, but meanwhile we shall concentrate on
developing the practical intuition.

Assuming that the method does indeed define a frame, we write it as

Fr ⟨ generators | relations ⟩,

and call this a *presentation* of the frame. We give a few examples to show how one
might reason with such a presentation (in fact Section 3.7 is a much bigger
example).

Example 4.2.1 Fr ⟨ | ⟩ (no generators, no relations). The only elements we can
generate are **true** and **false**. Our frame is therefore **2**.

Example 4.2.2 Fr ⟨ a, b | ⟩ (two generators, no relations). The finite meets (all
meets and joins here are going to be finite, of course) of the generators (subbasic
elements) are –

true, a, b and a∧b

and the joins of these are

false, the meets of generators themselves, and a∨b.

Any other join is already accounted for. We obtain this frame:

```
        • true
         ↑
          • a∨b
      a •◇• b
          • a∧b
         ↑
        • false
```

How do we know that this incorporates all the deductions that we were supposed to be making? Well, we calculated at most 6 elements that were all a and b could possibly generate. Plausibly, some of these might be forced to be equal by deductions that we've missed. But our diagram does in fact illustrate a frame (this just involves a bit of checking) containing 6 distinct elements including a and b, and it also satisfies all the relations (vacuously, because there aren't any). If we could deduce, just from frame laws and the relations, that two of the 6 expressions had to be equal, then they'd be equal in our diagram as well, and they're not. Therefore the diagram illustrates precisely the frame we were trying to construct.

Definition 4.2.3 A presentation with generators only, no relations, is called *free*. By extension, the algebra it presents is called free (on those generators).

Example 4.2.4 $\text{Fr}\langle\,a, b \mid a \leq b\,\rangle$ (two generators, one relation). Recall that we can recast inequalities as equalities, so this is the same as $\text{Fr}\langle\,a, b \mid a \wedge b = a\,\rangle$; but there is no reason why we shouldn't think in terms of the inequality during our reasoning.

Clearly we can start off with the frame of Example 4.2.2, and look for where the diagram collapses because of new equalities. We get $a \wedge b = a$ and $a \vee b = b$, leaving:

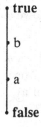

```
• true
↑
• b
• a
↑
• false
```

Again, this is a frame (in fact this doesn't even need checking: the ordering is linear, so we can use Example 3.4.6), it contains a and b, it satisfies the relation a ≤

b, and we haven't made any more identifications than we were forced to. It is therefore the frame we want.

In general, if $\mathbb{T}$ is any algebraic theory (described by operators and equational laws) for which this method works, then we write

$$\mathbb{T} \langle \text{ generators } | \text{ relations } \rangle$$

for the $\mathbb{T}$-algebra presented by the given generators and relations.

Example – Semilattice $\langle$ a, b | $\rangle$ has four elements, namely **true**, a, b and a∧b.

4.3 The universal characterization of presentations

As a preliminary, we quickly summarize the standard definitions of universal algebra.

Definition 4.3.1 Let $\mathbb{T}$ be an algebraic theory. It has some *operators*, each with an *arity* (the number of arguments it has), and some *laws*, each of the form $e_1 = e_2$, where e_1 and e_2 are expressions formed from a convenient stock of variables by applying the given operators. We define A to be a *$\mathbb{T}$-algebra* iff

(i)   A is a set (often known as the *carrier* of the algebra), and

(ii)   for each operator ω of $\mathbb{T}$ (say ω is an n-ary operator), A is equipped with a corresponding *operation*, a function $\omega: A^n \to A$.

Now suppose e is an expression formed using variables X_i ($i \in m$) and operators of $\mathbb{T}$. If we substitute an m-tuple of elements from A for the X_is, we can evaluate the expression in A. This gives us a corresponding function $e: A^m \to A$.

(iii)   If $e_1 = e_2$ is a law for $\mathbb{T}$, with free variables X_i ($i \in m$), then the two functions

$$e_1, e_2: A^m \to A$$

must be equal. In other words, however we substitute elements of A for the variables, the law holds in A.

Let A and B be two $\mathbb{T}$-algebras. A *($\mathbb{T}$-)homomorphism* from A to B is a function $f: A \to B$ such that if ω is any $\mathbb{T}$-operator (n-ary, say), then $f^n;\omega = \omega;f$. In other words – at least, if n is finite –, if $a_1, ..., a_n \in A$, then

$$\omega(f(a_1), ...,f(a_n)) = f(\omega(a_1, ..., a_n))$$

Examples 4.3.2

(i)   Semilattices. The theory has the two operators and four laws of Proposition 4.1.2, which says that the algebras and homomorphisms for the theory are precisely as defined in 4.1.1.

(ii)   Frames. The theory has a proper class of operators, **true**, $\wedge$ and $\bigvee_I$ (the I-ary join for each set I) and a proper class of laws: the four semilattice laws, and (exercise – prove these)

$$x_j \wedge \bigvee_I (x_i: i \in I) = x_j \qquad \text{if } j \in I,$$
$$y \wedge \bigvee_I (x_i: i \in I) = \bigvee_I (y \wedge x_i: i \in I)$$

Let us now try to be more precise about what it means for an algebra A to be presented as $\mathbb{T}\langle G \mid R \rangle$. First, A must contain elements corresponding G, and the relations in R must hold in A. We define this formally, and say that A must be a *model* for the presentation.

Definition 4.3.3 Let $\mathbb{T}\langle G \mid R \rangle$ be a presentation. A *model* for the presentation is an A satisfying the following conditions.

(i)   A is a $\mathbb{T}$-algebra.

(ii)   A is equipped with a function

$$[-]: G \to A, \qquad g \mapsto [g] \text{ or } [g]_A$$

(Often, by abuse of notation, we shall suppress the semantic brackets [and].)

This function can be extended to apply to any expression e built up from the generators and the $\mathbb{T}$-operators: replace the generators g by their interpretations $[g]$, and evaluate the expression in A to give $[e] \in A$.

(iii)   If $e_1 = e_2$ is a relation in R, then it must also hold in A – $[e_1] = [e_2]$.

Notice the two different uses of equations, in the laws that were part of $\mathbb{T}$ and in the relations in a presentation. In a law, an equation contains variables, and the equation must always hold, whatever values from an algebra are substituted for the variables. In a relation, the equation contains generators, and the equation must hold when the generators are given their particular values in a model.

To get the algebra A presented by a presentation, we still want to pin it down more precisely in two ways. First, we want it to be *generated* by the generators G – each of its elements can be formed as $[e]$ for some expression e involving the generators and the $\mathbb{T}$-operators. Second, we want to identify two such expressions only if we're forced to by the laws of $\mathbb{T}$-algebras and the given relations R. Thus if, for some two expressions e_1 and e_2, we have $[e_1] = [e_2]$ in A, then the same is also to hold in any model. This means that for any other model B, we can define a $\mathbb{T}$-homomorphism from A to B by $[e]_A \mapsto [e]_B$. Moreover, this is the only homomorphism for which $g_A \mapsto g_B$ for every generator g. We use this to give a more precise definition of what presentations present.

Definition 4.3.4 Let $\mathbb{T}$ be an algebraic theory. A $\mathbb{T}$-algebra A is *presented* by a presentation $\mathbb{T} \langle$ generators | relations $\rangle$ iff

(i)   it is a model for the presentation, and

(ii)   if B is any other model, then there is a unique homomorphism $\theta: A \to B$
        such that $\theta(g_A) = g_B$ for every generator g.

Because the second condition applies to all models B, relating them to A by homomorphisms, it is called a *universal* property. Notice carefully the word *unique*. It is an essential part.

In our informal justification of these ideas, we argued that these properties constitute some true facts about presentations. However, for a more rigorous development it would be convenient to take them as the definition, which is what we have in fact called it.

Now we have been trying to define *the* algebra presented by generators and relations, so we must ask what happens if two different algebras, A and A', both fit the definition. Letting A' play the role of B in the definition, we find a unique homomorphism $\theta: A \to A'$ mapping each g_A to $g_{A'}$, and similarly we find $\theta': A' \to A$ mapping each $g_{A'}$ to g_A. Therefore, $\theta;\theta'$ maps each g_A to itself and hence (letting A play the role of both A and B in the definition) is the unique such. But the identity homomorphism Id_A also does this, so $\theta;\theta' = Id_A$. Similarly, $\theta';\theta = Id_{A'}$.

As mutually inverse homomorphisms (*isomorphisms*), θ and θ' are structure-preserving bijections. Thus A and A', although not strictly equal, are structurally equivalent: they are *isomorphic*. Hence,

Proposition 4.3.5 The algebra presented by generators and relations, if it exists at all, is defined up to isomorphism by 4.3.4.   ]

Categorically speaking, $\mathbb{T} \langle$ G | R $\rangle$ is the initial model for the presentation. Also, we have a *forgetful* functor from the category of algebras to the category of sets, taking each algebra to its carrier set. If this functor has a left adjoint, then that takes each set G to an algebra $\mathbb{T} \langle$ G | $\rangle$ freely generated by it.

Now that we have shown uniqueness (up to isomorphism) of the algebra presented by generators and relations, we must look more carefully at whether it exists or not. The argument we gave at the beginning of Section 4.2, though informal, can be made to work rigorously, and with great generality.

Theorem 4.3.6 Let $\mathbb{T}$ be a *finitary* algebraic theory – i.e., one in which

(i)   the operators form a set (not a proper class), and
(ii)   each operator has finite arity.

Then every presentation $\mathbb{T} \langle\, G \mid R \,\rangle$ presents a $\mathbb{T}$-algebra.

Proof See Manes [76] for a full proof. We use four steps as before.

Step 1: Take the generators G.
Step 2: Derive from these all possible well-formed expressions using the generators and the operators of $\mathbb{T}$. $\mathbb{T}$'s finitariness ensures that these expressions form a set (not a proper class).
Step 3: Take the relations R. For a general theory $\mathbb{T}$, these have to be equations, because the operators of $\mathbb{T}$ may not allow us to define the partial ordering we have for semilattices.
Step 4: Deduce, just from the relations and the laws of $\mathbb{T}$, when any two given expressions must be equal. This, then, is an equivalence relation on the Step 2 expressions.

The equivalence classes of expressions then form the algebra we are trying to present.   ]

Thus for semilattices (and also for lattices and distributive lattices – see Exercise 1), we know that presentations present. Unfortunately, we still haven't settled the question for frames. We do this in the next Section.

A useful fact is that any algebra has presentations.

Proposition 4.3.7 Let $\mathbb{T}$ be a finitary algebraic theory, and let A be a $\mathbb{T}$-algebra. Then A has a presentation.

Proof For each element a of A, let there be a generator a'. For each n-ary operator ω, and each n-tuple $(a_i) \in A^n$, let there be a relation

$$\omega(a_1{}', \ldots, a_n{}') = \omega(a_1, \ldots, a_n)'$$

A model B for this has a function from A to B, and the fact that this respects the relations says precisely that the function is a homomorphism. Thus the models are the algebras equipped with homomorphisms from A. This says precisely that the presentation presents A.]

Finally, although the method of generators and relations is a very useful tool, it is often best used as a means to making universal constructions different from those described in Definition 4.3.4.

For instance, let S be a semilattice. Then we can construct a *universal distributive lattice* L over S. This means that L is a distributive lattice (and hence also a semilattice, by forgetting that it has joins as well as meets), there is a semilattice homomorphism f: S → L, and that if g: S → K is any other semilattice homomorphism from S to a distributive lattice K, then there is a *unique lattice homomorphism* h: L → K such that g = f;h. This is a universal property of L, characterizing it up to isomorphism. It is not hard to see that this universal property is satisfied by the distributive lattice presented as

$$\text{DL} \langle \, f(a): a \in S \mid f(\mathbf{true}) = \mathbf{true},\ f(a \wedge b) = f(a) \wedge f(b) : a, b \in S \, \rangle$$

(Each generator f(a) here is a formal symbol constructed out of a, but we have taken the liberty of making it agree with the functional notation for the homomorphism f.)

When we come to constructing lattice homomorphisms out of L, it may well be more convenient to use the new universal property rather than the one of Definition 4.3.4. We shall often use this kind of method implicitly.

With the power of the method of generators and relations comes a disadvantage. Although it tells us that certain algebras (with certain universal properties) exist, it does not tell us much about their structure. For instance, when we construct a universal distributive lattice as above, it is a fact that the homomorphism f is always 1-1; but it takes a little work to prove this. (Exercise: L can be constructed concretely as the set of lower closed subsets $\downarrow x_1 \cup \ldots \cup \downarrow x_n$ of S.)

4.4 Generators and relations for frames

The reader uninterested in technicalities can omit this section and take it for granted that presentations work. However, there are a few places in the remainder of the book where the details of the methods of this Section give more information than presentations on their own.

For infinitary theories, such as that of frames, there is a hitch. Step 2 of Theorem 4.3.6 tells us to form the set of all possible expressions using the generators and the operators, and at this stage the general theory doesn't use the algebraic laws to make any identifications between expressions (this comes in Step 4). This is fine for the finitary algebraic theories. However, for frames, we can make new expressions by forming joins of arbitrary sets of older expressions, and this can't be done in set theory. Technically, the "set" of all possible expressions would be a proper class: it is too big to be a valid set. This is a genuine problem. There are infinitary theories (such as that of *complete Boolean algebras* – see Johnstone [82]) where this is insuperable and presentations simply don't present algebras. For frames, fortunately, presentations do present, but we have to argue slightly carefully to show this. The trick is to import our knowledge of the frame laws into Step 2 and say that all possible expressions are joins of finite meets of generators. These do form a set.

To construct a frame presented by generators and relations, we first deal with the finite meets by constructing a semilattice, and then with the joins by constructing a frame out of the semilattice. The first part comes from Theorem 4.3.6 applied to semilattices and we shall concentrate on the second, using Johnstone's method of coverages.

Definition 4.4.1 Let S be a semilattice.

A *cover relation* in S is a formula U ⊣ a ("U *covers* a"), where a ∈ S and U ⊆ ↓a. This is intended to mean $\bigvee U = a$. A function f from S into a lattice is said to *transform the cover to a join* iff $\bigvee \{f(u): u \in U\} = f(a)$.

A *coverage* on S is a set C of cover relations such that if U ⊣ a is in C, and b ≤ a, then C also contains {b∧u: u ∈ U} ⊣ b. This corresponds to frame distributivity:

if $\bigvee U = a$ then $\bigvee \{b \wedge u: u \in U\} = b \wedge a = b$.

Clearly any set C' of cover relations generates a coverage given by the cover relations

{b∧u: u ∈ U} ⊣ b   for some U ⊣ a in C', b ≤ a

Suppose we want to present a frame with S as a basis, and a coverage C to define certain joins. Any element a can be expressed as a join of elements of S, and we can be complete in this expression by joining all the elements of S that are less than a. We can therefore identify the elements of the frame with certain subsets of S, namely (we shall prove) the *C-ideals*:

If C is a coverage on S, then a *C-ideal* in S is a subset I satisfying

(i)   I is lower closed.
(ii)   If U ⊣ a is a cover relation in C, and U ⊆ I, then a ∈ I.

We write C-Idl(S) for the set of C-ideals in S.

A *site* is a semilattice equipped with a coverage C.

Theorem 4.4.2 Let S be a semilattice, C' a set of cover relations and C the coverage it generates.

(i)   C-Idl(S) is a frame under the subset ordering (I ≤ J iff I ⊆ J).
(ii)   There is a function f: S → C-Idl(S) that preserves finite meets and transforms the covers of C' to joins.
(iii)   Any other such function from S to a frame factors uniquely as f followed by a frame homomorphism.

Proof
(i) First, we note that any intersection of C-ideals is still a C-ideal. Hence intersection is meet and C-Idl(S) is a complete lattice.

A union of C-ideals is not necessarily a C-ideal; but any subset X of S *generates* a C-ideal, namely the intersection of all the C-ideals that contain it. Let us write this as C-↓X. The join in C-Idl(S) is then $\bigvee_i I_i = $ C-↓ $\bigcup_i I_i$. It remains for us to prove distributivity, and we introduce some auxiliary notions.

Definition 4.4.2.1 Let X and Y be arbitrary subsets of S. Then we write

$$X \wedge Y = \{x \wedge y : x \in X, y \in Y\}$$
$$X/Y = \{z \in S : y \wedge z \in X \text{ for all } y \in Y\}$$

Proposition 4.4.2.2 For any subsets X, Y and $Z \subseteq S$,

(i) $Z \subseteq X/Y \Leftrightarrow Y \wedge Z \subseteq X \Leftrightarrow Y \subseteq X/Z$.
(ii)   If X and Y are C-ideals, then $X \wedge Y = X \cap Y$ (i.e. $X \wedge Y$ in C-Idl (S)).
(iii) If X is a C-ideal, then so is X/Y.   ]

Categorically, the poset $\wp S$ has all joins (unions) and hence all colimits. For each $Y \in \wp S$, the function $Z \mapsto Y \wedge Z$ preserves unions and hence has a right adjoint, $X \mapsto X/Y$. The adjunction is described by part (i) of Proposition 4.4.2.2. But then part (iii) allows us to turn the argument on its head: since $Z \mapsto Y \wedge Z$ has a right adjoint *within the system of C-ideals,* it preserves all joins and so frame distributivity is satisfied.

Returning to the proof of the Theorem, if we are given C-ideals I and J_i then we want

$$I \wedge \bigvee_i J_i \le \bigvee_i (I \wedge J_i) = K \text{ (say)} \qquad \text{(the reverse inequality is trivial),}$$
i.e. $\bigvee_i J_i \le K/I$
i.e. $\bigcup_i J_i \subseteq K/I$ because K/I is a C-ideal
i.e. $J_i \le K/I$ for all i
i.e. $I \wedge J_i \le K$ for all i, and this is clear.

(ii)   We map S into C-Idl (S) by $f(x) = $ C-↓ $\{x\}$.

Clearly f(**true**) = S, the top C-ideal. Now take $x, y \in S$. We want

$$f(x) \wedge f(y) \le f(x \wedge y)$$
i.e. $f(x) \le f(x \wedge y)/f(y)$
i.e. $\{x\} \subseteq f(x \wedge y)/f(y)$ because $f(x \wedge y)/f(y)$ is a C-ideal
i.e. $f(y) \le f(x \wedge y)/\{x\}$
i.e. $\{y\} \subseteq f(x \wedge y)/\{x\}$ because $f(x \wedge y)/\{x\}$ is a C-ideal
i.e. $\{x\} \wedge \{y\} = \{x \wedge y\} \subseteq f(x \wedge y)$,   which is clear.

Therefore, f preserves finite meets.

Finally, let $U \dashv a$ be a cover relation in C'. We want $f(a) \leq \bigvee \{f(u): u \in U\}$, i.e. a is in any C-ideal containing U. This comes straight from the definition of C-ideal. Note that f also transforms all the covers in C into joins.

(iii)   Let $g: S \to A$ be another such function into a frame. We want there to be a unique frame homomorphism h: C-Idl (S) $\to$ A such that f;h = g. Uniqueness is easy:

$$h(I) = h(\bigvee \{f(x): x \in I\}) = \bigvee \{h(f(x)): x \in I\} = \bigvee \{g(x): x \in I\}$$

It remains to show that this does indeed define a frame homomorphism, and that f;h = g.

$$h(\mathbf{true}) = \bigvee \{g(x): x \in S\} = g(\mathbf{true}) = \mathbf{true}$$

$$\begin{aligned}
h(I) \wedge h(J) &= \bigvee \{g(x): x \in I\} \wedge \bigvee \{g(y): y \in J\} \\
&= \bigvee \{g(x) \wedge g(y): x \in I, y \in J\} = \bigvee \{g(x \wedge y): x \in I, y \in J\} \\
&= \bigvee \{g(z): z \in I \wedge J\} = h(I \wedge J)
\end{aligned}$$

$$\bigvee_i h(I_i) = \bigvee_i \bigvee \{g(x): x \in I_i\} = \bigvee \{g(x): x \in \bigcup_i I_i\} = a, \text{ say.}$$

But $\{x \in S: g(x) \leq a\}$ is a C-ideal, because g transforms covers to joins, and hence contains $\bigvee_i I_i$. Therefore $a = \bigvee \{g(x): x \in \bigvee_i I_i\} = h(\bigvee_i I_i)$ as required.

To show that f;h = g, let $x \in S$. We must show

$$g(x) = \bigvee \{g(y): y \in \text{C-}{\downarrow}x\}$$

$\leq$ is obvious, so it remains to show that if $y \in \text{C-}{\downarrow}x$ then $g(y) \leq g(x)$. Define

$$I = \{y \in S: g(y) \leq g(x)\}$$

By the same argument as above, I is a C-ideal, containing x, and hence $I \supseteq \text{C-}{\downarrow}x$.]

We now put these together to get presentations of frames.

Theorem 4.4.3 In the theory of frames, any presentation by generators and relations presents a frame.

Proof We modify the presentation in stages until it is in a form suitable for the application of Theorem 4.4.2.

First, rewrite the relations in equational form $e_1 = e_2$, where each expression e_i is a join of finite meets of generators.

Second, for each relation $e_1 = e_2$ introduce a new generator x and replace the relation by $e_1 = x$ and $e_2 = x$.

Third, present a semilattice S as follows: its generators are those of the frame, and for each frame relation $\bigvee_i \bigwedge_j y_{ij} = x$ it has relations $\bigwedge_j y_{ij} \leq x$.

Fourth, generate a coverage C on S from the cover relations $\{\bigwedge_j y_{ij}\} \dashv x$ and take the frame C-Idl(S).

Now it is not hard to see that frame homomorphisms from C-Idl (S) to a frame A correspond to semilattice homomorphisms from S to A that transforms covers in C to joins, and that these correspond to functions from the generators to A that validate all the equations. This shows that C-Idl (S) is the frame we wished to present.   ]

Proposition 4.4.4 Let A be a frame. Then A has a presentation.
Proof For each element a of A, let there be a generator a'. Take as relations

   true = true'
   a'∧b' = (a∧b)'   (a, b ∈ A)
   $\bigvee_S$ (a': a ∈ S) = ($\bigvee$ S)'   (S ⊆ A)   ]

Notes
Generators and relations are nowadays a standard method in algebra, as well as being related to the axiomatic methods of logic. Johnstone [82] (Notes on chapter II) discusses the history of their application to frames; he himself introduced the method of coverages that we describe.

Actually, the coverage theorem is not necessary to justify the use of generators and relations. Once we know that free frame generated by the generators exists, the standard theory of congruences shows how to force the relations. A more particular role is described in Abramsky and Vickers [90]: the coverage theorem allows us to present frames as complete join semilattices (sup-lattices).

Technically, what makes universal algebra go wrong for complete Boolean algebras is that there is no free complete Boolean algebra on a countably infinite set of generators. This yields important counterexamples. For instance, one can deduce that for the free frame A on a countably infinite set of generators (which does exist) there is a proper class of non-isomorphic frame epimorphisms from A (the category of frames is not "co-well-powered"). Both these are proved in Johnstone [82]. Also, there can be no free cHa on a countably infinite set of generators: for if there were one, then the free complete Boolean algebra could be constructed as a quotient. This puts cHa's in stark contrast with frames, even though they are the same objects.

Exercises
1. Show that lattices can be described as algebras for a theory with four operators for binary and nullary meets and joins, the semilattice laws of Proposition 4.1.2 for both meets and joins, and the

absorptive laws: $x \wedge (x \vee y) = x$, $x \vee (x \wedge y) = x$

Clearly, distributive lattices are described using an extra algebraic law, distributivity.

2. The free semilattice on a set U is $\wp_{fin} U$, the set of all finite subsets of U, under the superset ordering: $X \leq Y$ iff $X \supseteq Y$.

3.   Show that Heyting algebras are described using the operators and laws for lattices, together with an extra operator $\rightarrow$ and laws

$$a \wedge (a \rightarrow b) = a \wedge b$$
$$c = c \wedge (a \rightarrow ((a \wedge c) \vee b))$$

From Exercise 7 of Chapter 3 Heyting algebras are distributive; prove this directly from the algebraic laws.

4. Consider the following two presentations of $\Omega 2^{*\omega}$ (see Section 3.7):

$A = Fr \langle$ 's_n=0', 's_n=1' : $n \in \mathbf{N}, n \geq 1$ |
    's_n=0' $\wedge$ 's_n=1'   =   **false**,
    's_{n+1}=0' $\vee$ 's_{n+1}=1' $\leq$ 's_n=0' $\vee$ 's_n=1' $\rangle$,

and

$B = Fr \langle$ **starts** l : l a finite list of bits |
    starts l $\leq$ **starts** m   if l $\sqsupseteq$ m
    starts l $\wedge$ **starts** m = **false**   if neither l nor m prefixes the other $\rangle$

Just using Definition 4.3.4, construct mutually inverse isomorphisms between A and B.

5. Let P be a poset, ordered by $\sqsubseteq$. Show that its Alexandrov topology can be presented as

$Fr \langle \uparrow x : x \in P$ |
    true $= \bigvee \{\uparrow x : x \in P\}$
    $\uparrow x \wedge \uparrow y = \bigvee \{\uparrow z : z \in P, z \sqsupseteq x, z \sqsupseteq y\} \rangle$

Hint: use 4.3.4 to define a homomorphism from the presented frame to the Alexandrov topology, and show that it is one-one and onto. Be careful to treat the generators $\uparrow x$ as formal symbols.

CHAPTER FIVE

TOPOLOGY: THE DEFINITIONS

In which we introduce Topological Systems, *subsuming topological spaces and locales.*

5.1 Topological systems

We have seen frames, as systems of finite observations, but with no formalization of what they might be observations of. We now remedy this. The notion that we define here is not a standard one, but it summarizes our approach and gives a convenient framework for discussing the traditional ideas.

Definition 5.1.1 Let A be a frame; we call its elements *opens*. Let X be a set; we call its elements *points*. Finally, let $\vDash$ be a subset of X×A. If $(x, a) \in \vDash$ then we write $x \vDash a$, and say x *satisfies* a.

   X and A, equipped with $\vDash$, form a *topological system* iff $\vDash$ matches the logic of finite observations. Formally,

- If S is a finite subset of A, then

$$x \vDash \bigwedge S \Leftrightarrow x \vDash a \text{ for all } a \in S$$

- If S is any subset of A, then

$$x \vDash \bigvee S \Leftrightarrow x \vDash a \text{ for some } a \in S$$

If $D = (X, A)$ is a topological system, then we write pt D for X, and ΩD for A:

$$D = (X, A) = (\text{pt } D, \Omega D)$$

We might also think of the points and opens as being *subjects* and *predicates*.
   It is easy to deduce that –

- $x \vDash$ **true** for all x
- $x \vDash$ **false** for no x
- if $x \vDash a \leq b$ then $x \vDash b$

Example 5.1.2 $X = $ some set of streams, $A = \Omega 2^{*\omega}$.

   $x \vDash$ **starts** l   iff the first few bits of the stream x are those specified in the list l.
   $x \vDash \bigvee_{l \in L}$ **starts** l   iff $x \vDash$ **starts** l for some $l \in L$.

Example 5.1.3 More concretely, with the same frame A, we can take X to be the set of programs in some language that generate streams. The program in the box here generates an infinite sequence 01010101..., so for example

```
while true do
    output 0;
    output 1
od
```
⊨ **starts** 01010

It is worth trying to think of this not as an abstract, set theoretic relation, but as a concrete sequence of actions. It says somebody has

1.   Typed the program in at a given computer,
2.   Pressed the GO button,
3.   Observed the initial output 01010.

Thus the opens are finite run-time observations. The computer is a black box referred to in the definition of ⊨.

However, if we have additional information, such as that the computer has been loaded with suitable interpreter, we can analyse the program and make predictions about it without actually running it (this is what we're doing here, of course). In fact, we can make more powerful predictions than just the finite run-time observations. A question of interest in computer science is how we can relate these two logics: the programmer's analytic logic and the customer's run-time observations.

The points here contain more information than can be observed through the frame A. For instance, the two programs

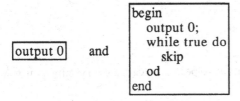

satisfy exactly the same opens. Each outputs a 0 and no more. However, whereas the left-hand program would normally also notify the user that it had finished, the right-hand one goes quietly into an infinite, unproductive loop. They are indistinguishable *using the opens that we have described,* which don't include observations of termination.

Example 5.1.4 X = set of programs, as in Example 5.1.3, but this time take the bigger A of Section 3.7 ("bits are read independently") in which 's$_2$=0' $\neq$ ('s$_1$=0'$\wedge$'s$_2$=0')$\vee$('s$_1$=1'$\wedge$'s$_2$=0')

We can use this A, but we may not want to. It makes distinctions that can't be observed in practice.

Example 5.1.5 Again, X is the set of programs, but try for A the frame $\Omega2^\omega$ of Definition 3.7.6 in which "time is not important" –

's$_n$=0'$\vee$'s$_n$=1' = **true**

This is no good, because in effect it assumes that the programs all output infinitely many bits. Programs that don't will make satisfaction go wrong. For instance, the program here goes immediately into an infinite, unproductive loop.

$$\boxed{\begin{array}{l} \text{while true do} \\ \quad \text{skip} \\ \text{od} \end{array}} \quad \begin{array}{l} \models \textbf{true} \\ \nvDash \text{ 's}_n\text{=0'}\vee\text{'s}_n\text{=1'} \end{array}$$

Example 5.1.6 Let X be any set, and let A be any topology on X, with

x $\models$ a iff x $\in$ a

5.2 Continuous maps

Suppose that (X, A) and (Y, B) are two topological systems, and that f: X $\rightarrow$ Y is a *computable* function in some sense. We shan't analyse precisely what functions are computable, but just accept that someone has given us a black box that transforms X-points into Y-points. Consider the following scenario.

1.   We take an X-point;
2.   We put it through the black box;
3.   We get to affirm a B-open b.

This ought to be a finite observation on X-points, because everything in it was done finitely. Let us write it ϕ(b), with

x $\models$ ϕ(b) iff f(x) $\models$ b,

and expect it to be already in A. Therefore ϕ is a function from B to A. Now for all points x, and subsets S of A,

x $\models$ $\phi(\bigvee S)$ $\Leftrightarrow$ f(x) $\models$ $\bigvee S$ $\Leftrightarrow$ f(x) $\models$ b for some b $\in$ S

$\Leftrightarrow$ x $\models$ ϕ(b) for some b $\in$ S $\Leftrightarrow$ x $\models$ $\bigvee$ {ϕ(b): b $\in$ S}

and similarly, if S is finite,

$$x \vDash \phi(\bigwedge S) \Leftrightarrow x \vDash \bigwedge \{\phi(b): b \in S\}$$

This isn't conclusive, but it strongly suggests that ideally ϕ should be a frame homomorphism.

Definition 5.2.1 Let D and E be topological systems. A *continuous map* f from D to E (we write f: D $\to$ E) is a pair (pt f, Ωf) where

pt f: pt D $\to$ pt E   is a function,
Ωf: ΩE $\to$ ΩD   is a frame homomorphism, and
$x \vDash \Omega f (b) \Leftrightarrow$ pt f(x) $\vDash$ b

Note the reversal of direction:

$$\text{pt D} \xrightarrow{\text{pt f}} \text{pt E}$$

$$\Omega D \xleftarrow{\Omega f} \Omega E$$

The continuous map is taken as going in the direction of its *points* part.

It is often convenient to omit 'pt' or 'Ω', and determine which is meant by the argument: so if x is a point then f(x) means pt f(x), and if a is an open then f(a) means Ωf(a). This convention will be used with caution.

A fruitful idea in computing is that, although not all continuous maps are computable, they are a useful generalization. In particular, if we don't want to consider how a function is computed then it is useful just to know that it is continuous.

Example 5.2.2 Let the points be bit streams, and the opens be those of $\Omega 2^{*\omega}$. We can define functions by structural recursion. For instance a function to complement all the bits of the stream can be defined by

complement (b::s) = (if b=0 then 1 else 0 fi)::complement (s)

Here ::, analogous to the cons operator of LISP, constructs a new stream b::s by putting the bit b in front of the stream s. The definition is really designed for infinite bit streams, but let us abuse notation by applying the function complement to finite lists of bits. Now

$s \vDash \Omega$complement(**starts** l) $\Leftrightarrow$ complement(s) $\vDash$ **starts** l
    $\Leftrightarrow s \vDash$ **starts** complement(l)

Therefore,

Ωcomplement($\bigvee_{l \in L}$ **starts** l) = $\bigvee_{l \in L}$ **starts** complement(l)

We can actually check that this is well-defined: that

if $\bigvee_{l \in L}$ **starts** $l = \bigvee_{m \in M}$ **starts** m, then
$\bigvee_{l \in L}$ **starts** complement(l) = $\bigvee_{m \in M}$ **starts** complement(m)

However, in computational systems, domain theoretic semantics of programming languages usually assure us that any computer program automatically gives a continuous map.

Definition 5.2.3 Let D be a topological system. The *identity* map $\text{Id}_D: D \to D$ is defined by

$\text{pt Id}_D = \text{Id}_{\text{pt D}}: \text{pt D} \to \text{pt D}$
$\Omega \text{ Id}_D = \text{Id}_{\Omega D}: \Omega D \to \Omega D$

Let D, E and F be topological systems, and let f: $D \to E$ and g: $E \to F$ be continuous maps. The *composite* f;g (or g∘f): $D \to F$ is defined by

$\text{pt (f;g)} = \text{(pt f);(pt g)}: \text{pt D} \to \text{pt F}$
$\Omega \text{ (f;g)} = \text{(}\Omega g\text{);(}\Omega f\text{)}: \Omega F \to \Omega D$

It is easy to check that these are continuous maps, and also that composition is associative, and that Id is an identity for it. Categorically speaking, topological systems with continuous maps form a category.

For algebras we saw that it is sometimes useful to consider two algebras as being essentially the same if they are isomorphic. The corresponding notion for topological systems is that of being *homeomorphic;* in terms of the rubber sheet geometry, a homeomorphism is a transformation that may stretch the space, but doesn't tear or break it. It can therefore be completely undone.

Definition 5.2.4 A continuous map f: $D \to E$ is a *homeomorphism* iff there is a map g: $E \to D$ such that f;g = Id_D and g;f = Id_E (so g is also a homeomorphism).

When there is a homeomorphism from D to E, we say D and E are *homeomorphic* and write $D \cong E$.

This means that the systems are structurally equivalent:

- pt D and pt E are isomorphic sets (i.e. in bijective correspondence),
- ΩD and ΩE are isomorphic frames,
- ⊢ is the same for both, when the correspondences are taken into account.

BEWARE! The words *homeomorphism* and *homomorphism* are different.

5.3 Topological spaces

Proposition 5.3.1 Let X and Y be topological spaces. Then continuous maps from X to Y are equivalent to functions f: X → Y such that if V is open in Y (V ∈ ΩY) then f^{-1}(V) is open in X.

Proof Let f be a continuous map. Then pt f is the function. The condition

$$x \vDash \Omega f(V) \Leftrightarrow pt\ f(x) \vDash V$$

says precisely that Ωf(V) = (pt f)$^{-1}$(V), which must thus be open.

This also tells us that for topological spaces a continuous map is completely determined by its points part. If the points part f is given, then f^{-1} always preserves meets and joins, so that (f, f^{-1}) is a continuous map iff f^{-1} maps ΩY to ΩX.

Note that all we really need to make this proof work is for X to be a topological space.]

A topological space is (as in Definition 3.6.1) commonly thought of as set X "equipped with" its frame ΩX of open sets. This means that the same symbol X is used both for the unstructured set of points and for the topological space with its structure. When we think of a space as a topological system, we distinguish between the system X, and the set pt X of points. To regain the standard notation, omit "pt" wherever it occurs and rewrite Ωf as f^{-1}.

As a prime example, we look at the real line.

Theorem 5.3.2 *Continuity for real numbers*
Let f: ℝ → ℝ be a function. Then f is the points part of a continuous map from (ℝ, Ωℝ) to itself iff "the graph of f has no jumps".

Proof How can we formalize the idea of having "no jumps in a graph"? The mathematical answer, after some centuries of uncertainty, was to formalize it by continuity! Therefore, the proof here can only be intuitive. We concentrate on jumps at 0, and assume for definiteness that f(0) = 0. The same argument applies more generally.

Some jumps are really blatant, such as in

$$f(x) = \begin{cases} 0 & \text{if } x \leq 0 \\ 1 & \text{if } x > 0 \end{cases}$$

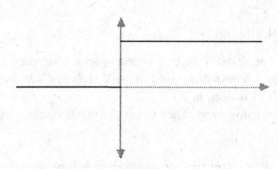

Others are more vacillatory, such as in

$$f(x) = \begin{cases} 0 & \text{if } x = 0 \\ \sin(1/x) & \text{if } x \neq 0 \end{cases}$$

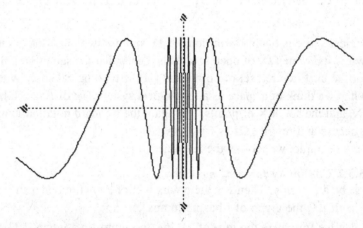

In both cases, however close x gets to 0, f(x) refuses to stay away from 1. There is thus a "jump" between 1 and f(0) = 0.

Suppose Ωf exists. Then – using the notation of Section 3.9 –

$\Omega f((0 \pm 1/2)) = \bigvee_i (q_i \pm \delta_i)$ for suitable q_i and δ_i

$f(0) = 0 \vDash (0 \pm 1/2)$

Therefore,

   $0 \vDash \Omega f((0 \pm 1/2))$, and
   $0 \vDash (q_i \pm \delta_i)$ for some i.

But some x in this region has f(x) close to 1: say

   $f(x) \vDash (1 \pm 1/2)$, and $x \vDash (q_i \pm \delta_i) \leq \Omega f((0 \pm 1/2))$

Therefore,

$$f(x) \vDash (0 \pm 1/2) \wedge (1 \pm 1/2) = \textbf{false}.$$

This is a contradiction, and so such a jump is impossible. More generally, if Ωf exists then there are no jumps.

For the converse, suppose that Ωf does not exist, so for some open U, $f^{-1}(U)$ is not open: it contains a boundary point x (say). $f(x) \in U$, so for some $\delta > 0$,

$$f(x) - \delta < y < f(x) + \delta \Rightarrow y \in U$$

x is a boundary point for $f^{-1}(U)$, so however closely we look at x, it has neighbouring points outside $f^{-1}(U)$. For such a point, w, say, $f(w) \notin U$, so either $f(w) \le f(x) - \delta$ or $f(w) \ge f(x) + \delta$.

Thus, "However close w gets to x, f(w) refuses to stay within δ of f(x)."

We can take this as a jump from $f(x) \pm \delta$ to f(x), so if Ωf doesn't exist then f has a jump. **]**

Spatialization

We stick with topological spaces if we take the view that there is no reason to distinguish between two opens when they're satisfied by exactly the same points. This is reasonable for fixed points like the real numbers, but perhaps it is less so when we're not quite sure what the points are, like the streams.

If we want to, we can always convert a topological system D into a topological space, by comparing opens entirely by the points that satisfy them.

Definition 5.3.3 For each open a, its *extent* in D is $\{x \in \text{pt } D: x \vDash a\}$.

By the definition of $\vDash$, joins and finite meets of opens correspond to unions and finite intersections of their extents. Hence the extents of opens form a topology $\Omega pt \, D$ on pt D. (Note that $\Omega pt \, D$ depends on ΩD as well as pt D, although we have suppressed this fact from the notation.)

Theorem 5.3.4

(i)   (pt D, $\Omega pt \, D$) is a topological space, the *spatialization* Spat D of D.

(ii)   There is a natural continuous map e: Spat D $\to$ D defined by

$$\text{pt } e(x) = x \qquad\qquad \Omega e(a) = \text{extent of a in D}$$

(iii)   Any other continuous map from a topological space into D factors uniquely
        via e:

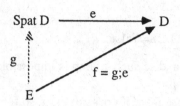

Proof (i) and (ii) are clear.

(iii) characterizes spatialization up to homeomorphism by a universal property, just as we had for presentations by generators and relations.

If g exists, then it must have pt g(y) = pt e(pt g(y)) = pt f(y). Thus the points part is uniquely defined, and because we are dealing with spaces, the opens part is also uniquely defined, as g^{-1}. Now if $U \in \Omega$pt D, say $U = \Omega$e(a), then $g^{-1}(U) = \Omega$f(a) is open in E, so g is continuous.   ]

It is often more helpful to know not that a topological system *is* a topological space, but that it is homeomorphic to one. We say that such a system is *spatial*.

Proposition 5.3.5 The following are equivalent for a topological system D:

(i)   D is spatial

(ii) $\forall a, b \in \Omega D. ((\forall x \in \text{pt } D. x \vDash a \leftrightarrow x \vDash b) \rightarrow a = b)$

(iii) $\forall a, b \in \Omega D. ((\forall x \in \text{pt } D. x \vDash a \rightarrow x \vDash b) \rightarrow a \leq b)$

Proof (iii) $\Rightarrow$ (ii) is easy; for (ii) $\Rightarrow$ (iii), if for all points x we have x $\vDash$ a $\Rightarrow$ x $\vDash$ b, then for all points x we have x $\vDash$ a∧b $\leftrightarrow$ x $\vDash$ a, and hence by (ii) a∧b = a and a $\leq$ b.

(ii) $\Rightarrow$ (i):   (ii) says precisely that if two opens have the same extent, then they're equal, i.e. that Ωe is 1-1. We know anyway that Ωe is onto, so (ii) says that Ωe is a frame isomorphism, i.e. e is a homeomorphism, and hence D is spatial.

(i) $\Rightarrow$ (ii):   If f is a homeomorphism from a space E to D, then we can use the diagram of Theorem 5.3.4 (iii). Ωf = Ωe;Ωg is 1-1, so Ωe is also 1-1, i.e. (ii) holds.]

Categorically, the functor Spat: **Topological Systems** → **Topological Spaces** is right adjoint to the forgetful functor.

5.4 Locales

Just as in spatialization we thought of an open as being a set of points, in other words a function (the characteristic function of the set) from the points to 2, we can also think of a point as being a function from the opens to **2**:

$$x(a) \text{ (i.e. "} x \vDash a \text{ treated as a Boolean value")} = \begin{cases} \textbf{true} & \text{if } x \vDash a \\ \textbf{false} & \text{otherwise} \end{cases}$$

The axioms for $\vDash$ say precisely that each x, treated as a function, is actually a frame homomorphism from the opens to **2**.

Definition 5.4.1 Let A be a frame. The *locale* corresponding to A is the topological system D defined by

$\Omega D = A$
$\text{pt } D = \{\text{frame homomorphisms } x\colon A \to \textbf{2}\}$
$x \vDash a \quad \text{iff } x(a) = \textbf{true}$

By abuse of language, we shall sometimes refer to "the locale A" rather than inventing a new symbol D.

A topological system is *localic* iff it is homeomorphic to a locale.

Proposition 5.4.2 Let D and E be locales. Then continuous maps from D to E are equivalent to frame homomorphisms from ΩE to ΩD (note the reversal of direction).

Proof Given such a frame homomorphism Ωf, pt f must be defined by

$$\text{pt } f(x)(b) = \textbf{true} \Leftrightarrow \text{pt } f(x) \vDash b \Leftrightarrow x \vDash \Omega f(b) \Leftrightarrow x \circ \Omega f(b) = \textbf{true}$$

Hence pt $f(x) = x \circ \Omega f$, and this does in fact pair with Ωf to give a continuous map.

   ]

Locales and continuous maps between them are thus determined precisely by their frames and frame homomorphisms between them, except that continuous maps and frame homomorphisms go in *opposite directions*. In fact, the usual definition says that a locale *is* a frame, which means that the same symbol A is used both for a locale and for its frame (our ΩA) of its opens. A continuous map between locales is usually defined simply as a frame homomorphism in the opposite direction, but with a notational distinction to avoid confusion. If f: A → B is a continuous map between locales, then Johnstone writes f*: B → A for the corresponding frame homomorphism, our $\Omega f\colon \Omega B \to \Omega A$.

True locale theory is a rather clever trick. Frames are not equivalent to topological spaces, but the language of locales makes them appear to be so and turns theorems about spaces into conjectures about frames. Often enough, these conjectures turn out to be true, but as a rule of thumb, this is more likely if one can avoid mentioning points (categorically speaking, global elements are in general not enough) – thus one tries to do "pointless topology".

Our formulation of locales, with its explicit mention of the points, is counter to the spirit of pointlessness. However, it puts both locales and topological spaces into a common framework, and this seems to have pedagogical virtues. Even more important to us is its use in domain theory. Here we alternate between spatial and logical reasoning (see the next Section), so it is never clear whether a domain ought best to be a space or a locale. Our answer is to make them spatial, localic topological systems.

Categorically speaking, the category of locales is opposite to the category of frames.

Our terminology is equivalent to that of Johnstone. Some authors, following Joyal and Tierney [84], call our frames *locales,* and our locales *spaces.*

Localification

Spatialization reduced opens to open sets, and correspondingly, localification reduces points to points of locales.

Theorem 5.4.3 Let D be a topological system. Then –

(i)   Its *localification* is the locale Loc D corresponding to the frame ΩD (i.e., in the usual language, it *is* the locale ΩD).

(ii)   There is a natural continuous map, the localification map, p: D $\rightarrow$ Loc D defined by

$$\text{pt } p(x)(a) = \textbf{true} \quad \text{iff} \quad x \vDash a, \qquad\qquad \Omega p(a) = a$$

(iii)   Any other continuous map from D to a locale E factors uniquely via p:

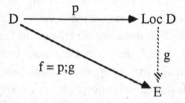

Proof As for spatialization, we just prove (iii), the universal characterization of localification.

Ωg has to be defined by $\Omega g(b) = \Omega p(\Omega g(b)) = \Omega f(b)$. This is a frame homomorphism, and hence defines a unique continuous map between the locales.]

Categorically, the functor Loc: **Topological Systems** $\rightarrow$ **Locales** is left adjoint to the forgetful functor.

In localifying D, p gives each "concrete point", in pt D, a value as an "abstract point", in pt Loc D.

Example 5.4.4 We have already defined the frame $\Omega 2^{*\omega}$; let us write $2^{*\omega}$ for the corresponding locale, and find its points pt $2^{*\omega}$. A point x is determined by its values on the basic observations **starts** l, so it suffices to find

$$S = \{ \text{ l: } x \vDash \textbf{starts } l \}$$

If l, m are both in S, then $x \vDash \textbf{starts } l \wedge \textbf{starts } m = \textbf{false}$, unless one of l and m is a prefix of the other. Therefore S is linearly ordered by the prefix ordering. There are now two cases.

1.   S may have a longest element l. Then the rest are all the prefixes of l.
2.   S may have no longest element: it has arbitrarily long lists. But then they build up into an infinite list (remember that we only use finite lists in the predicates **starts** l).

A point therefore can be thought of as a sequence s of bits, with

$$s \vDash \bigvee\nolimits_{l \in L} \textbf{starts } l \text{ iff some } l \in L \text{ is a prefix of s}$$

s may be either an infinite sequence (a complete bit-stream, an element of 2^ω) or a finite one (a partial or incomplete bit-stream, an element of 2^*).

We call this locale the *Kahn domain* $2^{*\omega}$ on the set $2 = \{0, 1\}$ of bits. We may similarly define the Kahn domain $X^{*\omega}$ on any set X of symbols.

The points of $2^{*\omega}$ are *abstract streams*. A different locale A may have different points, and hence a different notion of abstract streams. For instance, the locale 2^ω corresponding to the frame $\Omega 2^\omega$ has for its points the complete, infinite streams only [exercise].

If we have any topological system with the same frame $\Omega 2^{*\omega}$ of opens, for example the one whose points are the programs that produce streams, then its points can be thought of as *concrete streams*. The localification map forgets the concrete details of how the streams are produced. It gives each concrete stream an abstract meaning: this is a simple case of *denotational semantics*. The more elaborate denotational semantics that is used for proper programming languages seeks its abstract meanings in *domains,* which are in effect locales.

Different ways of describing points of locales

If A is a frame, we have defined a point x of its locale as a frame homomorphism from A to **2**. Clearly, this is equally well described by its

true-kernel, $\{a: x(a) = \textbf{true}\}$,

or its

false-kernel, {a: x(a) = **false**}.

We therefore ask what subsets of A are **true**-kernels or **false**-kernels of points.

Definition 5.4.5 Let A be a frame and let $F \subseteq A$ be upper closed.

(i)   F is a *filter* iff it is closed under finite meets:

> if $S \subseteq F$, S finite, then $\bigwedge S \in F$

Note the case when $S = \emptyset$, which guarantees that **true** $\in$ F.

(ii)   A filter F is *prime* iff it is "inaccessible by finite joins" –

> if $S \subseteq A$, S finite, and $\bigvee S \in F$, then $s \in F$ for some $s \in S$ (*)

Note the case $S = \emptyset$, which guarantees that **false** $\notin$ F, and hence that F is a *proper* filter (one not equal to the whole of A).

(iii) A filter F is *completely prime* iff it is "inaccessible by joins", i.e. (*) holds without restricting S to be finite.

(iv)   An element $p \in A$ is *prime* iff –

> if $S \subseteq A$, S finite, and $\bigwedge S \leq p$, then $s \leq p$ for some $s \in S$

Note the case $S = \emptyset$, which guarantees that $p \neq$ **true**.

Lemma 5.4.6 Let A be a frame, and let F, $I \subseteq A$.

(i)   F is the **true**-kernel of a point of the locale of A iff F is a completely prime filter.

(ii)   I is the **false**-kernel of a point of the locale of A iff $I = \downarrow p$ for some prime element p of A.]

Proposition 5.4.7 There are three ways of describing points of a locale D:

(i)   as frame homomorphisms from ΩD to **2**;

(ii)   as completely prime filters of ΩD;

(iii) as prime elements of ΩD.   ]

It is also useful to look at the case where ΩD is presented by generators and relations. The universal characterization of presentations shows that a point of D is equivalent to a function from the generators to **2** (i.e. a subset of the generators) that makes all the relations hold. These are often quite easy to describe in more concrete terms.

5.5 Spatial locales or sober spaces

We know that a continuous map between spatial topological systems is completely determined by its function part; while a continuous map between localic topological systems is completely determined by its frame part. Therefore if the systems are both spatial and localic, there is a complete duality ("duality" implies the order reversal) between the continuous functions and the frame homomorphisms.

Categorically speaking, we have functors

Loc: **Topological spaces → Locales**

Spat: **Locales → Topological spaces**

and localification is left adjoint to spatialization. This restricts to an equivalence between localic spaces and spatial locales, or a duality between localic spaces and the frames whose locales are spatial.

The point of this is that we move freely between two rather different ways of reasoning.

On the points side, arguments are set theoretic with some extra notions for topology. For instance if U and V are open sets, then we show $U \subseteq V$ by showing that if x is a point in U then it's also in V.

On the frame side, arguments are logical or algebraic. To show that $U \leq V$ in a frame, we show that it follows from the relations with which we present the frame. Thinking of the relations as logical axioms, this amounts to a logical proof that U entails V.

Clearly, the theories of spatial, localic, topological systems, of spatial locales and of localic topological spaces are all equivalent. However, they give rather different viewpoints.

In locale theory, we can think of the axioms and algebra as giving the syntax of a frame, and the points as giving the semantics (each point is a model).

The syntax is automatically sound (if $U \leq V$ then extent(U) $\subseteq$ extent(V)), but completeness is equivalent to spatiality (if extent(U) $\subseteq$ extent(V) then $U \leq V$). Therefore,

A proof of spatiality of a locale shows completeness of a logical system.

Topology gives us a rather more obscure viewpoint (which shows the benefits of locale theory). A topological space X is localic iff the localification map p from X to Loc X is a homeomorphism, in other words iff each abstract point (of Loc X) comes from a unique concrete point (of X). Using Proposition 5.4.7, this says that for each prime open set $q \in \Omega X$ there is a unique point $x \in pt\ X$ such that

$$x \vDash a \Leftrightarrow a \nleq q$$

for all open sets a. This is usually expressed in terms of closed sets.

Definition 5.5.1 Let X be a topological space.

A closed set $F \subseteq$ pt X is *irreducible* iff it is the complement of a prime open set, i.e. if whenever G_i $(1 \le i \le n)$ are closed sets with $F \subseteq \bigcup_i G_i$, then $F \subseteq G_i$ for some i.

If F is a closed set and $x \in$ pt X, then x is a *generic point* for F iff $F = Cl\{x\}$,

i.e.   for all closed sets G, $x \in G \Leftrightarrow F \subseteq G$,

i.e.   for all open sets U, $x \in U \Leftrightarrow U \cap F \ne \emptyset$,

i.e. $x \vDash a \Leftrightarrow a \le F^c$,

i.e.   the locale point pt p(x) corresponds to the prime open set F^c.

X is *sober* iff every irreducible closed set has a unique generic point.

Our discussion shows that for a topological space, sober and localic mean the same. Localification of a space is usually called *soberification*.

Sobriety, as a property of topological spaces, is not very illuminating. If you are making essential use of sobriety, it shows that you probably ought to be thinking in terms of locales.

Mainstream topology avoids this by using an even stronger property, the Hausdorff separation axiom, that is well tailored to spatiality – in fact it is difficult to formulate it in purely localic terms. This course is not open to us, because we want to deal with spaces that are sober, but definitely not Hausdorff. However, Hausdorff spaces are still worth looking at.

Definition 5.5.2 A topological space X is *Hausdorff*, or T_2, iff for any two distinct points x and y, there are open sets U and V with $x \in U$, $y \in V$ and $U \cap V = \emptyset$.

Example – the real line, or indeed any metric space (exercise). Hence a non-Hausdorff topology cannot arise from a metric.

Proposition 5.5.3 Hausdorff spaces are sober.

Proof Let q be a prime open set. $q \ne$ **true**, so, by spatiality, there is at least one point not in q. Suppose there are more, say x and y. Choose disjoint open sets U and V containing them. Then $U \cap V \subseteq q$, but neither U nor V is contained in q, contradicting primeness. Therefore there is a unique point x not satisfying q. Using spatiality again, $a \le q \Leftrightarrow x \nvDash a$, so pt p(x) is the locale point corresponding to q.]

In a topological system that is both spatial and localic, we can argue either on the points side or the frame side, whichever is most convenient for us, and with completely equivalent effect. We shall see this in action in the chapter on domain theory.

It is helpful to know that spatial locales / sober spaces can easily be obtained either by localifying spaces or spatializing locales. We know already, of course, that you don't change a space when you spatialize it, nor a locale when you localify it.

Proposition 5.5.4

(i)   If X is a topological space, then Loc X is spatial (and localic).

(ii)   If D is a locale, then Spat D is localic (and spatial).

Proof (i) If two opens are different then they are distinguishable using the concrete points of X, and so they are distinguishable using the abstract points of Loc X.

(ii) We have continuous maps e: Spat D $\to$ D and p: Spat D $\to$ Loc Spat D. Since D is localic, and by part (i) Loc Spat D is spatial, we can use the universal properties of Loc and Spat (Theorems 5.4.3 (iii) and 5.3.4 (iii)) to get maps

   f: Loc Spat D $\to$ D,   g: Loc Spat D $\to$ Spat D

such that e = p;f and f = g;e. Hence p;g;e = e, and by the universal properties again p;g = $Id_{Spat\ D}$, p;g;p = p, and g;p = $Id_{Loc\ Spat\ D}$. Hence Spat D is homeomorphic to the locale Loc Spat D.   ]

5.6 Summary

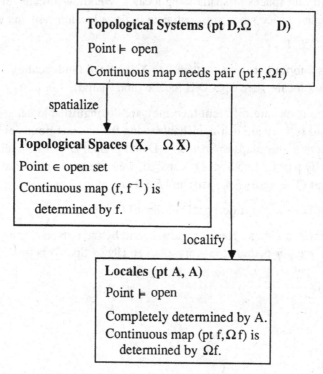

We are also in a position now to state three equivalent ways of describing a topological system, given a set X and a frame A:

- With ⊨ as in the definition;
- By a frame homomorphism from A to ℘X;
- By a function from X to the locale points of A.

Notes

The "topological systems" described in this section are new. My justification for introducing them is, first, that it seems pedagogically useful to have a single framework in which to treat both spaces and locales and, second, that with domains – which are both spaces and locales – it is useful not to have commit oneself to making them concretely either one or the other.

Although the results are new in the sense that they use topological systems, they are essentially no more than rephrasings of the established connections between spaces and locales, as described in Johnstone [82].

Exercises

1. For the continuous map

   complement: $2^{*\omega} \to 2^{*\omega}$

of Example 5.2.2, define Ωcomplement by applying the universal property of presentations (Definition 4.3.4) to those in Exercise 4 of Chapter 4.

2. The locale $2^{*\omega}$ is spatial.

3. Given a continuous map f: $D \to E$, use the universal properties of Spat and Loc to define maps

   Spat f: Spat D $\to$ Spat E,   Loc f: Loc D $\to$ Loc E

such that e;f = (Spat f);e and p;Loc f = f;p. Show that Spat and Loc are *functorial*, i.e. (for Spat) Spat Id_D = $Id_{Spat\ D}$ and, given g: $E \to F$, Spat(f;g) = Spat f;Spat g.

4. Define the following topological systems and continuous maps:

$(1, \mathbf{2})$	is the discrete topology on a single point
$(\emptyset, \mathbf{2})$	has the same opens but no points
$\alpha: (\emptyset, \mathbf{2}) \to (1, \mathbf{2})$	is the unique continuous map
$(2, \mathbf{3})$	is the locale with three opens, linearly ordered
$(2, \mathbf{2})$	has the same points, with the indiscrete topology
$\beta: (2, \mathbf{3}) \to (2, \mathbf{2})$	is the identity on points

   Various parts of an arbitrary topological system D can be described as continuous maps.

   (i)   Points of D are equivalent to continuous maps from $(1, \mathbf{2})$ to D.
   (ii)   Points of Loc D are equivalent to continuous maps from $(\emptyset, \mathbf{2})$ to D.
   (iii)   D is localic iff every continuous map from $(\emptyset, \mathbf{2})$ to D factors uniquely via α.
   (iv)   Opens of D are equivalent to continuous maps from D to $(2, \mathbf{3})$.
   (v)   D is spatial iff each continuous map from D to $(2, \mathbf{2})$ factors in at most one way via β.

5. (Truly pointless topology.) Show that locales and continuous maps between them correspond 1-1 with topological systems with empty point sets, and continuous maps between them.

CHAPTER SIX

NEW TOPOLOGIES FOR OLD

In which we see some ways of constructing topological systems, and some ways of specifying what they construct.

Given some topological systems already constructed, we are now going to look at how we might construct subsystems, and also sums (disjoint unions) and products. On the points side, the process is usually obvious, but we still need to find a counterpart on the frame side. Two ideas are going to be useful. First, we can use "universal properties" (category theory) to state *what* we are constructing, without going into the details of *how* it is done (like the relation between a specification and a computer program). Second, presentations by generators and relations enable us to define the frames in a painless way, and they are often easy to relate to the universal properties.

6.1 Subsystems

Suppose D is a topological system, and $Y \subseteq$ pt D. Then trivially, we can make a topological system $D' = (Y, \Omega D)$ with the same $\vDash$ (restricted to Y).

Now if D is spatial, there is no reason why D' should be too – consider, for example, when $Y = \emptyset$. Therefore in topology we should want to replace D' by its spatialization, given by mapping each $U \in \Omega D$ to its extent $U \cap Y$ in Y.

Definition 6.1.1 Let D be a topological space, and $Y \subseteq$ pt D.
$\{U \cap Y : U \in \Omega D\}$ is the *subspace topology* on Y. It is the finest topology on Y such that the inclusion function $Y \to$ pt D is continuous.

More generally, we shall be interested in situations where a space D' is not an actual subspace of D, but homeomorphic to one. The composite map from D' to D via the subspace is then called an *embedding,* and it is easy to show that a continuous map i: $D' \to D$ between topological spaces is an embedding iff pt i is injective and Ωi is surjective.

Note that for locales D and E, if i: $E \to D$ has Ωi surjective, then pt i is automatically injective. For let y and y' be two points of E such that $i(y) = i(y')$. If $b \in \Omega E$, then $b = \Omega i(a)$ for some a, so

$$y(b) = y \circ \Omega i(a) = \text{pt } i(y)(a) = \text{pt } i(y')(a) = y' \circ \Omega i(a) = y'(b)$$

Therefore $y = y'$.

Definition 6.1.2 A continuous map i is an *embedding* iff pt i is injective and Ωi is surjective.

6.2 Sublocales

The results of this section are not used in the rest of the book, so it could be omitted on first reading.

For an embedding of spaces there is a canonical representative of the class of homeomorphic embeddings, namely the subspace. Can we find a similar canonical representative for homeomorphism classes of locale embeddings? Such a thing would be a *sublocale*. We therefore look at various ways of elucidating the structure of a frame homomorphic surjection f: A $\rightarrow$ B (so B is a *frame homomorphic image* of A).

We shall also want to consider order amongst sublocales. Our reference point is: if a locale C embeds in a locale B, then C should be considered a smaller locale than B.

There is, quite generally, a categorical preorder on homomorphic images:

Definition 6.2.1 Let f: A $\rightarrow$ B and g: A $\rightarrow$ C be two surjective homomorphisms. Then we write f $\leq$ g iff there is some [necessarily unique] h: B $\rightarrow$ C such that f;h = g. This is a preorder.

Categorically, this preorder can be defined on *epimorphisms* with domain A, which may be different from surjective homomorphisms (see Exercise 2).

The h in the definition is the frame surjection needed to embed the locale C in the locale B, so if f $\leq$ g then f corresponds to a bigger sublocale.

Extra relations
First, we can see B as being made out of A by imposing extra relations.

Proposition 6.2.2 Let A and B be two frames, with A = Fr $\langle$ G | R $\rangle$. Then B is a frame homomorphic image of A iff B can be presented as

$$B = Fr \langle G | R' \rangle$$

with R $\subseteq$ R'.
Proof $\Leftarrow$: B is a model for the presentation Fr $\langle$ G | R $\rangle$, and so there is a homomorphism f: A $\rightarrow$ B, defined by f(g$_A$) = g$_B$. B is generated by its elements g$_B$ and so must be equal to the image of f, which is a subframe.
$\Rightarrow$: Let f: A $\rightarrow$ B be a surjective frame homomorphism, and define R' to be the set of equations e = e' such that f([e]$_A$) = f([e']$_A$). Let B' = Fr $\langle$ G | R' $\rangle$. R $\subseteq$ R', and so by the first part we get a homomorphism θ: A $\rightarrow$ B'. If we interpret the

generators in B by $g_B = f(g_A)$, then B is a model for both presentations, and so we
get a homomorphism f': B' → B with θ;f' = f.

On the other hand, we can define a homomorphism g: B → B' as follows. If b
∈ B, then b = f(a) for some a, so b = f([e]$_A$) for some expression e. Define g(b) =
[e]$_{B'}$. By definition of R', this is independent of choice of e, and so g is well-
defined. By some routine checking, or a standard piece of universal algebra, g is a
homomorphism, and g and f are mutually inverse and hence isomorphisms.]

If R' is extended to R", with corresponding surjections f: A → B and g: A → C,
then it is easy to see that f ≤ g. The converse, showing that R' ⊆ R", holds if that
R' and R" are the complete sets of relations defined in the ⇒ part of the proof.

Congruences

Up to isomorphism, B is defined entirely by the *congruence* ≡ on A that has a ≡ a'
iff f(a) = f(a'). Universal algebra gives a general account of these. A congruence on
an algebra A is a subset ≡ of A×A that is both an equivalence relation and a sub-
algebra of A×A, and then the set A/≡ of equivalence classes can be made into an
algebra, a homomorphic image of A.

It is easy to see that if surjections f and f' have congruences ≡ and ≡', then

$$f \leq f' \quad \text{iff} \quad \equiv \subseteq \equiv'$$

Congruence preorders

For algebras, like frames, whose algebraic structure is determined by a partial
order, it is often more useful to consider the preorder ≲ on A defined by

$$a \leq b \quad \text{iff} \quad f(a) \leq f(b)$$

Let us call this a *congruence preorder*.

Proposition 6.2.3 Let A be a frame. A subset ≲ of A×A is a frame congruence
preorder iff

(i)   if a' ≤ a ≲ b ≤ b' then   a' ≲ b'
(ii)   if a ≲ b for all a ∈ S (S ⊆ A) then ∨S ≲ b
(iii)   if a ≲ b for all b ∈ S (S ⊆ A, S finite) then a ≲ ∧S
(iv)   if a ≲ b and b ≲ c then a ≲ c
(v)   a ≲ a

Inclusion of congruences corresponds to inclusion of congruence preorders.
Proof ⇒: If ≲ is the congruence preorder corresponding to f: A → A/≡, then (i) –
(v) follow by considering properties of ≤ in B.

⇐: Define ≡ by

$$a \equiv b \quad \text{iff} \quad a \leq b \text{ and } b \leq a$$

This is a congruence, and ≤ is the corresponding congruence preorder.
The final part is easy.　]

C-ideals

From 6.2.3 (i), we see that ≤ is a lower closed subset of A×Aᵒᴾ. We next show that it is actually a C-ideal for an appropriate coverage C. To avoid confusion, we write aᵒᴾ for the element of Aᵒᴾ corresponding to a ∈ A. C contains the following cover relations:

(i) $\{(a, b^{op}): a \in S\} \dashv (\bigvee S, b^{op})$ (S ⊆ A)

(ii) $\{(a, b^{op}): b \in S\} \dashv (a, (\bigwedge S)^{op})$ (S ⊆ A, S finite)

(iii) $\emptyset \dashv (a, b^{op})$ (a, b ∈ A, a ≤ b)

(iv) $\{(a, (b \vee c)^{op}), (a \wedge b, c^{op})\} \dashv (a, c^{op})$ (a, b, c ∈ A)

Propositions 6.2.4 The congruence preorders of A are the C-ideals of A×Aᵒᴾ.
Proof First, one should check that C actually is a coverage.

Next, let ≤ be a congruence preorder. We have already remarked that it is lower closed; we also want it to be closed under cover relations: if U ⊣ (a, bᵒᴾ) is in C, and u ≤ v for all (u, vᵒᴾ) in U, then a ≤ b. For relations of the form (i), (ii) or (iii) it follows from Proposition 6.2.3, (ii), (iii), or (i) and (v). For a relation (iv), suppose a ≤ b∨c and a∧b ≤ c. Then

$$a \equiv a \wedge (b \vee c) = (a \wedge b) \vee (a \wedge c) \leq c$$

Finally, let I be a C-ideal. Clauses (i), (ii), (iii) and (v) in Proposition 6.2.3 follow from lower closure and consideration of relations of the form (i), (ii) and (iii). For clause (iv), suppose (a, bᵒᴾ), (b, cᵒᴾ) ∈ I. By lower closure, (a, (b∨c)ᵒᴾ) and (a∧b, cᵒᴾ) ∈ I, and we can now apply closure under a cover relation (iv).　]

Corollary 6.2.5 The homeomorphism classes of frame homomorphic images of A form a frame.
Proof Use Theorem 4.4.2.　]

Nuclei

For frames, each congruence class has a canonical representative, namely its join. We now investigate the function that takes each frame element a to this join: define

$$va = \bigvee \{a': f(a') = f(a)\}$$

v is called the *nucleus* of f. Then f(va) = f(a), and in fact f(a') = f(a) iff va = va'; so up to isomorphism a frame surjection is determined by its nucleus.

Proposition 6.2.6 We order nuclei pointwise, i.e. $v \leq v'$ iff $va \leq v'a$ for all a.
   Let surjections f and f' have nuclei v and v'. Then $f \leq f'$ iff $v \leq v'$.
Proof $f \leq f'$ means that for all a and b in A, if f(a) = f(b) then f'(a) = f'(b), i.e. for all a, f'(a) = f'(va), i.e. for all a, v'va = v'a, i.e. for all a, $va \leq v'a$.   ]

Theorem 6.2.7 Let A be a frame. A function $v: A \to A$ is the nucleus of a frame homomorphic surjection from A iff for all a and b in A,

- $a \leq va = v^2 a$
- $v(a \wedge b) = va \wedge vb$

Proof Clearly nuclei do satisfy these conditions; our goal is to show that all such functions are nuclei.
   We can present A using a semilattice (A itself) and a coverage $(X \dashv \bigvee X$ for each $X \subseteq A)$. A homomorphic image of A, with nucleus v, can presented using the same presentation together with extra cover relations to say that $\{a\} \dashv va$. Given v, we thus define the appropriate coverage and show that this presents a homomorphic image with nucleus v. Our site has –

- semilattice A
- cover relations $X \dashv \bigvee X$ for each $X \subseteq A$
- cover relations $\{a\} \dashv b$ whenever $a \leq b \leq va$

Lemma 6.2.7.1 These cover relations already form a coverage, C (say).
Proof If $X \dashv \bigvee X$ and $c \leq \bigvee X$, then

$$\{x \wedge c: x \in X\} \dashv \bigvee\{x \wedge c: x \in X\} = \bigvee X \wedge c = c.$$

If $a \leq b \leq va$ and $c \leq b$, then $a \wedge c \leq c \leq va \wedge vc = v(a \wedge c)$, so $\{a \wedge c\} \dashv c$.   ]

   The site presents a homomorphic image of A, because all the meets and joins in the frame can be calculated in A: the generators generate no new elements.
   Suppose I is a C-ideal. I is closed under all joins and also under v. Thus it has a greatest element a, say, and a = va. Conversely, if a is any element for which a = va, then $\downarrow a = \{b \in A: b \leq a\}$ is a C-ideal. Thus the C-ideals correspond to the fixpoints of v.
   Now for any a, the C-ideal it generates is $\downarrow va$, so a and a' generate the same C-ideal iff va = va'. This shows that v is the nucleus of the homomorphic image that the site presents.   ]

Categorically speaking, a frame has all colimits and a frame homomorphism f preserves them, and we can apply the Adjoint Functor Theorem to show that f has a right adjoint g. The nucleus v is the composite f;g. The condition $a \le va = v^2a$ follows from the adjunction; and because f preserves finite meets and g (as a right adjoint) preserves all meets (limits), v preserves finite meets.

Sublocales

Our final step is to pursue the observation that the C-ideals in Theorem 6.2.7 – and hence the elements of the homomorphic image – correspond to the fixpoints of v. We call the set B of these the *sublocale* corresponding to v, and treat this as the underlying set of the frame homomorphic image we want to construct. Its frame structure is given by

$\bigvee X$ [join in B] $= v(\bigvee X)$ [join in A]   for $X \subseteq B$
$\bigwedge X$ [meet in B] $= \bigwedge X$ [meet in A]   for finite $X \subseteq B$

Proposition 6.2.8

(i)   Let nuclei v and v' correspond to sublocales B and B'. Then $v \le v'$ iff $B \supseteq B'$.

(ii)   A subset $B \subseteq A$ is a sublocale iff

- B is closed under *all meets*, and
- if $a \in A$ and $x \in B$ then $a \rightarrow x \in B$.

(Recall the Heyting arrow from Section 3.10. The operations mentioned here are all performed in A.)

Proof (i) $\Rightarrow$: Let $x \in B'$. Then $x \le vx \le v'x = x$, so $x \in B$.
$\Leftarrow$: Let $a \in A$. $v'a \in B' \subseteq B$, so $va \le vv'a = v'a$.
(ii) $\Rightarrow$: Let $X \subseteq B$. If $x \in X$ then $v(\bigwedge X) \le vx = x$. Therefore $v(\bigwedge X) \le \bigwedge X$, so $\bigwedge X \in B$. Now take $x \in B$ and $a \in A$.

$$a \wedge v(a \rightarrow x) \le va \wedge v(a \rightarrow x) = v(a \wedge (a \rightarrow x)) \le vx = x$$

Therefore $v(a \rightarrow x) \le a \rightarrow x$, and so $a \rightarrow x \in B$.
$\Leftarrow$:   Given B, define

$$va = \bigwedge\{x \in B: a \le x\} \ge a.$$

Closure under meets tells us that $va \in B$, and we deduce that B is the set of fixpoints for v and that $va = v^2a$.
If $a, b \in A$ then clearly $v(a \wedge b) \le va \wedge vb$. For the reverse inclusion, we have

$$a \wedge b \le x \in B \Rightarrow a \le b \rightarrow x \in B \Rightarrow va \le b \rightarrow x \Rightarrow va \wedge b \le x$$
$$\Rightarrow b \le va \rightarrow x \in B \Rightarrow vb \le va \rightarrow x \Rightarrow va \wedge vb \le x$$

We deduce that

$$va \wedge vb \leq \bigwedge \{x \in B : a \wedge b \leq x\} = v(a \wedge b) \qquad]$$

Notice the big difference between a sub*frame,* a subset of the frame that is closed under the frame operations of finite meets and arbitrary join, and a sub*locale,* a subset of the frame whose closure properties are defined using the distinctly untopological operations (but which still happen to be there) of arbitrary meet and the Heyting arrow. In summary,

Theorem 6.2.9 The following constructs out of a frame A are equivalent:

(i)   Frame homomorphic surjections of A (up to isomorphism), preordered by $\geq$ (Definition 6.2.1);

(ii)   Frames presented by some presentation of A together with some new relations (but no new generators) (up to isomorphism; Proposition 6.2.2);

(iii)   Frame congruences on A, ordered by $\supseteq$;

(iv)   Frame congruence preorders on A, ordered by $\supseteq$ (Proposition 6.2.3);

(v)   C-ideals for a certain coverage C on $A \times A^{op}$, ordered by $\supseteq$ (Proposition 6.2.4; see also Exercise 1);

(vi)   Nuclei on A, ordered pointwise by $\geq$ (Proposition 6.2.6, Theorem 6.2.7);

(vii)   Sublocales of A, ordered by $\subseteq$ (Proposition 6.2.8).   ]

Note the reversals of the ordering:

big homomorphic image
    = (categorically) small surjection
    = few relations
    = small congruence or congruence preorder or C-ideal
    = small nucleus
    = big sublocale.

Corollary 6.2.5 says that the sublocales form a frame, but taking the order reversals into account we should say that –

the *nuclei* form a frame,
the *sublocales* form the opposite of a frame

6.3 Topological sums

From set theory we know various ways of constructing new sets from old, including the disjoint union (or sum) X+Y and Cartesian product X×Y of two sets X and Y. It is natural to ask if we can perform similar constructions on topological systems.

First, sums. If D and E are topological systems, is there a natural way of combining their frames to make a topological system with points pt D + pt E? Take subbasic opens from $\Omega D + \Omega E$:

u $\vDash$ a $\in$ ΩD iff u $\in$ pt D and u $\vDash$ a in D
u $\vDash$ b $\in$ ΩE iff u $\in$ pt E and u $\vDash$ b in E

Thinking spatially, the open sets in pt D and pt E are still open in the sum:

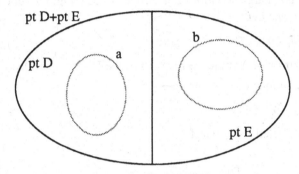

Within the old frames we want meets and joins to be calculated as before, and for a $\in$ ΩD and b $\in$ ΩE we want a$\wedge$b = **false**. It follows that every open generated from this subbasis has the form a$\vee$b for some a $\in$ ΩD and b $\in$ ΩE. Writing $\langle a, b \rangle$ for this a$\vee$b, we can see that the frame operations are computed componentwise: thus the resulting frame is the Cartesian product $\Omega D \times \Omega E$. Generalizing this, we give –

Definition 6.3.1 Let $\{D_\lambda\}$ be a family of topological systems. Their *topological* (or *disjoint*) *sum*, $\Sigma_\lambda D_\lambda$, is defined by

pt $\Sigma_\lambda D_\lambda = \Sigma_\lambda$ pt D_λ,   the disjoint union of the points sets,
$\Omega \Sigma_\lambda D_\lambda = \Pi_\lambda \Omega D_\lambda$,   the Cartesian product of the frames,
u $\vDash \langle a_\lambda \rangle$ iff u $\vDash a_\mu$ where u $\in$ pt D_μ

This says *how* the topological sum is constructed; but it is not especially clear *what* it does. For this we give, as with spatialization and localification, a universal property that characterizes the topological sum up to homeomorphism. As usual with universal properties, we need to look at continuous maps, as they are how we compare our construction with all other topological systems; in particular we shall use a family of *injections*, embeddings from the D_λs into the sum. The injection

$i_\mu: D_\mu \to \Sigma_\lambda D_\lambda$

is defined by

$$\text{pt } i_\mu(x) = x, \quad \Omega i_\mu (\langle a_\lambda \rangle) = a_\mu$$

That is to say, pt i_μ is the μth set theoretic injection into the disjoint union, and Ωi_μ is the μth projection from the product.

Theorem 6.3.2 *The Universal Characterization of the Topological Sum*

(i)   Given D_λ as above, the topological sum $\Sigma_\lambda D_\lambda$ is indeed a topological system, and the maps i_μ are embeddings.

(ii)   (The actual characterization. Categorically speaking, the topological sum is a *coproduct*.) Let

$$f_\mu : D_\mu \to E$$

be any family of continuous maps from the D_μs to a single system E. Then there is a unique continuous map

$$f : \Sigma_\lambda D_\lambda \to E$$

such that for all μ, $f_\mu = i_\mu ; f$.

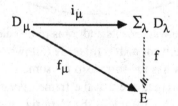

Proof (i) is easy checking.

(ii) First, we prove uniqueness. If f exists, then for $u \in \text{pt } \Sigma_\lambda D_\lambda$, specifically $u \in \text{pt } D_\mu$,

$$\text{pt } f(u) = \text{pt } f \circ \text{pt } i_\mu(u) = \text{pt } f_\mu(u)$$

and for $c \in \Omega E$

$$\Omega f(c) = \langle \Omega i_\lambda (\Omega f(c)) \rangle = \langle \Omega f_\lambda(c) \rangle$$

For existence, it is easy to show that f defined in this way is indeed a continuous map.]

Since our topological systems are a non-standard notion, we must now say how the topological sum as defined here relates to the standard theories of topology and locales.

Proposition 6.3.3

(i)   A topological sum of spatial systems is still spatial.

(ii)   A topological sum of localic systems is still localic.

(iii)   In either of these two cases, the sum still satisfies the same universal property with respect to continuous maps into a space or a locale as appropriate.

Proof (i) The extent of $\langle a_\lambda \rangle$ is the disjoint union of the extents of the a_λs, so different tuples $\langle a_\lambda \rangle$ have different extents.

(ii)   We have a continuous localification map

$$p: \Sigma_\lambda\, D_\lambda \to \text{Loc}\,(\Sigma_\lambda\, D_\lambda)$$

and we wish to show that it is a bijection on points.

First, for each μ, define a function $j_\mu: \Omega D_\mu \to \prod_\lambda \Omega D_\lambda$ by

$$j_\mu(a)_\lambda = \begin{cases} a & \text{iff } \lambda = \mu \\ \textbf{false} & \text{iff } \lambda \neq \mu \end{cases}$$

This is almost a frame homomorphism; it preserves all joins and finite, non-empty meets. If $\mu \neq \mu'$, then $j_\mu(a) \wedge j_{\mu'}(a') = \textbf{false}$.

To show pt p is 1-1, suppose pt $p(u) = $ pt $p(u')$ where $u \in$ pt D_μ and $u' \in$ pt $D_{\mu'}$. u satisfies $j_\mu(\textbf{true})$, so u' does too, and we deduce that $\mu = \mu'$. Now $u = u'$, follows from the fact that $\Omega(i_\mu;p)$ is surjective, so that (as in Section 6.1) pt $(i_\mu;p)$ is injective.

To show that pt p is onto, take $z \in$ pt Loc $(\Sigma_\lambda\, D_\lambda)$. Then $z \vDash \textbf{true} = \bigvee_\lambda j_\lambda(\textbf{true})$, so for some μ, $z \vDash j_\mu(\textbf{true})$. It follows that if $\lambda \neq \mu$ then $z \nvDash j_\lambda(\textbf{true})$. Now thinking of z as a frame homomorphism to **2**, the composite $x = j_\mu;z$ is also a frame homomorphism and hence a point of D_μ.

If $c = \langle c_\lambda \rangle \in \prod_\lambda \Omega D_\lambda$, then we can calculate that

$$c = \bigvee_{\lambda \neq \mu} j_\lambda(c_\lambda) \vee j_\mu(c_\mu)$$

Therefore $z \vDash c$ iff $z \vDash j_\mu(c_\mu)$, i.e. $x \vDash c_\mu$, so $z = $ pt $p(x)$.

(iii)   This follows easily, given (i) and (ii).   ]

We started our discussion with the binary topological sum of two systems, and generalized this to arbitrary topological sums. It is useful to consider two trivial, but easily overlooked cases. First, the unary sum, of a single system, is just that system.

More interestingly, the nullary sum, of no systems at all, is the system $0 = (\emptyset, \textbf{1})$ with no points and a single, inconsistent open. The universal property of sums then says that *for any topological system there is a unique continuous map into it from 0.* [Exercise: describe this map.] Categorically speaking, 0 is an *initial* topological system. As a trivial observation, or as a corollary of Proposition 6.3.3, it is both spatial and localic.

Finally, we describe how to decompose topological systems as sums.

Proposition 6.3.4 Let D be a topological system. Then, up to homeomorphism, decompositions $D \cong E+E'$ correspond to complementary pairs of opens of D, i.e. pairs a, b $\in \Omega D$ such that $a \wedge b =$ **false** and $a \vee b =$ **true**.

Proof If $\Omega D = \Omega E \times \Omega E'$, then $\langle$**true, false**$\rangle$ and $\langle$**false, true**$\rangle$ are complementary.

Now suppose a $\in \Omega D$. $\downarrow$a is a frame (it is almost a subframe of ΩD, but not quite, because **true** in $\downarrow$a is a, not **true** in ΩD), and the map $x \mapsto x \wedge a$ is a frame homomorphism from ΩD to $\downarrow$a.

If a has a complement b, we get a frame homomorphism θ from ΩD to $\downarrow$a $\times \downarrow$b, $x \mapsto \langle x \wedge a, x \wedge b \rangle$, and we show that this is an isomorphism. It is 1-1, for if $\theta(x) = \theta(y)$ then

$$x = x \wedge (a \vee b) = x \wedge a \vee x \wedge b = y \wedge a \vee y \wedge b = y \wedge (a \vee b) = y$$

It is also onto, for suppose a' $\le$ a and b' $\le$ b, and let $x = a' \vee b'$. Then

$$x \wedge a = a' \wedge a \vee b' \wedge a = a' \quad \text{(because } b \wedge a = \text{false)}$$

and similarly $x \wedge b = b'$. Finally, pt $D = \text{extent}(a) + \text{extent}(b)$.   ]

6.4 Topological products

We now ask the same question of Cartesian products: given systems D and E, is there a natural frame with which we can make a topological system whose points are pairs, in pt D $\times$ pt E? (And, categorically speaking, does it construct products?) The sub-basic opens with which we start are of the form a' (a $\in \Omega D$) and b" (b $\in \Omega E$) where

$$\langle x, y \rangle \vDash a' \text{ iff } x \vDash a, \qquad \langle x, y \rangle \vDash b'' \text{ iff } y \vDash b$$

For the finite conjunctions of these we have $a_1' \wedge a_2' = (a_1 \wedge a_2)'$ and similarly for the b's, so the general finite conjunction is of the a'$\wedge$b". We write this as $a \otimes b$. Then

$$a' = a \otimes \text{true} \quad \text{and} \quad b'' = \text{true} \otimes b$$

so that we can forget about the notation using a' and b".

Basic opens are pairs from $\Omega D \times \Omega E$, written $a \otimes b$.

Comparing the two expressions

$$a_1 \otimes b_1 \wedge a_2 \otimes b_2 \quad \text{and} \quad (a_1 \wedge a_2) \otimes (b_1 \wedge b_2)$$

we see they at least have the same extent, so let us insist they are equal in our frame.

Meets of expressions a⊗b are computed componentwise.

If joins were also computed componentwise, then we'd end up with the product frame $\Omega D \times \Omega E$ again; however, this doesn't happen. Comparing

$$a_1 \otimes b_1 \vee a_2 \otimes b_2 \quad \text{and} \quad (a_1 \vee a_2) \otimes (b_1 \vee b_2)$$

we see that

$$\langle x, y \rangle \vDash a_1 \otimes b_1 \vee a_2 \otimes b_2 \qquad \text{iff} \qquad \left(\begin{array}{c} x \vDash a_1 \text{ and } y \vDash b_1 \\ \text{or} \\ x \vDash a_2 \text{ and } y \vDash b_2 \end{array} \right)$$

$$\langle x, y \rangle \vDash (a_1 \vee a_2) \otimes (b_1 \vee b_2) \quad \text{iff} \quad \left(\begin{array}{c} x \vDash a_1 \text{ or } x \vDash a_2 \\ \text{and} \\ y \vDash b_1 \text{ or } y \vDash b_2 \end{array} \right)$$

$$\text{i.e. iff} \qquad \left(\begin{array}{c} x \vDash a_1 \text{ and } y \vDash b_1 \\ \text{or} \\ x \vDash a_2 \text{ and } y \vDash b_2 \\ \text{or} \\ x \vDash a_1 \text{ and } y \vDash b_2 \\ \text{or} \\ x \vDash a_2 \text{ and } y \vDash b_1 \end{array} \right)$$

We therefore want

$$(a_1 \vee a_2) \otimes (b_1 \vee b_2) = a_1 \otimes b_1 \vee a_1 \otimes b_2 \vee a_2 \otimes b_1 \vee a_2 \otimes b_2 \geq a_1 \otimes b_1 \vee a_2 \otimes b_2$$

We can be more precise in two special cases, namely when $a_1 = a_2$ or $b_1 = b_2$:

$$a \otimes b_1 \vee a \otimes b_2 = a \otimes (b_1 \vee b_2)$$
$$a_1 \otimes b \vee a_2 \otimes b = (a_1 \vee a_2) \otimes b$$

All this means the general open, of the form $\bigvee_i a_i \otimes b_i$, can be rather complex. We shall use our general theory of generators and relations to analyse the situation.

Definition 6.4.1 Let A and B be two frames. We define their *tensor product*, A⊗B, to be the frame presented as

$$\text{Fr} \langle a \otimes b \colon a \in A, b \in B \quad |$$
$$\bigwedge_i (a_i \otimes b_i) = (\bigwedge_i a_i) \otimes (\bigwedge_i b_i)$$
$$\bigvee_i (a_i \otimes b) = (\bigvee_i a_i) \otimes b$$
$$\bigvee_i (a \otimes b_i) = a \otimes (\bigvee_i b_i) \quad \rangle$$

We also define two *injections* $i_A \colon A \to A \otimes B$ and $i_B \colon B \to A \otimes B$ by

$$i_A(a) = a \otimes \mathbf{true} \qquad \text{(a' in our previous, temporary notation)}$$
$$i_B(b) = \mathbf{true} \otimes b \qquad \text{(b'')}$$

These are both frame homomorphisms.

Proposition 6.4.2 (Categorically: tensor products are coproducts of frames.)

Let f: A → C and g: B→ C be frame homomorphisms. Then there is a unique frame homomorphism h: A⊗B→ C such that f = i_A;h and g = i_B;h.

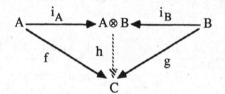

Proof h is defined by its action on the generators, and so if it exists then

$$h(a \otimes b) = h(a \otimes \textbf{true} \wedge \textbf{true} \otimes b) = h(i_A(a)) \wedge h(i_B(b)) = f(a) \wedge g(b) \qquad (*)$$

This proves uniqueness. For existence, we must use the universal property of presentations, Definition 4.3.4. The frame homomorphism h is defined uniquely by (*), provided the relations still hold in C when f(a) ∧ g(b) is substituted for each generator a⊗b. We have

$$\bigwedge_i (f(a_i) \wedge g(b_i)) = (\bigwedge_i f(a_i)) \wedge (\bigwedge_i g(b_i))$$
$$\bigvee_i (f(a_i) \wedge g(b)) = (\bigvee_i f(a_i)) \wedge g(b)$$
$$\bigvee_i (f(a) \wedge g(b_i)) = f(a) \wedge (\bigvee_i g(b_i))$$

Finally, with this definition of h, we have

$$h(i_A(a)) = h(a \otimes \textbf{true}) = f(a) \wedge g(\textbf{true}) = f(a)$$

Thus f = i_A;h, and similarly g = i_B;h.   ]

As an immediate corollary, the points of the locale for A⊗B, frame homomorphisms to **2**, correspond to pairs ⟨x, y⟩ of points from the locales for A and B.

Thinking of joins as sums and meets as products, there is a precise analogy between the tensor product of frames and the tensor product of commutative rings. This is brought out well in Joyal and Tierney [84].

The following technical lemma will be used in Chapter 8 to get a more precise description of the tensor product.

Lemma 6.4.3 The elements of A⊗B can be represented uniquely in the form $\bigvee$ {a⊗b: ⟨a, b⟩ ∈ I}, where I ⊆ A×B satisfies

- if a' ≤ a, b' ≤ b and ⟨a, b⟩ ∈ I, then ⟨a', b'⟩ ∈ I;
- if ⟨x, b⟩ ∈ I for all x ∈ X ⊆ A, then ⟨$\bigvee$X, b⟩ ∈ I; and
- if ⟨a, y⟩ ∈ I for all y ∈ Y ⊆ B, then ⟨a, $\bigvee$Y⟩ ∈ I.

Proof In terms of sites, $A \otimes B$ can be presented using the semilattice $A \times B$ (meets computed componentwise) and covering relations $\{\langle x, b \rangle : x \in X\} \dashv \langle \bigvee X, b \rangle$ etc. Our subsets I are then the C-ideals for this coverage. ▌

Definition 6.4.4 Let D and E be topological systems. The *topological product* D×E is the system defined by

$$pt\,(D \times E) = pt\,D \times pt\,E$$
$$\Omega\,(D \times E) = \Omega D \otimes \Omega E$$
$$\langle x, y \rangle \vDash \bigvee_i a_i \otimes b_i \quad \text{iff for some i, } x \vDash a_i \text{ and } y \vDash b_i.$$

The *projections*

$$p: D \times E \to D \text{ and } q: D \times E \to E$$

are defined by

$$pt\,p(\langle x, y \rangle) = x \qquad \text{(pt p is the projection function)}$$
$$\Omega p(a) = a \otimes \textbf{true} \qquad \text{(}\Omega p \text{ is the injection homomorphism } i_{\Omega D}\text{)}$$

and similarly for q.

Theorem 6.4.5 (Categorically: the topological product is a product of topological systems.)

(i)   D×E is indeed a topological system, and p and q are continuous maps.

(ii)   If f: F → D and g: F → E are continuous maps, then there is a unique continuous map h: F → D×E such that f = h;p and g = h;q.

Proof (i) This does require proof. Although we have purported to define the satisfaction relation in Definition 6.4.4, it is conceivable that we might have two different ways of writing an open as $\bigvee_i a_i \otimes b_i$, and that we get different answers when we ask whether $\langle x, y \rangle$ satisfies it. We use the corollary to Proposition 6.4.2. Each pair $\langle x, y \rangle$ of points gives rise to a pair of locale points of ΩD and ΩE, and hence a locale point of $\Omega D \otimes \Omega E$. As mentioned in Section 5.6, this function from pt D × pt E to the locale points of $\Omega D \otimes \Omega E$ defines $\vDash$.

That p and q are continuous is easily checked.

(ii)   If h exists, it satisfies

$$pt\,h(z) = \langle pt\,f(z), pt\,g(z) \rangle \quad \text{and} \quad \Omega h(a \otimes b) = \Omega f(a) \wedge \Omega g(b)$$

This gives uniqueness; existence – that h is thus well-defined – can be verified using Proposition 6.4.2. ▌

As before, we must investigate how the product works for spaces and locales.
For locales, it is simple.

Proposition 6.4.6

(i)   A topological product of localic systems is still localic.
(ii)   In this case, the product still satisfies the same universal property with
         respect to continuous maps from a locale.

Proof (i) is immediate from the corollary to Proposition 6.4.2; (ii) is immediate.
]

A topological product of spatial systems is *not* necessarily spatial. This means
that the relations used in presenting A⊗B can be *logically incomplete* – not enough
to prove all the relations that hold between open sets in the product. The counterexamples (Johnstone [82] gives one in paragraph II.2.14) are generally complicated,
and we shall see in Theorem 8.5.7 that products of commonly encountered spatial
systems are still spatial. However in general, to get a product *space,* we must
spatialize.

Proposition 6.4.7 Let D and E be spatial topological systems. Then Spat (D×E)
satisfies the same universal property (categorically: it is the product) with respect to
topological spaces as D×E does with respect to topological systems.
Proof Just combine Theorems 6.4.5 and 5.3.4.   ]

For topological spaces X and Y, the *product space* X×Y is what we are writing
here as Spat(X×Y). The basic open sets in the product space are the rectangles such
as U×V here:

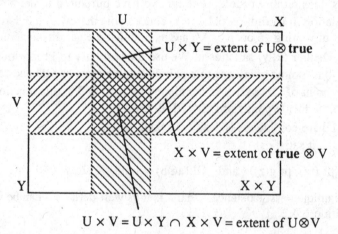

$$U \times V = U \times Y \cap X \times V = \text{extent of } U \otimes V$$

Any other open set is a union of these.

General products

We have concentrated on binary products because the product is more complicated than the sum, but in fact the product can be defined for an arbitrary family of topological systems and it satisfies a universal property analogous to that in Theorem 6.4.5.

The nullary product is $(1, \mathbf{2})$, the *final* topological system. From any other topological system there is a unique continuous map into $(1, \mathbf{2})$.

The product of more than two, but still finitely many, topological systems can be found by iterating the binary product. Although this apparently depends on the order of the iteration, we can in fact work with unbracketed generators like $a_1 \otimes a_2 \otimes \ldots \otimes a_n$ (with meets computed componentwise) and relations like

$$a_1 \otimes a_2 \otimes \ldots \otimes \bigvee_j a_{ij} \otimes \ldots \otimes a_n = \bigvee_j a_1 \otimes a_2 \otimes \ldots \otimes a_{ij} \otimes \ldots \otimes a_n$$

However, this doesn't work for infinitely many systems, and so we give a few remarks on how to generalize the construction. The Cartesian product of infinitely many sets of points is well-known, but there remains the tensor product of infinitely many frames A_i. Recall that the subbasic opens for the binary product $A \otimes B$ were of the form $a \otimes \mathbf{true}$ and $\mathbf{true} \otimes b$, and these can be treated as elements of $A \times B$. In the general case we have subbasic elements of the form $\langle a_i \rangle \in \prod_i A_i$ where all except one of the components a_i are **true**. The finite meets of these, the basic opens, are those sequences $\langle a_i \rangle$ for which *all but finitely many* of the components are **true**. Such sequences form a sub-semilattice of $\prod_i A_i$. The relations are formed, as above, from terms that agree on all but one component.

Notes

As stated, for topological systems, these results are of course new; but they do no more than put together what is already established for spaces and locales.

Many proofs have been given of Corollary 6.2.5, that the sublocales of a locale form a frame. As far as I know, the one here in terms of C-ideals is new.

Exercises

1. (Joyal and Tierney, [84]) Given a frame A, show that the frame described in Corollary 6.2.5 can be presented as

$$A' = \text{Fr} \langle \ a, b^c \colon a, b \in A \quad | $$

   all the relations holding in A hold for the a's,

   $$a \vee a^c = \mathbf{true}$$
   $$a \wedge a^c = \mathbf{false} \quad \rangle$$

Show that the locale for A' has the same points as that for A.

2. Let A be a frame, and A' the frame as in Exercise 1. Define a homomorphism

   i: A $\to$ A'   a $\longmapsto$ a

   Show that i satisfies the following universal property:

(i)   i(a) has a complement for every a $\in$ A;
(ii)   if j: A $\to$ B is a frame homomorphism such that every j(a) has a
         complement, then there is a unique homomorphism ϕ: A' $\to$ B such that j
         = i;ϕ.

   Show that i is 1–1 but not generally onto. Show also that if f, g are
homomorphisms from A' to another frame, B, and i;f = i;g, then f = g. Categorically,
i is both mono and epi in the category of frames, but not an isomorphism. Frame epimorphisms need
not be surjections (the surjections are the *regular* epimorphisms, i.e. those that can be described as
coequalizers).

3. Let A be a frame, and let $\neg$: A $\to$ A be the Heyting negation. Show that the
double negation $\neg \circ \neg$ is a nucleus. The fixpoints of this nucleus, the opens in the
corresponding sublocale, are the *regular* opens. In a topological space, an open U is
regular iff U = Int(Cl(U)) (see Exercise 4 of Chapter 3).

4. (H. Simmons) Let A be the frame $\Omega 2^{*\omega}$. Show that every open **starts** l is
regular. If s $\in$ pt $2^{*\omega}$ (s is a finite or infinite list of bits), show that $\downarrow$s = {t $\in$ pt
$2^{*\omega}$: t $\sqsubseteq$ s} is closed, i.e. that its complement, U, say, is open. Show that $\neg$U (the
interior of $\downarrow$s) is empty, and hence that $\neg\neg$U = **true**. Thus s $\models$ $\neg\neg$U, but s$\not\models$ U.
Deduce that the locale for A/$\neg\neg$ has no points and hence is a non-spatial sublocale
of the spatial locale $2^{*\omega}$.

5. Let D be a topological system, and let Y $\subseteq$ pt D. Then the corresponding
subspace is the system (Y, ΩD/$\leq$) where the congruence preorder $\leq$ is defined by

   a $\leq$ b   iff   extent(a) $\cap$ Y $\subseteq$ extent(b) $\cap$ Y   (*)

   If D is spatial, and Y is an open set U, then (*) amounts to

   a $\leq$ b   iff   a $\wedge$ U $\leq$ b

This definition makes sense in an arbitrary frame, and defines the *open* sublocale
o(U) corresponding to U. Show that Ωo(U) is isomorphic as a poset to {a $\in$ ΩD: a
$\leq$ U}, and this isomorphism preserves all meets and joins except the empty meet
true (**true** in Ωo(U) corresponds to U in ΩD). It is made out of ΩD by imposing
the extra relation U = **true**.

   If D is spatial and Y is a closed set U^c, then (*) amounts to

$$a \le b \quad \text{iff} \quad a \le b \vee U$$

Again, this makes sense in an arbitrary frame, and defines the *closed* sublocale c(U) corresponding to U. Show that Ωc(U) is isomorphic as a poset to $\{a \in \Omega D: U \le a\}$, and this isomorphism preserves all meets and joins except the empty join **false** (**false** in Ωc(U) corresponds to U in ΩD). It is made out of ΩD by imposing the extra relation U = **false**.

How are open and closed sublocales defined in terms of the other descriptions of sublocales in Theorem 6.2.9?

6. Nuclei form a frame. How are the consequent meets and joins, and also the Heyting operations, expressed in terms of the various representations of sublocales? (Some answers are in Johnstone [82], Proposition II.2.5.)

7. Show that for frames A, B and C we have

$$A \otimes B \cong B \otimes A$$
$$A \otimes 2 \cong A$$
$$(A \otimes B) \otimes C \cong A \otimes (B \otimes C)$$

Categorically speaking, one can use these isomorphisms to make a symmetric monoidal category out of frames (see MacLane [71]).

8. Taking X to be the plane of 2-dimensional Euclidean geometry, formalize the definition of open set suggested in Chapter 1 and show that this space is homeomorphic to the product space $\mathbb{R} \times \mathbb{R}$.

9. Show that $\wp X \otimes \wp Y \cong \wp(X \times Y)$, and hence that the product of discrete spaces is a discrete space.

10. Let the frames A_λ be presented as

$$A_\lambda = \text{Fr} \langle G_\lambda \mid R_\lambda \rangle$$

with the generating sets G_λ assumed to be disjoint. Show that the tensor product can be presented by "putting the presentations for the A_λs side by side with no interaction":

$$\otimes_\lambda A_\lambda = \text{Fr} \langle \cup_\lambda G_\lambda \mid \cup_\lambda R_\lambda \rangle$$

11. Let the locale 2^ω be defined by

$$\Omega 2^\omega = \text{Fr} \langle \text{ `}s_n = 0\text{'}, \text{ `}s_n = 1\text{'}: n \in \omega, n \ge 1 \mid$$
$$\text{`}s_n = 0\text{'} \wedge \text{`}s_n = 1\text{'} = \textbf{false}$$
$$\text{`}s_n = 0\text{'} \vee \text{`}s_n = 1\text{'} = \textbf{true} \qquad \rangle$$

as in Definition 3.7.6. This is a spatial sublocale of the Kahn domain $2*^\omega$; its points
are the infinite bit streams. It is the product of countably many copies of 2, the
discrete space on two points. Products of copies of 2 are known as *Cantor spaces*.

12.   A topological system D is *connected* iff it cannot be non-trivially decomposed
in the manner of Proposition 6.3.4, i.e. iff its only complementary pair of opens is
{**false**, **true**}. In spatial terms, this means that **false** and **true** are its only clopens.

(i)   Let $I \subseteq pt\ \mathbb{R}$. Show that, as a subspace of $\mathbb{R}$, I is connected iff it is an
          interval (i.e. if $x < y < z$ and x and z are in I, then so is y). (Hint. Suppose I
          is an interval, $U, V \in \Omega\mathbb{R}$, $I \subseteq U \cup V$, $U \cap V \cap I = \emptyset$ and $x \in U \cap I$. If $x < y$
          $\in I$, consider the interval

$$S = \{z: x \le z \le y \wedge \forall w.\ (x \le w \le z \to w \in U)\}$$

          If z_0 is its right-hand endpoint, then $y = z_0 \in S$; deduce that $V \cap I = \emptyset$.)
          Hence the only clopen subsets of $\mathbb{R}$ are $\emptyset$ and $\mathbb{R}$.

(ii) $2*^\omega$ is connected.

(iii) 2^ω is not connected. In fact, if x and y are distinct points then there is a
          clopen containing x but not y (the space is *totally separated*).

The following two exercises require some knowledge of category theory.

13.   Show that limits can be constructed in **Topological Systems** by taking
limits of the sets of points, and colimits of the frames of opens. Show that a colimit
of frames can be presented by combining presentations of the frames to present the
coproduct (see Exercise 10) and imposing additional relations to ensure that the
injections commute with the morphisms in the diagram.
      Use Exercise 4, Chapter 5 to show that a limit in **Topological Systems** of
locales is still localic and hence is a limit in **Locales**; what happens with limits of
spaces?

14.   Show that colimits can be constructed in **Topological Systems** by taking
colimits of the sets of points and limits of the frames of opens. Use Exercise 4,
Chapter 5 to show that a colimit in **Topological Systems** of topological spaces is
still spatial and hence is a colimit in **Topological Spaces**; what happens with
colimits of locales?

CHAPTER SEVEN

POINT LOGIC

In which we seek a logic of points *and find an ordering and a weak disjunction.*

The satisfaction relation x ⊨ a is supposed to describe some finitely observable relationship between points and opens, and so far we have been thinking of a as the observation and x as what is observed. However, for x and a in isolation, there is no óverriding reason for this; why can't we think of x as being the open, making an observation about a as a point?

The answer, of course, is that x and a are not in isolation. a is just one element of a whole logical system, and satisfaction has to respect the logic. We therefore ask how much logic we can put on the points x, making them into a logical system that satisfaction respects. It turns out that this "point logic", although not as full as the frame logic, has an ordering, representing entailment, and certain "directed" disjunctions. Moreover, although conjunctions are not immediately present, considering them leads in the next chapter to the notion of *compact set*.

We work in some fixed topological system D.

7.1 The specialization preorder

Definition 7.1.1 Let x and y be two points. We say y *specializes* x, and write x ⊑ y, iff for every open a, if x ⊨ a then y ⊨ a.

In other words, y satisfies at least all the opens satisfied by x; or we can say more about y than about x; or y represents a superior, or more refined state of information than x. This leads to various synonyms for specialization:

	y *specializes* x	
or	x ⊑ y	
or	x *approximates* y	
or	y *refines* x	
or	x *implies* y	(thinking of x and y as properties of opens).

Example 7.1.2 Let D be the system $2^{*\omega}$. The points are finite and infinite sequences of bits. Then for sequences s and t, s ⊑ t iff s is a prefix of t (our previous use of the symbol ⊑).

For the ⟸ direction, suppose s is a prefix of t, and s ⊨ **starts** l. Then l is a prefix of s, hence also of t, and so t ⊨ **starts** l. Thus s implies t for the basic opens **starts** l.

For a more general open $\bigvee_{l \in L}$ **starts** l, if s ⊨ $\bigvee_{l \in L}$ **starts** l then s ⊨ some **starts** l, so t ⊨ **starts** l, so t ⊨ $\bigvee_{l \in L}$ **starts** l. (See Exercise 1.)

For the ⇒ direction, suppose that s is not a prefix of t, and let l be the initial part where s and t agree. Then l is finite, it is a prefix of both s and t, and l ≠ s. Let l' be l together with the next bit from s.

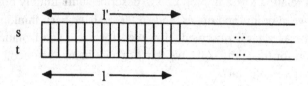

Then s ⊨ **starts** l' but t ⊭ **starts** l', so s ⋢ t.   ]

Now the *finite* sequences occur both as points s, with s ⊑ t iff s prefixes t, and in basic opens **starts** l, with **starts** l ≤ **starts** m iff m prefixes l: they have the opposite ordering on the two sides.

The rest of the points (the infinite sequences) are formed from the finite sequences as limits.

Points:

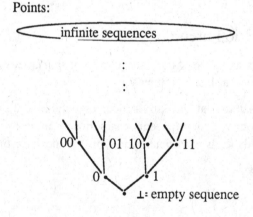

The rest of the opens are formed as joins (see also Exercise 2).

Opens:

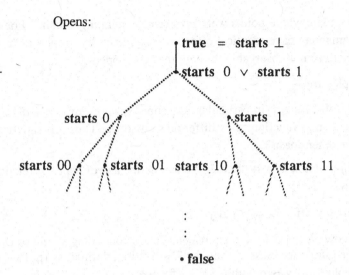

Proposition 7.1.3 In any Hausdorff topological space, $x \sqsubseteq y$ iff $x = y$ (the specialization ordering is *discrete*).

Proof Suppose $x \neq y$. We want an open set U containing x but not y. But by the Hausdorff property, we can actually find disjoint open sets U containing x and V containing y – so $y \notin U$.]

As an immediate example, in the real line $\mathbb{R}$, $x \sqsubseteq y$ iff $x = y$. Note that the specialization ordering is very different from the usual ordering on the reals.

T_0, T_1 and T_2 systems

We required that the opens should form a poset under $\leq$, so we ask whether the points are a poset under $\sqsubseteq$. $\sqsubseteq$ is preorder (reflexive and transitive), but not in general antisymmetric. Antisymmetry means –

> if $x \sqsubseteq y$ and $y \sqsubseteq x$ then $x = y$;

i.e. if $x \neq y$ then either $x \not\sqsubseteq y$ or $y \not\sqsubseteq x$;

i.e. if $x \neq y$ then there is some open a satisfied by one of x or y but not the other.

Definition 7.1.4 A topological system D is T_0 iff $\sqsubseteq$ is antisymmetric, i.e. iff pt D is a poset under $\sqsubseteq$.

Some non-examples of T_0 systems are –

- Any indiscrete topological space with at least two points.

- The example where points were *programs* generating streams. For different programs may have identical effect, or may differ by properties (e.g. termination) not observable through the given opens.

Some examples are –

- Any localic system (in particular, any sober space). For if x and y are distinct points, then as functions they differ on some open. Thus one satisfies the open and the other doesn't.

- The *T_0-ification* of a system D. We can define an equivalence relation ~ on pt D by

$$x \sim y \text{ iff } x \sqsubseteq y \text{ and } y \sqsubseteq x$$

If we now write [x] for the equivalence class containing x, and pt D/~ for the set of equivalence classes, then the T_0-ification, defined as (pt D/~, ΩD), is a T_0 topological system with [x] ⊨ a iff x ⊨ a.

- If $\sqsubseteq$ is discrete, i.e. $x \sqsubseteq y$ iff $x = y$, then the system is called *T_1*. Any T_1 system is T_0.

- We have already seen that any Hausdorff topological space is T_1, and hence T_0; alternatively, we have already seen that any Hausdorff space is sober (localic) and hence T_0. Hausdorff spaces are sometimes called *T_2*.

7.2 Directed disjunctions of points

If we can define a disjunction $\vee$ S of points S $\subseteq$ pt D, then it must satisfy

$$\vee S \vDash a \text{ iff } x \vDash a \text{ for some } x \in S$$

Unfortunately, in general it is impossible for this to define a point, because it won't interact correctly with *con*junctions of opens. Consider two incomparable points x and y. We can find opens a and b such that x ⊨ a, y ⊭ a, y ⊨ b and x ⊭ b. Then if x∨y exists it satisfies both a and b, but not a∧b.

Of course, if x and y are comparable, then they do have a disjunction: it is the larger of the two. We therefore consider a special kind of disjunction in which, in effect, the incomparable disjunctions have already been done for us. What is left is a limiting process.

Definition 7.2.1 Let $\sqsubseteq$ be a preorder on a set X. A subset S $\subseteq$ X is *directed* iff every finite subset of S has an upper bound in S. (Note that S cannot be empty, because it must contain an upper bound for the empty set.)

The prime example is a linearly ordered subset of X. For then any finite subset has a greatest element, which is an upper bound. This covers the common case of a sequence

$$x_1 \subseteq x_2 \subseteq x_3 \subseteq \ldots$$

We are going to look for *directed* disjunctions $\bigvee^{\uparrow} S$, where the use of the arrow $\uparrow$ is to imply that the set S is directed. If F is a finite subset of S, with upper bound x, then the part $\bigvee F$ of the disjunction is already taken care of by x, and this is how directed joins avoid the problematic incomparable disjunctions.

For the opens we represented disjunction by joins, and we made sure that this worked by imposing conditions on $\vdash$. Since $\vdash$ is now already given to us, for points we must be careful to distinguish between *disjunctions* $\bigvee S$, defined by

$$\bigvee S \vdash a \ \text{ iff } \ x \vdash a \text{ for some } x \in S,$$

and *joins* $\bigsqcup S$, defined as least upper bounds with respect to $\sqsubseteq$ (it doesn't actually matter that $\sqsubseteq$ is only a preorder).

Proposition 7.2.2 Any disjunction of points is a join.
Proof Let $x = \bigvee S$ be a disjunction. Suppose $y \in S$. If $y \vdash a$, then $x \vdash a$, so $y \sqsubseteq x$ and x is an upper bound of S. Now let x' be any other upper bound. If $x \vdash a$ then $y \vdash a$ for some $y \in S$, and $y \sqsubseteq x'$, so $x' \vdash a$. Thus $x \sqsubseteq x'$, so x is a least upper bound.
]

The converse is however not true. The first counterexample is simply a manifestation of our problems with incomparable disjunctions. Take D to be the system with these posets:

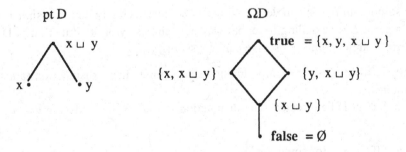

This is to be a topological space. It is routine to check –

- ΩD is a subframe of $\wp(\text{pt } D)$ (it is the Alexandrov topology).
- The specialization order $\sqsubseteq$ on pt D is as shown in the poset diagram.
- $x \sqcup y$ is the join of x and y.

- $x \sqcup y$ is not the disjunction of x and y: $x \sqcup y$ satisfies $\{x \sqcup y\}$, but neither x nor y does.

The second counterexample shows that even directed joins need not be disjunctions. Our frame ΩD is the ordinal $\omega+3$ with ω omitted: its elements are the natural numbers together with two transfinite ordinals, $\omega+1$ and $\omega+2$. However, we give it the opposite ordering from usual. pt D is $\omega+2$ with the usual ordering, but with ω again omitted.

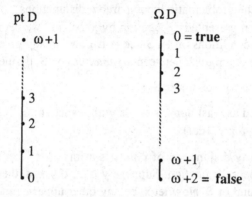

These make up a topological system, with $x \vDash a$ iff $x \geq a$ (treating x and a as ordinals with the usual ordering), and the specialization ordering on pt D is as shown. Now $\omega+1$ in pt D is the directed join $\bigsqcup^{\uparrow} \{n: n \in \omega\}$, but it's not the disjunction:

$\omega+1 \vDash \omega+1$, but $n \nvDash \omega+1$ ($n \in \omega$).

The solution to this is simple. The directed set does actually have a disjunction, namely a point corresponding to ω, but we have carelessly omitted it from pt D. To avoid these "careless omissions", we can just soberify.

Theorem 7.2.3 In a locale D, any directed set of points has a disjunction (and hence a join).
Proof Let $S \subseteq$ pt D be directed. The disjunction $x = \bigvee^{\uparrow} S$, if it exists, must be defined by

$x \vDash a$ iff $y \vDash a$ for some $y \in S$

We must therefore show that this defines a point. If $T \subseteq \Omega D$, then

$x \vDash \bigvee T \Leftrightarrow y \vDash \bigvee T$ for some $y \in S$
$\Leftrightarrow y \vDash a$ for some $y \in S, a \in T$
$\Leftrightarrow x \vDash a$ for some $a \in T$

Thus x preserves joins, and it follows that x is monotone.

To show that x preserves finite meets, let $T \subseteq \Omega D$ be finite, and suppose $x \vdash a$ for all $a \in T$. For each $a \in T$, there is some $y_a \in S$ with $y_a \vdash a$. Using directedness, we can find an upper bound $z \in S$ for the y_as; then $z \vdash a$ for all $a \in T$, so $z \vdash \bigwedge T$, so $x \vdash \bigwedge T$.   ]

    We note also the following property:

Lemma 7.2.4 Continuous maps preserve disjunctions of points.
Proof Suppose f: D → E is continuous, and the disjunction $\bigvee S$ exists in pt D.

$$\text{pt } f(\bigvee S) \vdash b \Leftrightarrow \bigvee S \vdash \Omega f(b) \Leftrightarrow x \vdash \Omega f(b) \text{ for some } x \in S$$
$$\Leftrightarrow \text{pt } f(x) \vdash b \text{ for some } x \in S$$

Therefore, pt $f(\bigvee S)$ is a disjunction $\bigvee \{\text{pt } f(x): x \in S\}$.   ]

7.3 The Scott topology

Suppose we are given a poset X with ordering $\sqsubseteq$, which we take as defining an abstract point logic on X. Can we make X the points of a topological system in which this becomes the actual point logic? We want not only that $\sqsubseteq$ should be recovered as the specialization ordering, but also that the directed joins that already exist in X should become disjunctions. Since the points X are all-important, the system will be a topological space, and clearly an open set U must be –

- upper closed, and
- *inaccessible by directed joins*, i.e. if $\bigsqcup^{\uparrow} S \in U$, then $x \in U$ for some $x \in S$.

Such sets we shall call *Scott open* subsets of X (with respect to $\sqsubseteq$).

Theorem 7.3.1

(i)   The Scott open sets form a topology on X, the *Scott* topology.
(ii)   The specialization ordering is the original $\sqsubseteq$.
(iii)   It is the finest topology that makes all directed joins (with respect to $\sqsubseteq$) into disjunctions.
(iv)   If X and Y are two posets, then a function from X to Y is Scott continuous iff it preserves all directed joins.

Proof (i) – easy.
(ii) Write, temporarily, $\sqsubseteq'$ for the specialization ordering. If $x \sqsubseteq y$ then $x \sqsubseteq' y$ by upper closure of the Scott open sets. If $x \not\sqsubseteq y$, then let U be the set $\{z \in X: z \not\sqsubseteq y\}$. This is Scott open and contains x but not y, so $x \not\sqsubseteq' y$.

(iii) Let A be such a topology. We reasoned above that all its open sets must be inaccessible by directed joins. For upper closure, suppose $y \sqsupseteq x \vDash a \in$ A. Then $y = \bigsqcup^{\uparrow} \{x, y\}$ which satisfies a because it is a disjunction. Therefore every open set from A is Scott open.

(iv) $\Rightarrow$: Lemma 7.2.4 says that continuous maps preserve disjunctions, and all directed joins here are disjunctions.

$\Leftarrow$: This is just a matter of checking that if V is Scott open in Y then $f^{-1}(V)$ is Scott open in X. Note that f must be monotone, for if $x \sqsubseteq x'$ then

$$f(x') = f(\bigsqcup^{\uparrow} \{x, x'\}) = \bigsqcup^{\uparrow} \{f(x), f(x')\},$$

so $f(x) \sqsubseteq f'(x)$.   ]

Corollary 7.3.2 In a locale, the extent of any open is Scott open with respect to the specialization order.]

Part (iv) of the Theorem tells us, as we would expect, that for Scott topologies continuity is determined solely by the poset structure.

Example 7.3.3 Let D be the bit-stream system $2^{*\omega}$. D is a spatial locale, and so by Corollary 7.3.2 ΩD is *coarser* than the Scott topology. But any Scott open set U is already in ΩD, for if s is an infinite sequence of bits then s is the directed join of its finite prefixes, so $s \vDash U$ iff some finite prefix is in U. Thus U is determined by the finite sequences in it, and in fact

$$U = \bigvee \{\textbf{starts } l: l \text{ finite}, l \in U\} \in \Omega D.$$

This example is rather typical of domain theory, where points may represent finite or infinite runs of programs. Some, like the finite bit sequences, give out all their information in a finite time, while others, like the infinite bit sequences, are best considered as limits – or directed joins.

If $x \sqsubseteq y$, then y contains *more information* than x (it satisfies more observations), and a computable function f that uses these points as input shouldn't gratuitously throw away this extra information: we expect that $f(x) \sqsubseteq f(y)$, in other words that f is monotone.

Moreover, if f is applied to a limit, it shouldn't give any more information than you get by applying f to the finite approximations and taking the limit of the answers. If f were to give such extra information, then we couldn't get it except by waiting until the Crack of Doom (when all the infinite computations have been completed), and that is too late. Formally then, f should preserve directed joins.

We can summarize this by saying that if computing is described in the abstract by information states, with an ordering of relative information content ($\sqsubseteq$), then we can put this into a topological setting by using the Scott topology.

Exercises

1. Let D be a topological system, and suppose some subbasis is given for ΩD. For two points x and y, show that $x \sqsubseteq y$ iff for every subbasic open a,

if $x \vDash a$ then $y \vDash a$.

2. With reference to the diagram of opens in Example 7.1.2, show that there are no opens between **starts** $0 \vee$ **starts** 1 and **true** (where there is a solid line in the diagram). Find unmentioned opens in the places where there are broken lines.

3. In the discrete topology on X, $x \sqsubseteq y$ iff $x = y$. In the indiscrete topology, $x \sqsubseteq y$ for all x and y.

4. In the real line, or indeed any T_1 space, all subsets are Scott open.

5. A set is closed in the Scott topology iff it is lower closed, and closed under directed joins.

CHAPTER EIGHT

COMPACTNESS

In which we define conjunctions of points and discover the notion of compactness.

8.1 Scott open filters

In the last chapter we developed a logic of points up as far as an ordering and directed disjunctions. The natural question now is to investigate conjunctions: given two points x and y, is it reasonable to look for a conjunction $x \wedge y$? It must be defined by

$$x \wedge y \vDash a \quad \text{iff} \quad x \vDash a \text{ and } y \vDash a \qquad (*)$$

Just as for the general disjunctions of points, which were incompatible with conjunctions of opens, we find that our conjunction of points is incompatible with disjunctions of opens (Exercise – work this out). We might try to develop some idea of directed conjunctions of points, but our arguments – in the proof of Theorem 7.2.3 – only show that these would be compatible with *finite* disjunctions of opens, and this is not in the spirit of frame theory. We therefore try a different tack.

Given x and y, (*) defines a function $x \wedge y$ from the opens to **2**. Our problem is that this is not a point, because although it preserves finite meets, it doesn't preserve all joins. However, it does preserve directed joins:

$$x \wedge y \vDash \bigvee^{\uparrow} S \Leftrightarrow x \vDash \bigvee^{\uparrow} S \text{ and } y \vDash \bigvee^{\uparrow} S$$
$$\Leftrightarrow x \vDash s \text{ and } y \vDash t \quad \text{for some } s, t \in S$$
$$\Leftrightarrow x \vDash u \text{ and } y \vDash u \quad \text{for some } u \in S \text{ (choose } u \text{ an upper bound for } s \text{ and } t)$$
$$\Leftrightarrow x \wedge y \vDash \text{ some } u \in S$$

Proposition 8.1.1 Let A be a frame. Then there is a 1-1 correspondence between

(i)   functions from A to **2** that preserve finite meets and directed joins, and

(ii)   subsets of A that are both filters and open in the Scott topology on A (*Scott open filters*).

Proof c.f. Proposition 5.4.7. The Scott open filters are the **true**-kernels of the functions.]

Thus our conjunction of points defines a Scott open filter. If F and F' are Scott open filters, then we extend the notation for points by writing

F ⊦ a iff a ∈ F

F ⊑ F' iff for all a, if F ⊦ a then F' ⊦ a (i.e. F ⊆ F').

This allows us to be vague about whether a particular F is defined as an actual Scott open filter (subset of A) or as its characteristic function from A to **2**.

Although the definition mentions only the interaction of F with directed joins, in fact it gives us information about all joins of opens:

Proposition 8.1.2 If A is a frame, then the following conditions on a monotone function F: A → **2** are equivalent:

(i)   F preserves directed joins;

(ii)   if X ⊆ A and F ⊦ $\bigvee$ X then F ⊦ $\bigvee$ X' for some finite X' ⊆ X.

Proof (i) ⇒ (ii): Let Y be the set {$\bigvee$ X': X' is a finite subset of X}. Then Y is directed, and $\bigvee^\uparrow$Y = $\bigvee$X. F ⊦ $\bigvee^\uparrow$Y, so F satisfies some element of Y.

(ii) ⇒ (i): If F ⊦ $\bigvee^\uparrow$X, then F ⊦ $\bigvee$ X' for some finite X' ⊆ X. By directedness X' has an upper bound x in X, so F ⊦ x.   ]

Proposition 8.1.3 Let D be a topological system.

(i)   A finite set C of points of D gives rise to a Scott open filter in ΩD, its *conjunction* $\bigwedge$C, defined by

$\bigwedge$C ⊦ a   iff   x ⊦ a for all x ∈ C, i.e. C ⊆ extent (a)

In other words, as a filter, $\bigwedge$C is the intersection of the completely prime filters corresponding to the points in C.

(ii)   If C ⊆ C' then $\bigwedge$C ⊒ $\bigwedge$C'.

Proof (i) has essentially been proved already. Note the particular case of the empty conjunction $\bigwedge$Ø, which satisfies every open (including **false**!).

(ii) is immediate.   ]

However, not all Scott open filters arise as finite conjunctions of points. The first, superficial reason is that there might be points missing. To overcome this, we localify. The second, much deeper reason is that *finite* conjunctions are not enough (we shall see later that the real line provides counterexamples). We therefore look at all possible sets C that work.

Definition 8.1.4 A set C of points is *compact* iff $\bigwedge$C, defined as in Proposition 8.1.3, is a Scott open filter.

$\wedge$C preserves meets for any C, so the essence of compactness is preserving directed joins. Reformulating along the lines of Proposition 8.1.2, and thinking spatially, we get the usual definition (the *Heine-Borel property*), that

> *C is compact iff any open cover has a finite subcover.*

In other words, if S is a family of open sets covering C (C $\subseteq \cup_{a \in S}$ extent(a), i.e. $\wedge$C $\vDash \vee$S), then there is a finite subcover S' $\subseteq$ S.

BEWARE! There is a well-established usage, hallowed by Bourbaki, in which "compact", applied to an entire space, means "*Hausdorff* and satisfying the Heine-Borel property". Our compactness is then called "quasicompact". Although this usage is falling out of fashion, it is still commonly encountered.

The following useful result says that compactness is preserved by continuous maps.

Proposition 8.1.5 Let f: D $\to$ E be a continuous map, and let C $\subseteq$ pt D be compact. Then so is its image f(C) = {pt f(x): x $\in$ C}.
Proof Let T $\subseteq \Omega$E be a directed set covering f(C). Then {Ωf(b): b $\in$ T} is a directed cover of C, so for some b $\in$ T we have C contained in the extent of Ωf(b), whence f(C) is contained in the extent of b.]

8.2 The Hofmann–Mislove Theorem

We now have the language to relate Scott open filters to compact sets. To ensure that all the necessary points are present, we assume we are working in a locale.

- If we want to construct Scott open filters as conjunctions of sets of points, the compact sets are the best we can do. Are they enough? YES.
- When do two compact sets give equal, or comparable conjunctions? We can answer this in terms of how $\sqsubseteq$ relates the points in the two sets.
- Each compact set has a *saturation,* the greatest compact set with the same conjunction. It is the intersection of the extents of the opens satisfied by the conjunction.
- Thus there is a 1-1 correspondence between Scott open filters and saturated compact sets of points, and it is order reversing: $\wedge$C $\sqsubseteq \wedge$C' iff C $\supseteq$ C'.

This is the Hofmann–Mislove Theorem. The first part shows that any locale has enough points to describe all its Scott open filters, and the result is not constructive: for a given Scott open filter it says that suitable points exist without showing how to construct them. Our proof uses the axiom of choice in the form of Zorn's Lemma.

Lemma 8.2.1 *Zorn's Lemma.*

Let P be a non-empty poset in which every non-empty, linearly ordered subset has an upper bound. Then P has a (not necessarily unique) maximal element x, i.e. one for which

$$x \leq y \Rightarrow x = y.$$

Proof A proof can be found in many introductions to axiomatic set theory, such as Halmos [60]. Note the distinction between *maximal* and *greatest* elements. A greatest element is greater than every other and is unique. There may be more than one maximal element, mutually incomparable.]

Lemma 8.2.2 Let D be a locale, and F a Scott open filter on ΩD. Let

$$C = \{x \in \text{pt } D: F \subseteq x\} = \bigcap \{\text{extent}(a): F \vDash a\}$$

Then $F = \bigwedge C$ (and consequently C is compact).

Every Scott open filter is a conjunction of some compact set of points.

Proof Clearly $F \subseteq \bigwedge C$. For the reverse inequality, suppose $F \nvDash a$ We want to show that $\bigwedge C \nvDash a$, i.e. $x \nvDash a$ for some $x \in C$. By Proposition 5.4.7, x can be equivalently described by a prime element p of ΩD, and we seek that: it must satisfy $a \leq p$ ($x \nvDash a$) and $F \nvDash p$ ($F \subseteq x$). Let

$$P = \{b \in \Omega D: a \leq b \text{ and } F \nvDash b\}$$

If $T \neq \emptyset$ is any linearly ordered (hence directed) subset of P, then $F \nvDash \bigvee^\uparrow T$ and so $\bigvee^\uparrow T$ is an upper bound for T in P. We can therefore apply Zorn's lemma to find a maximal element p of P.

Suppose now that S is some finite subset of ΩD, and for each $b \in S$, $b \nleq p$, so that $b \vee p > p$ and by maximality of p, $F \vDash b \vee p$. Then

$$F \vDash \bigwedge \{b \vee p: b \in S\} = (\bigwedge S) \vee p, \quad \text{so } \bigwedge S \nleq p$$

Therefore p is prime, and it describes the point x that we want.]

Lemma 8.2.3 Let D be a topological system, and let C and C' be subsets of pt D (not necessarily compact). Then the following are equivalent.

(i) $\bigwedge C \subseteq \bigwedge C'$

(ii)   For every $y \in C'$ there exists $x \in C$ with $x \subseteq y$.

(This relation between subsets is written $C \subseteq_U C'$ and is the *upper* or *Smyth* preorder on subsets.)

(iii) $\uparrow C \supseteq \uparrow C'$.

In this context, the upper closure $\uparrow C$ is commonly known as the *saturation* of C.
Proof (ii) $\Leftrightarrow$ (iii) is obvious.
(ii) $\Rightarrow$ (i): Suppose $\wedge C \vDash a$ and $y \in C'$, and $x \in C$ with $x \sqsubseteq y$. Then $x \vDash a$, so $y \vDash a$. Hence $\wedge C' \vDash a$.
(i) $\Rightarrow$ (ii): Let $y \in C'$, and let $p = \vee \{a \in \Omega D: y \nvDash a\}$ be the corresponding prime open. $y \nvDash p$, so $\wedge C' \nvDash p$, so $\wedge C \nvDash p$, so $x \nvDash p$ for some $x \in C$, and then $x \sqsubseteq y$.]

As a corollary,

$$\wedge C = \wedge C' \Leftrightarrow C \sqsubseteq_U C' \text{ and } C' \sqsubseteq_U C \text{ (write } C \equiv_U C')$$
$$\Leftrightarrow \uparrow C = \uparrow C'.$$

Lemma 8.2.4 Let D be a topological system and C a set of points. Then

(i)   There is a greatest set of points with the same conjunction as C, namely
           $\uparrow C$.
(ii) $\uparrow C$ is the intersection of the extents of the opens satisfied by $\wedge C$.

Proof (i) Obvious.
(ii) $\wedge C \vDash a$ iff C is contained in the extent of a. Each extent is upper closed, so if it contains C then it also contains $\uparrow C$, so

$$\uparrow C \subseteq \cap \{\text{extent}(a) : \wedge C \vDash a\} = C' \text{ (say).}$$

For the reverse inclusion,

$$y \in C' \Leftrightarrow \forall a. (\wedge C \vDash a \rightarrow y \vDash a) \Leftrightarrow \wedge C \sqsubseteq y$$

Therefore $\wedge C \sqsubseteq \wedge C'$, so $\uparrow C \supseteq \uparrow C' = C'$.   ]

Theorem 8.2.5 *The Hofmann–Mislove (Scott Open Filter) Theorem*
Let D be a locale. Then there is a 1-1 order reversing correspondence between Scott open filters of ΩD and compact, saturated sets of points of D:

$$F \longmapsto \{x \in \text{pt } D: F \sqsubseteq x\} = \cap \{\text{extent}(a): F \vDash a\}$$
$$C \longmapsto \wedge C \qquad\qquad\qquad\qquad\qquad\qquad]$$

Notice that although this result deals very much with points, it does not rely on spatiality. It just states a relation between what points there are, and the Scott open filters.

Theorem 8.2.6 *Summary of Logic of Compactness.*
Let D be a locale. We write QD for the set of Scott open filters of ΩD.

(i)   QD under $\sqsubseteq$ has finite meets and directed joins, and the finite meets
           distribute over directed joins.

(ii)   The finite meets and directed joins for both QD and ΩD are logical
        conjunctions and disjunctions with respect to $\vDash$:

$$x \vDash \wedge S \quad \Leftrightarrow x \vDash a \text{ for all } a \in S$$
$$x \vDash \vee^\uparrow S \quad \Leftrightarrow x \vDash a \text{ for some } a \in S$$

$$\sqcap T \vDash a \quad \Leftrightarrow F \vDash a \text{ for all } F \in T$$
$$\sqcup^\uparrow T \vDash a \quad \Leftrightarrow F \vDash a \text{ for some } F \in T$$

In other words, the pairing $\vDash: QD \times \Omega D \to \mathbf{2}$ preserves finite meets and
directed joins for each argument.

(iii)   Treating the Scott open filters concretely as subsets of ΩD, $\sqsubseteq$, $\sqcap$ and $\sqcup^\uparrow$
        become $\subseteq$, $\cap$ and $\cup^\uparrow$.

(iv)   Identifying the Scott open filters with saturated compact sets of points, $\sqsubseteq$,
        $\sqcap$ and $\sqcup^\uparrow$ become $\supseteq$, $\cup$ and $\cap^\downarrow$ (with $\downarrow$ to show that the intersection is
        downward directed, reflecting the order reversal).

(v)   In terms of arbitrary compact sets of points, $\sqsubseteq$ and $\sqcap$ are represented by
        $\sqsubseteq_U$ and $\cup$.

Proof (i) Define the meets and joins in QD as conjunctions and disjunctions as in
(iii) and show that the results are still Scott open filters.
(ii), (iii) By definition in part (i).
(v) We already know that $\wedge C \sqsubseteq \wedge C'$ iff $C \sqsubseteq_U C'$, and if T is a finite set of subsets
of pt D, then it is easy to see that

$$\wedge (\cup T) = \sqcap \{\wedge C: C \in T\}$$

Note that this shows that a finite union of compact sets is compact.
(iv) Again, we already know that $\sqsubseteq$ corresponds to $\supseteq$, and, given (iv), the meet
must correspond to union. If T is a directed set of Scott open filters, then the
saturated compact set corresponding to the join is, after Lemma 8.2.4 (ii),

$$\cap \{\text{extent } (a): \sqcup^\uparrow T \vDash a\} = \cap \cup_{F \in T} \{\text{extent } (a): F \vDash a\}$$
$$= \cap_{F \in T} \cap \{\text{extent } (a): F \vDash a\}$$

i.e. the intersection of the individual compact saturated sets.

Note that as a corollary, a directed intersection of compact saturated subsets is
still compact.   ]

We thus see that the use of compact sets redistributes the logic: instead of having
a strong logic (finite meets and all joins) in the frame and a weak logic (directed
joins) on the points, we have a medium logic (finite meets and directed joins) on
both sides.

8.3 Compactness and the reals

We just give a hint of the richness of the theory on the real line. Any standard introduction to topology will give much more detail. The first step is to identify the compact subsets of $\mathbb{R}$. Note that because the specialization order is discrete, all compact sets are saturated.

Theorem 8.3.1 *Heine-Borel*

Let $x \le y$ be real numbers. Then the closed interval

$$[x, y] = \{z: x \le z \le y\}$$

is compact.

Proof Let $T \subseteq \Omega\mathbb{R}$ be an open cover of $[x, y]$, and consider

$$S = \{z \in [x, y]: [x, z] \text{ is covered by a finite subset of } T\}$$

S is an interval containing x, so if w is its right-hand endpoint (the join of S when $\mathbb{R}$ is given its usual order) then S is either $[x, w]$ or $[x, w) = \{z: x \le z < w\}$. We want to show that $w = y$, and $w \in S$. Since $w \in [x, y]$, we can find $w \in U$ for some $U \in T$.

If $w = x$, then $w \in S$. Otherwise, $w > x$ and we can find $\delta > 0$ such that $w - \delta \in S$ and U contains $[w - \delta, w]$. Then the finite subset of T that covers $[x, w - \delta]$, together with U, covers $[x, w]$, so again $w \in S$.

If $w \ne y$ then $w < y$, and we can find $\delta > 0$ such that $w < w + \delta \le y$ and $[w, w + \delta] \subseteq U$. But then $[x, w + \delta]$ is covered by a finite subset of T, which contradicts the definition of w. Therefore $w = y$.]

Incidentally, this shows that not all compact sets are finite. We use this Theorem to characterize all compact subsets of $\mathbb{R}$, using two important lemmas.

Lemma 8.3.2 In a compact topological space (i.e. it is compact as a set of points), all closed subsets are compact.

Proof Let X be the space and F closed in it. If T is an open cover of F, then $T \cup \{F^c\}$ is an open cover of X and hence has a finite subcover. Even if F^c is in this subcover, we can drop it and get a finite subset of T covering F.   ]

Lemma 8.3.3 In a Hausdorff topological space, all compact subsets are closed.

Proof Let X be the space, and F a compact subset. Suppose $y \notin F$. For each $x \in F$, we can find disjoint open sets U_x and V_x containing x and y respectively. Then the U_xs form an open cover of F and hence have a finite subcover; and the intersection of the corresponding V_xs is an open set containing y and not meeting F. Therefore F^c is open.   ]

Thus in a compact Hausdorff space (i.e. a compact space in the Bourbaki sense), closed and compact mean the same. The real line, though Hausdorff, is not compact; but the Heine-Borel theorem tells us about enough compact subspaces for our needs.

Theorem 8.3.4 A subset of $\mathbb{R}$ is compact iff it is closed and bounded.

(A subset is *bounded* iff it is included in some finite interval [x, y].)

Proof $\Leftarrow$: A closed, bounded subset is a closed subset of a compact space [x, y], and hence compact.

$\Rightarrow$: Suppose F is compact. $F \subseteq \mathbb{R} = \bigcup^{\uparrow}\{(-n, n)\colon n$ a natural number$\}$, so for some n

$\quad F \subseteq (-n, n) \subseteq [-n, n]$ and F is bounded. F is closed by Lemma 8.3.3.   ]

This characterization is extremely useful in the theory of real valued functions, and we give two sample applications.

Proposition 8.3.5 A non-empty compact subset of $\mathbb{R}$ has a greatest and a least element.

Proof Let F be the subset. A more primitive property of $\mathbb{R}$ says that any bounded non-empty subset has a least upper bound, so F has one, m, say. But any open set containing m meets F (otherwise we could find a smaller upper bound), and we can deduce that m must be in F: it is the greatest element. The least element exists by symmetry.   ]

Theorem 8.3.6 Let x and y be real numbers, and let f: [x, y] $\to \mathbb{R}$ be continuous. Then "f is bounded and attains its bounds":

$\quad$ for some $z_0 \in [x, y]$, if $x \leq z \leq y$ then $f(z) \leq f(z_0)$.

Proof By Proposition 8.1.5, f([x, y]) is compact, and so it has a greatest element $f(z_0)$.]

8.4 Examples with bit streams

We consider the locale $2^{*\omega}$.

Proposition 8.4.1 A set $U \subseteq$ pt $2^{*\omega}$ is compact and open iff it is of the form $\uparrow S$ where S is a finite set of finite points (points that are finite sequences).

Proof If S is any finite set, then $\uparrow S$ is compact. If l is a finite point, then $\uparrow l$ = **starts** l is open, so if S is a finite set of finite points then

$\quad \uparrow S = \bigcup \{$**starts** l: $l \in S\}$

is open.

Conversely, we have seen that for any open set U,

U = ∪ {**starts** l: l ∈ U, l finite}.

If U is compact, then there is a finite subcover, and U is the upper closure of the corresponding set of l's.]

Here we have lots of compact open sets. This is in contrast with the reals, where a compact open set must be also closed, and so is either ∅ or ℝ (see Exercise 12 of Chapter 6); but ℝ is not bounded, so *the only compact open subset of ℝ is ∅*.

Proposition 8.4.2 The set 2^ω of infinite bit sequences is compact in $2^{*\omega}$.
Proof We define the compact open

$$U_n = \vee \ \{\textbf{starts } l: \text{length } l = n\}$$

Then **true** = $U_0 \geq U_1 \geq U_2 \geq \ldots$. The set of infinite bit sequences is $\cap_n U_n$, a downward directed intersection of compact upper closed sets, and hence compact.
   ]

Although we have proved this for sequences of bits, in fact it works for sequences of any symbols taken from any *finite* alphabet.

8.5 Compactness and products

Tychonoff's Theorem
This theorem, important in standard topology, proves that a product of compact topological spaces is still compact. Surprisingly, in view of the idea that compactness somehow means small (or a generalization of finiteness), it remains true even for infinite products and a proof of this may be found in standard texts such as Kelley [55]. Since the infinite case is less elementary, we give here a proof for binary – and hence finite – products. A space is said to be compact when its entire set of points is compact.

Theorem 8.5.1 *Tychonoff's Theorem*
Let X and Y be compact topological spaces. Then their spatial product X×Y is also compact.
Proof Recall that the spatial product is the spatialization of the product as topological systems.
   Since the sets a×b (a ∈ ΩX, b ∈ ΩY; a×b is the extent of a⊗b) form a basis for the product topology, it suffices to consider joins of basic sets covering the product. We can therefore suppose we have I ⊆ ΩX × ΩY where

pt X × pt Y = ∪ {a×b: ⟨a, b⟩ ∈ I}.

Fix $x \in$ pt X. For each $y \in$ pt Y, there is some $\langle a, b \rangle \in I$ such that $x \in a$ and $y \in b$. By compactness of Y, there is some finite subset I_x of these pairs such that

$$\text{pt } Y = \bigcup \{b: \exists a. \langle a, b \rangle \in I_x\}$$
$$x \in \bigcap \{a: \exists b. \langle a, b \rangle \in I_x\} = a_x, \text{ say}$$

Now by compactness of X, there is a finite subset $S \subseteq$ pt X such that

$$\text{pt } X = \bigcup \{a_x: x \in S\}$$

Let $I' = \bigcup \{I_x: x \in S\}$, a finite subset of I. If $x \in$ pt X and $y \in$ pt Y, then $x \in a_{x'}$ for some $x' \in S$, and so $x \in a$, $y \in b$ for some $\langle a, b \rangle \in I_{x'} \subseteq I'$. Thus I' is a finite subcover of I.]

Corollary 8.5.2 A subset of $\mathbb{R}^n$ is compact iff it is closed and bounded.]

Johnstone [82], Theorem III.1.7, also proves by rather different methods that any product of compact *locales* is compact. I know of no generalization to topological systems.

Spatiality of products

The tensor product of frames was a complicated object, and a particular problem was that of whether a product of spatial systems was still spatial. This is a problem of *completeness*. The construction rules of $A \otimes B$ allow us to deduce certain syntactic entailments

$$\bigvee_i a_i \otimes b_i \leq \bigvee_j a_j' \otimes b_j'$$

and the inference rules are semantically *sound*: we can validly infer a corresponding inclusion between open sets

$$\bigcup_i a_i \times b_i \subseteq \bigcup_j a_j' \times b_j'$$

The converse question is that of *completeness*: can all such inclusions between open sets be deduced from the construction rules of $A \otimes B$? In general the answer is No, but we shall see how a technical application of compactness allows us to answer Yes in a wide range of cases.

Recall from Lemma 6.4.3 how the elements of a tensor product $A \otimes B$ were represented canonically in the form

$$\bigvee \{a \otimes b: \langle a, b \rangle \in I\}$$

for certain subsets I of $A \times B$, the C-ideals for an appropriate coverage C. Let us call these *bilinear ideals* of $A \times B$ and write $\bigvee I$ for $\bigvee \{a \otimes b: \langle a, b \rangle \in I\}$.

Lemma 8.5.3 Let A and B be frames, let C and D be compact sets of points from the locales of A and B, and let I be a bilinear ideal of $A \times B$. Then

$\wedge(C{\times}D) \vDash \vee I$ iff $\wedge C \vDash a$ and $\wedge D \vDash b$ for some $\langle a, b \rangle \in I$.

Proof Of course, this is trivial if C and D are singletons, i.e. actual points. Therefore, if $x \in C$ and $y \in D$ then we can find $\langle a_{xy}, b_{xy} \rangle \in I$ with $x \vDash a_{xy}$ and $y \vDash b_{xy}$.

Fixing y, we have $\wedge C \vDash \vee_{x \in C} a_{xy}$, and so for some finite $C' \subseteq C$,

$$\wedge C \vDash \vee_{x \in C'} a_{xy}.$$

Write

$$a_{Cy} = \vee_{x \in C'} a_{xy}, \quad b_{Cy} = \wedge_{x \in C'} b_{xy}$$

Then $\langle a_{xy}, b_{Cy} \rangle \in I$ for each x, and so $\langle a_{Cy}, b_{Cy} \rangle \in I$, with $\wedge C \vDash a_{Cy}$ and $y \vDash b_{Cy}$.

Now $\wedge D \vDash \vee_{y \in D} b_{Cy}$ and so for some finite $D' \subseteq D$,

$$\wedge D \vDash \vee_{y \in D'} b_{Cy}.$$

Write

$$a = \wedge_{y \in D'} a_{Cy}, \quad b = \vee_{y \in D'} b_{Cy}$$

Then $\langle a, b_{Cy} \rangle \in I$ for each y, and so $\langle a, b \rangle \in I$, with $\wedge C \vDash a$ and $\wedge D \vDash b$.   ]

Definition 8.5.4 A topological space X is *locally compact* iff for every point x and open a with $x \vDash a$, we can find a compact set C and an open b such that

$x \vDash b$,
$b \subseteq C$ (i.e. for all points y, if $y \vDash b$ then $y \in C$), and
$C \subseteq a$ ($\wedge C \vDash a$).

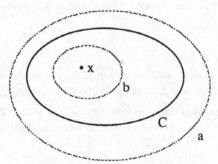

Examples 8.5.5

(i)   The real line $\mathbb{R}$. For if a point x is in an open set a, then we can find $\delta > 0$ such that the open interval $(x{-}\delta, x{+}\delta)$ is contained in a; then we can take C to be $[x{-}\delta/2, x{+}\delta/2]$ (which is compact by Heine-Borel) and $b = (x{-}\delta/2, x{+}\delta/2)$.

(ii)   The spatial system $2^{*\omega}$. For if $s \vDash a$, then for some finite l we have $s \vDash \mathbf{starts}\ l \leq a$. $\mathbf{starts}\ l$ is both compact and open, so we can use it for both C and b.

We digress with some lemmas about locally compact spaces.

Lemma 8.5.6 Let D be a locally compact space, K a compact subset of pt D, and T a finite subset of ΩD such that $K \subseteq \bigvee T$. Then for each $b \in T$ we can find an open set U_b and a compact set K_b such that $U_b \subseteq K_b \subseteq b$ and $K \subseteq \bigcup_b U_b$.

Proof Each $x \in K$ is in some $b_x \in T$, and then by local compactness we can find open U_x and compact K_x such that $x \in U_x \subseteq K_x \subseteq b_x$. $K \subseteq \bigcup_x U_x$, so by compactness K has a finite subset K' such that $K \subseteq \bigcup \{U_x : x \in K'\}$. Now for each $b \in T$, let

$U_b = \bigcup \{U_x : x \in K', b_x = b\}$,
$K_b = \bigcup \{K_x : x \in K', b_x = b\}$ (still compact)

These are the sets required.   ]

Note that in the case where T has just one element, this says roughly for compact sets what the definition says for points: that if $K \subseteq b$, then we can interpolate an open and a compact set between them.

The intuition behind local compactness is that there are enough compact sets to describe the structure of the open sets, and in fact we can make this precise. Let D be a spatial locale. For each $a \in \Omega D$, the set $E(a) = \{F \in QD : F \vDash a\}$ (a generalized extent of a) is a Scott open filter of QD – this follows from the concrete representation of $\sqcap$ and $\bigsqcup^\uparrow$ as $\cap$ and $\bigcup^\uparrow$ on filters. The function $a \longmapsto E(a)$ is monotone, and by spatiality it is one-one.

Theorem 8.5.7 If D is a locally compact spatial locale, then the function E defined above is an order isomorphism between ΩD and the set of Scott open filters of QD.

Proof After the preliminary remarks above, we just need to prove that E is onto. Let G be a Scott open filter in QD, and define

$a = \bigcup \{K : K \text{ saturated compact}, \wedge K \in G\}$.

We show that a is an open set, and that $G = E(a)$. First, suppose K is saturated compact and $\wedge K \in G$. If $K \subseteq c \in \Omega D$, then by Lemma 8.5.6 we can find $b \in \Omega D$ and L saturated compact such that $K \subseteq b \subseteq L \subseteq c$. K is the downward directed intersection of such c's, and hence

$K = \bigcap^\downarrow \{L : L \text{ saturated compact and } \exists b \in \Omega D. \ K \subseteq b \subseteq L\}$

With respect to QD, this makes K a directed join. Hence by Scott openness of G we can find b and L such that $K \subseteq b \subseteq L$ and $\wedge L \in G$. We deduce that

$a = \bigcup \{b \in \Omega D : \exists L \text{ saturated compact. } b \subseteq L \text{ and } \wedge L \in G\}$

which is open. Clearly $G \subseteq E(a)$.

Now suppose K is compact and $K \subseteq a$. By compactness we can find a finite subset T of ΩD such that $K \subseteq \bigcup T$, and for each $b \in T$ there is some compact L_b with $b \subseteq L_b$ and $\bigwedge L_b \in G$. Then $\bigwedge K \sqsupseteq \bigcap \{\bigwedge L_b : b \in T\} \in G$. This proves $E(a) \subseteq G$.   ]

We now return to the promised application to products.

Theorem 8.5.8 Let X and Y be topological spaces, and suppose X is locally compact. Then their product X×Y (as topological systems, i.e. before spatialization to make their product as spaces) is already spatial.

Proof Let I be a bilinear ideal in $\Omega X \times \Omega Y$, and write $c \subseteq \mathrm{pt}\, X \times \mathrm{pt}\, Y$ for the extent of $\bigvee I$. We show that if $a \times b \subseteq c$ then $\langle a, b \rangle \in I$, which shows that any element of $\Omega X \otimes \Omega Y$ is determined by its extent.

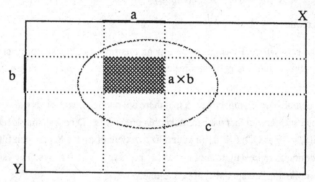

Suppose $x \in a$. By local compactness, we can choose a compact K_x and open d_x such that

$$x \vdash d_x \subseteq K_x \subseteq a$$

If $y \in b$, then $K_x \times \{y\} \subseteq a \times b \subseteq c$, so $\bigwedge(K_x \times \{y\}) \vdash \bigvee I$. By Lemma 8.5.3, we can find $a_{xy} \in \Omega X$ and $b_{xy} \in \Omega Y$ such that

$$\langle a_{xy}, b_{xy} \rangle \in I, \bigwedge K_x \vdash a_{xy} \text{ and } y \vdash b_{xy}.$$

We see that $d_x \leq a_{xy}$, so $\langle d_x, b_{xy} \rangle \in I$, so $\langle d_x, b \rangle \in I$ (because $b \leq \bigvee_{y \in b} b_{xy}$), so $\langle a, b \rangle \in I$ (because $a \leq \bigvee_{x \in a} d_x$).   ]

8.6 Local compactness and function spaces

The prime application of local compactness is to function spaces: if D is locally compact, then for other systems E, the set of continuous maps from D to E can be given a nice topology. Most of the rest of this section is devoted to formalizing this. However, the full generality of the treatment is not used in the remainder of the book, and on first reading you are invited to skip this section, just noting parts (ii) and (iii) of Theorem 8.6.2, which define the appropriate order structure of the function space. (See also Exercise 4.)

In Section 3.7 we introduced subbasic opens [x→b] for the set [D→E] of continuous maps from D to E: x ∈ pt D, b ∈ ΩE, and f ⊢ [x→b] iff pt f(x) ⊢ b (or x ⊢ Ωf(b)). This defines a topology on [D→E] (the *pointwise* topology), and – at least if D and E are spatial locales – it is fine enough to distinguish between different continuous maps: the topology is T_0. If f ≠ g, then for some x ∈ pt D, pt f(x) ≠ pt g(x). Without loss of generality, we can find b ∈ ΩE such that pt f(x) ⊢ b but pt g(x) ⊬ b: then f ⊢ [x, b], but g ⊬ [x, b].

Unfortunately, this topology is still too coarse for some purposes, and we define a finer *compact-open* topology. (Note however that for the domains treated in Chapter 10, the pointwise and compact-open topologies coincide: the pointwise topology is fine enough. See Theorem 10.5.3.) Our touchstone is the evaluation function

$$ev: D×[D→E] → E, \langle x, f\rangle \mapsto f(x)$$

By the arguments of Section 5.2, this ought to be continuous.

Example 8.6.1 If [ℝ→ℝ] is given the pointwise topology, then ev: ℝ×[ℝ→ℝ] → ℝ is not continuous.

Proof Suppose it is continuous, and consider $ev^{-1}((-1, 1))$. This contains the pair $\langle 0, k_0\rangle$, where k_0 is the constant zero function. We can therefore find basic neighbourhoods (−ε, ε) of 0 and $\bigwedge_i[x_i→a_i]$ of k_0 (so 0 ∈ a_i for all i) such that

$$(-ε, ε) × \bigwedge_i [x_i→a_i] \subseteq ev^{-1}((-1, 1))$$

Since the meet is finite, we can find x' ∈ (−ε, ε) distinct from each x_i, and it is easy to define a continuous f with $f(x_i) = 0$ for all i, but f(x') = 2. Then

$$\langle x', f\rangle \in (-ε, ε) × \bigwedge_i [x_i→a_i],$$

but ev $(\langle x', f\rangle) \notin (-1, 1)$ – contradiction.]

For stronger observations we take those of the form [K, b], where K is a compact subset of pt D and b an open for E, and f ⊢ [K→b] iff pt f(K) ⊆ b (or K ⊆ Ωf(b)). (We shan't consider how we might set up K to make this observation.) Since open sets are upper closed, it makes no difference to [K, b] if we replace K by its saturation, and if D is a locale then we can work equally well with the Scott open filters of ΩD. We assume for simplicity that D and E are both spatial locales.

In Theorem 8.6.2 we give five relation schemes that will hold for these generators [K, b]. 1) to 4) follow from the logic of compactness (Theorem 8.2.6), and the fact that the frame parts of continuous maps preserve finite meets and directed joins. However, these do not include the information that frame parts Ωf also preserve finite joins. For a point x, we have [x→⋁T] = ⋁{[x→b]: b ∈ T}, because x must be contained in some disjunct of Ωf(⋁T) = ⋁{Ωf(b): b ∈ T}. A general K may split into different parts, contained in different disjuncts. Suppose for each b in T we have a compact set K_b such that K ⊆ $\bigcup_b K_b$ (K ⊒ $\bigsqcap_b K_b$). Then from the relations 8.6.2 1) to 4),

$$\bigwedge\{[K_b{\to}b]: b \in T\} \le \bigwedge\{[K_b{\to}\bigvee T]: b \in T\} = [\textstyle\prod_b K_b{\to}\bigvee T] \le [K{\to}\bigvee T]$$

so that

$$[K{\to}\bigvee T] \ge \bigvee\ \{\bigwedge\{[K_b{\to}b]: b \in T\}: K \sqsupseteq \textstyle\prod\{K_b: b \in T\}\} \qquad (T \subseteq \Omega E, \text{ T finite})$$

To get equality here, we assume that D is locally compact. Then if f satisfies the left-hand side, i.e. $K \subseteq \bigcup\ \{\Omega f(b): b \in T\}$, we can use Lemma 8.5.6 to find compact sets $K_b \subseteq \Omega f(b)$ such that $K \subseteq \bigcup\ \{K_b: b \in T\}$.

Theorem 8.6.2 Let D and E be spatial locales, with D locally compact. Define a locale F by

$$\Omega F = \text{Fr}\ \langle\ [K{\to}b]: K \in QD, b \in \Omega E \mid$$

1) $[K{\to}\bigwedge T]\ = \bigwedge\ \{[K{\to}b]: b \in T\}$ $(T \subseteq \Omega E, \text{ T finite})$

2) $[K{\to}\bigvee^{\uparrow} T]\ = \bigvee^{\uparrow} \{[K{\to}b]: b \in T\}$ $(T \subseteq \Omega E, \text{ T directed})$

3) $[\textstyle\prod S{\to}b]\ = \bigwedge\ \{[K{\to}b]: K \in S\}$ $(S \subseteq QD, \text{ S finite})$

4) $[\bigsqcup^{\uparrow} S{\to}b]\ = \bigvee^{\uparrow} \{[K{\to}b]: K \in S\}$ $(S \subseteq QD, \text{ S directed})$

5) $[K{\to}\bigvee T]\ = \bigvee\ \{\bigwedge\{[K_b{\to}b]: b \in T\}: K \sqsupseteq \textstyle\prod\{K_b: b \in T\}\}$

                                              $(T \subseteq \Omega E, \text{ T finite})\quad\ \rangle$

(i)   The points of F can be identified with the continuous maps from D to E, with

$$f \vdash [K, b] \Leftrightarrow \text{pt } f(K) \subseteq b \Leftrightarrow K \vdash \Omega f\ (b)$$

(ii)   The specialization order on pt F is defined by

$$f \sqsubseteq g \Leftrightarrow \forall x \in \text{pt D. pt } f(x) \sqsubseteq \text{pt } g(x) \Leftrightarrow \forall b \in \Omega E.\ \Omega f(b) \le \Omega g(b)$$

(iii)   If Z is a directed set of points of F, then

$$\text{pt }(\bigsqcup^{\uparrow} Z)(x) = \bigsqcup^{\uparrow} \{\text{pt } f(x): f \in Z\}, \quad \Omega(\bigsqcup^{\uparrow} Z)(b) = \bigvee^{\uparrow} \{\Omega f(b): f \in Z\}$$

Proof (i) We have already shown that each continuous map gives a point, and that different maps give different points. It remains to show that each point $f': \Omega F \to \mathbf{2}$ gives a map.

First, note that if x is a point of D, then

$$[x{\to}\bigvee T] = \bigvee\ \{\bigwedge\{[K_b{\to}b]: b \in T\}: x \sqsupseteq \textstyle\prod\{K_b: b \in T\}\}$$
$$= \bigvee\ \{[x{\to}b]: b \in T\}$$

because if $x \sqsupseteq \textstyle\prod\{K_b: b \in T\}$ then $x \sqsupseteq K_c$ for some $c \in T$. It follows from relation schemes 1), 2) and 5) that $\{b: f' \vdash [x{\to}b]\}$ is a completely prime filter of ΩE, and hence corresponds to a point pt f(x), say, of E.

On the other hand, if $b \in \Omega E$, then $\{K: f' \vdash [K{\to}b]\}$ is a Scott open filter of QD (by relation schemes 3) and 4)) and hence by Theorem 8.5.7 defines an open $\Omega f(b)$, say, of D. Now

$$\text{pt } f(x) \vdash b \Leftrightarrow f' \vdash [x{\to}b] \Leftrightarrow x \vdash \Omega f(b)$$

It follows that pt f and Ωf form the two parts of a continuous map f. Moreover,

$$f \vDash [K \to b] \Leftrightarrow K \vDash \Omega f(b) \Leftrightarrow f' \vDash [K \to b]$$

so f defines the same point as f'.

(ii) $f \sqsubseteq g \Leftrightarrow \forall K \in QD, b \in \Omega E. (K \vDash \Omega f(b) \to K \vDash \Omega g(b))$
     $\Leftrightarrow \forall x \in pt\ D, b \in \Omega E. (x \vDash \Omega f(b) \to x \vDash \Omega g(b))$

The required conditions follow from this, using spatiality.

(iii)   If the definition given does in fact define a map, then by part (ii) it must be the required directed join. Now

$$\bigsqcup{}^{\uparrow} \{pt\ f(x): f \in Z\} \vDash b \Leftrightarrow \exists f \in Z.\ pt\ f(x) \vDash b$$
$$\Leftrightarrow \exists f \in Z.\ x \vDash \Omega f(b) \Leftrightarrow x \vDash \bigvee{}^{\uparrow} \{\Omega f(b): f \in Z\}$$

It follows that $\Omega(\bigsqcup{}^{\uparrow} Z)$ is the inverse image map of pt $(\bigsqcup{}^{\uparrow} Z)$, and, using spatiality, the two parts form a continuous map.   ]

Of course, Spat F is the function space [D→E]. In the contexts of Chapter 10, F itself will be spatial, but we shall not say anything about its spatiality in general.

Finally, we return to our touchstone.

Proposition 8.6.3 Let D and E be spatial locales, with D locally compact. If the function space [D→E] is given the compact-open topology, then the evaluation map ev: D×[D→E] → E is continuous.

Proof We have not said here whether × is supposed to represent the product of topological systems, or the spatial product. In fact, Theorem 8.5.8 says these are the same.

Suppose $x \in pt\ D$ and $f \in pt\ [D \to E]$ with pt $f(x) \vDash b \in \Omega E$. By local compactness, we can find $a \in \Omega D$ and K a compact set of points of D such that

$$x \in a \subseteq K \subseteq \Omega f(b).$$

Then $f \vDash [K \to b]$ and $ev(a \times [K \to b]) \subseteq b$.   ]

Notes

Section 8.2: The correspondence of Theorem 8.2.5 appears to have been first set out in Hofmann and Mislove [81]. Although it was there stated only for sober spaces, the proof works for general locales – hence it can be used to prove spatiality results such as Theorem 9.2.4. Set theoretic irrelevancies (for instance, whether a point is an element of an open or – identifying the point with the filter – the other way round) can make the result somewhat obscure, but its application is quite straightforward. It is often easier to construct Scott open filters than completely prime ones, and the

theorem tells us that this is good enough. Smyth [83] first pointed out the importance of the theorem in power domains, stating the theorem for sober spaces.
Section 8.5: Local compactness has considerably more importance than is apparent here, and Johnstone [82] gives a good account. Briefly, a locally compact sober space has a frame of opens that is a *continuous lattice* in a certain technical sense, and conversely a distributive continuous lattice is a frame whose locale is spatial and locally compact. This shows us both a good class of spatial locales (in fact it generalizes the spectral locales of chapter 9) and a link with the active theory of continuous lattices (Gierz et al. [80]).

Theorem 8.5.8 is folklore, according to Johnstone.
Section 8.6: Theorem 8.6.2 here is just part of Hyland's theorem ([81], described in Johnstone [82]; see also Robinson [87]), which says that a locale is *exponentiable* in a certain category theoretic sense if and only if it is locally compact. Hyland shows that the locale F (he presents it slightly differently – see Exercise 3) satisfies the property that there is a natural 1-1 correspondence between continuous maps from E' to F and those from E'×D to E, for any other locale E'.

Exercises

1. Show that for subsets of 2^ω (as in Proposition 8.4.2), compact $\Leftrightarrow$ closed.

2. Let f: D $\rightarrow$ E be a continuous map between locales. By Proposition 8.1.5 pt f preserves compactness, and this suggests that we should get a function Qf: QD $\rightarrow$ QE.

If K $\in$ QD, show that $(\Omega f)^{-1}(K) = \{b \in \Omega E: K \vDash \Omega f(b)\}$ is a Scott open filter; let this be Qf(K). K $\vDash \Omega f(b) \Leftrightarrow$ Qf(K) $\vDash$ b, analogous to the relation between Ωf and pt f. If K = $\bigwedge$C, show that Qf(K) = $\bigwedge\{$pt f(y): y $\in$ C$\}$.

Show that Qf preserves finite meets and directed joins, and that Q is functorial (c.f. Exercise 3 of Chapter 5).

3. Let D be a locally compact spatial locale. If a and b are opens for D, define a « b (a is *way below* b) iff a $\subseteq$ K $\subseteq$ b for some compact set K of points of D. (This is not the fundamental definition of the way below relation – see Johnstone [82] for an account of it –, but happens to be equivalent in our case.) Show that the locale F of Theorem 8.6.2 can also be presented by

   $\Omega F = \text{Fr} \langle$ w(a, b): a $\in \Omega$D, b $\in \Omega$E $|$
      w(**false**, b) = **true**
      w(a$_1$ $\vee$ a$_2$, b) = w(a$_1$, b)$\wedge$w(a$_2$, b)
      w(a, b) $\leq$ w(a, b')   (b $\leq$ b')

$$w(a, \textbf{true}) = \textbf{true} \qquad\qquad (a \ll \textbf{true})$$
$$w(a, b_1) \wedge w(a, b_2) \leq w(a', b_1 \wedge b_2) \quad (a' \ll a)$$
$$w(a, b) = \bigvee \{w(a', b): a \ll a'\}$$
$$w(a, \vee^\uparrow T) = \vee^\uparrow \{w(a, b): b \in T\} \qquad (T \subseteq \Omega E, \ T \text{ directed})$$
$$w(a, \textbf{false}) = \textbf{false} \qquad\qquad (a \neq \textbf{false})$$
$$w(a, b_1 \vee b_2) = \bigvee \{w(a_1, b_1) \wedge w(a_2, b_2): a \leq a_1 \vee a_2\} \quad)$$

The isomorphism uses

$$w(a, b) = \bigvee \{[K \rightarrow b] : a \subseteq K\}, \quad [K \rightarrow b] = \bigvee \{w(a, b) : K \subseteq a\}$$

4. Let D and E be topological systems. Define two preorders on the continuous maps from D to E:

$$f \sqsubseteq_{pt} g \quad \text{iff} \quad \forall x \in \text{pt } D. \ \text{pt } f(x) \sqsubseteq \text{pt } g(x)$$
$$f \sqsubseteq_\Omega g \quad \text{iff} \quad \forall b \in \Omega E. \ \Omega f(b) \leq \Omega g(b)$$

Show that if $f \sqsubseteq_\Omega g$ then $f \sqsubseteq_{pt} g$, and that the converse holds if D is spatial.

In general, we *define* $f \sqsubseteq g$ iff $f \sqsubseteq_\Omega g$.

Show that $\sqsubseteq_{pt}$ is the specialization preorder for the pointwise topology, and $\sqsubseteq_\Omega$ is the specialization preorder for the topology with subbasic open sets $[U \leftarrow b]$ (U a Scott open subset of ΩD, $b \in \Omega E$), with $f \vDash [U \leftarrow b]$ iff $\Omega f(b) \vDash U$.

Suppose in addition that D is a locally compact space. Show that every open for D is a directed join of opens way below it and hence that every Scott open subset of ΩD is a union of Scott open filters, and deduce that the topology described by the subbasics $[U \leftarrow b]$ is the compact open topology.

5. Let D and E be locales (or, more generally, T_0 topological systems that have disjunctions of all directed sets of points). If Z is a set of continuous maps from D to E that is directed with respect to the order $\sqsubseteq$ defined in Exercise 4, show that Z has a join defined as in Theorem 8.6.2 (iii). Show that composition preserves these directed joins: if f: D' $\rightarrow$ D and h: E $\rightarrow$ E' are continuous, then

$$f; \sqcup^\uparrow Z = \sqcup^\uparrow \{f;g: g \in Z\}, \qquad (\sqcup^\uparrow Z);h = \sqcup^\uparrow \{g;h: g \in Z\}$$

CHAPTER NINE

SPECTRAL ALGEBRAIC LOCALES

In which we see a category of locales within which we can do the topology of domain theory.

9.1 Algebraic posets

We saw in Theorem 7.2.3 that the points of a locale have all directed joins – they form a *directed complete poset,* or *dcpo*. This is not true for an arbitrary poset, so we ask how we might complete it to a dcpo. The answer is to treat its directed sets as being formal representatives of their joins.

Definition 9.1.1 Let P be a poset.

An *ideal* of P is a lower closed, directed subset of P.

The *ideal completion* of P, written Idl(P), is the poset of ideals of P, ordered by inclusion.

An element $x \in P$ is *compact* iff whenever S is a directed subset of P and $x \leq \bigvee^\uparrow S$, then $x \leq y$ for some $y \in S$ – i.e. iff $\uparrow x$ is Scott open. (For instance, the compact opens for a topological space X are the compact elements of ΩX.) We write KP for the set of compact elements of P. The word *finite* is commonly used instead of *compact* here.

Proposition 9.1.2 Let P be a poset.

(i)   Idl(P) is a dcpo.

(ii)   P can be mapped into Idl(P) by $x \mapsto \downarrow x$, and $\downarrow x \subseteq \downarrow y$ iff $x \leq y$.

(iii)   The ideals $\downarrow x$ are precisely the compact elements of Idl(P).

(iv)   Every element of Idl(P) is the directed join of the compact elements less than it.

(v)   Let f: P $\to$ D be a monotone function into a dcpo. Then f extends uniquely to a Scott continuous map from Idl(P) to D.

Proof (i) A directed union of ideals is still an ideal, so it must be the directed join.
(ii) is obvious.
(iii) If $x \in P$ and $\downarrow x \leq \bigvee^\uparrow S = \bigcup^\uparrow S$, then $x \in$ some $J \in S$ and so $\downarrow x \leq J$.

Conversely, suppose that I is a compact element of Idl(P). $I = \bigvee^\uparrow \{\downarrow x: x \in I\}$, and so by compactness $I = \downarrow x$ for some $x \in I$.
(iv) $I = \bigvee^\uparrow \{\downarrow x: x \in I\} = \bigvee^\uparrow \{\downarrow x: \downarrow x \leq I\}$.
(v) Assume that an extension g exists. Then

$$g(I) = g(\bigvee^\uparrow \{\downarrow x \colon x \in I\}) = \bigvee^\uparrow \{g(\downarrow x) \colon x \in I\} \qquad \text{by Scott continuity}$$
$$= \bigvee^\uparrow \{f(x) \colon x \in I\} \qquad \text{(we use monotonicity to show that this join is}$$
directed)

This proves uniqueness. It remains to show that this g is Scott continuous.

$$g(\bigvee^\uparrow S) = g(\bigcup^\uparrow S) = \bigvee^\uparrow \{f(x) \colon x \in \bigcup^\uparrow S\} = \bigvee^\uparrow_{J \in S} \bigvee^\uparrow \{f(x) \colon x \in J\}$$
$$= \bigvee^\uparrow_{J \in S} g(J)$$

]

Definition 9.1.3 A dcpo is *algebraic* iff every element is a directed join of compact elements less than it.

It is quite important that the join involved should be directed.

Proposition 9.1.4 Let D be an algebraic dcpo and P = KD be its set of compact elements. Then D is isomorphic to Idl(P).
Proof An ideal I in P corresponds to the element $\bigvee^\uparrow I \in D$, and every element of D is of this form. We show that $I \subseteq J$ iff $\bigvee^\uparrow I \le \bigvee^\uparrow J$. Suppose the latter, and take $x \in I$. Then $x \le \bigvee^\uparrow J$, so $x \le y$ for some $y \in J$, and $x \in J$. Thus $I \subseteq J$.]

We thus have three characterizations of algebraicity: the intrinsic characterization is that of the definition, the extrinsic characterization says that it is isomorphic to an ideal completion, and the universal characterization is that of Proposition 9.1.2 (v).

We now show how if a poset P has some extra structure, then sometimes that can be lifted to Idl(P).

Theorem 9.1.5 Let P be a poset.

(i)   If P has finite meets, then Idl(P) has finite meets and directed joins, and the meets distribute over the directed joins.
(ii)   If P has finite joins, then Idl(P) has all joins.
(iii)   If P is a distributive lattice, then Idl(P) is a frame.
(iv)   In any of (i), (ii) or (iii), the injection of P into Idl(P) preserves the meets and joins listed for P. Suppose in addition:

   D is a poset with the properties listed for Idl(P),
   f: P → D preserves the meets and joins listed for P, and
   g is the extension of f to Idl(P).

Then g preserves the meets and joins listed for Idl(P).
e.g. for (iii), if D is a frame and f: P → D is a distributive lattice homomorphism, then g: Idl(P) → D is a frame homomorphism.

Proof (i) **true** in Idl(P) is $P = {\downarrow}\textbf{true}$. $I{\wedge}J$ is $\{x{\wedge}y: x \in I, y \in J\} = I{\cap}J$.

$I{\wedge}\bigvee^{\uparrow} S = I{\cap}\bigcup^{\uparrow} S = \bigcup_{J\in S}^{\uparrow} I{\cap}J$ by set theory.

For part (iv), ${\downarrow}x{\wedge}{\downarrow}y = {\downarrow}(x{\wedge}y)$, and

$$g(\textbf{true}) = f(\textbf{true}) = \textbf{true}$$
$$g(I{\wedge}J) = \bigvee^{\uparrow} \{f(x){\wedge}f(y): x \in I, y \in J\} = \bigvee^{\uparrow} \{f(x): x \in I\}{\wedge} \bigvee^{\uparrow} \{f(y): y \in J\}$$
$$= g(I){\wedge}g(J)$$

(ii) Note that a poset has all joins iff it has finite joins and directed joins: for the join of an infinite set is the directed join of the joins of the finite subsets. Also, if a poset has finite joins, then the ideals are the non-empty lower closed subsets that are also closed under binary joins.

false in Idl(P) is $\{\textbf{false}\} = {\downarrow}\textbf{false}$. $I{\vee}J$ is ${\downarrow}\{x{\vee}y: x \in I, y \in J\}$.

For part (iv), ${\downarrow}x{\vee}{\downarrow}y = {\downarrow}(x{\vee}y)$, and

$$g(\textbf{false}) = f(\textbf{false}) = \textbf{false}$$
$$g(I{\vee}J) = \bigvee^{\uparrow} \{f(x){\vee}f(y): x \in I, y \in J\} = \bigvee^{\uparrow} \{f(x): x \in I\}{\vee} \bigvee^{\uparrow} \{f(y): y \in J\}$$
$$= g(I){\vee}g(J)$$

(iii) After (i) and (ii), we just need to show finite distributivity. If $z \in I{\wedge}\bigvee S$, with S finite, then for each $J \in S$ we can find $y_J \in J$ such that $z \le \bigvee_{J\in S} y_J$: then

$$z = \bigvee_{J\in S} (z{\wedge}y_J) \in \bigvee_{J\in S} (I{\wedge}J). \qquad \rrbracket$$

Categorically, consider a number of categories of posets. For each one the objects are the posets with the listed meets and joins for which the listed meets distribute over the listed joins, and the morphisms are the functions that preserve those meets and joins.

C_1:   finite meets (i.e. meet semilattices)
C_1':   finite meets and directed joins
C_2:   finite joins (join semilattices)
C_2':   all joins (complete join semilattices)
C_3:   finite meets and finite joins (distributive lattices)
C_3':   finite meets and all joins (frames)

Then for $i = 1, 2$ or 3, the forgetful functor from C_i' to C_i has a left adjoint given concretely by Idl.

We conclude this section with a useful Proposition.

Proposition 9.1.6 In any poset, finite joins of compact elements are compact.

Proof Let P be a poset, let S be finite subset of compact elements with a join, let T be a directed subset with a join, and suppose $\bigvee S \le \bigvee^{\uparrow} T$. If $s \in S$ then by compactness we can find $t_s \in T$ such that $s \leq t_s$. If t is an upper bound in T for $\{t_s: s \in S\}$, then $\bigvee S \leq t$.]

9.2 Spectral locales

Reasoning that finite joins are nicer than infinite ones, we now investigate frames that can be presented without infinite joins. It turns out that this is related to algebraicity of the frame. In the next section we shall introduce algebraicity also for the dcpo of points, so that it is present on both sides.

Definition 9.2.1 A presentation of a frame is *coherent* iff there are no infinite joins in its relations.

Theorem 9.2.2 Let A be a frame. The following are equivalent.

(i)   A has a coherent presentation.
(ii) $A \cong Idl(K)$ for some distributive lattice K.
(iii) As a poset A is algebraic, and also KA is a sublattice (it suffices that KA should be closed under finite meets).

Proof First, let K be any distributive lattice presented by generators and relations. We can use the same generators and relations to present a frame A_0, and we show that this is isomorphic to $A = Idl(K)$. Using the appropriate universal properties, we construct a series of functions:

1.   A distributive lattice homomorphism f: $K \to A_0$, taking each generator of K to the corresponding generator of A_0.
2.   A frame homomorphism f': $A = Idl(K) \to A_0$ extending f (by Theorem 9.1.5).
3.   A frame homomorphism g: $A_0 \to A$, taking each generator of A_0 to the corresponding generator of K (contained in A).

Now f';g restricted to K is the identity on K (it brings each generator back to itself), so f';g is the identity on A. Likewise, g;f' is the identity on A_0 (again, it brings each generator back to itself). Therefore A is isomorphic to A_0.

Now if we have a coherent presentation of a frame, then the generators and relations present a distributive lattice, and the frame is its ideal completion.

Conversely, suppose $A = Idl(K)$. By Proposition 4.3.7, K has a presentation as a distributive lattice, and then A is presented coherently as a frame by the same generators and relations. This completes the proof of (i) $\Leftrightarrow$ (ii). (ii) $\Leftrightarrow$ (iii) comes from Theorem 9.1.5.   ]

Definition 9.2.3 A frame is *coherent* iff it satisfies any of the equivalent conditions of Theorem 9.2.2.

A locale D is *spectral* iff ΩD is coherent.

A topological system is *spectral* iff it is homeomorphic to a spectral locale.

If K is a distributive lattice, then its *spectrum*, Spec K, is the locale of the frame Idl K. Hence a topological system D is spectral iff it is homeomorphic to Spec KΩD.

Theorem 9.2.4 Spectral locales are spatial and locally compact.

Proof Let D be a spectral locale.

Suppose a and b are opens with $a \not\leq b$. We want a point x such that

$$x \vDash a, \text{ but} \quad x \nvDash b.$$

We can find $e \in$ KΩD with $e \leq a$, $e \not\leq b$, and then it suffices to find x with $x \vDash e$, $x \nvDash b$. Equivalently, we can assume that $a \in$ KΩD.

By compactness, $\uparrow a$ is a Scott open filter in ΩD. Now let

$$C = \{x \in \text{pt D}: \uparrow a \subseteq x\} = \{x \in \text{pt D}: x \vDash a\} = \text{extent of a}$$

By the Hofmann–Mislove Theorem, $\uparrow a = \bigwedge C$, i.e.

$$a \leq b \Leftrightarrow (x \vDash a \Rightarrow x \vDash b) \Leftrightarrow \text{extent of a} \subseteq \text{extent of b}$$

This proves spatiality. For local compactness, if $x \vDash b$, then $x \vDash a \leq b$ for some compact open a.]

As we have remarked before, if the coherent presentation is seen as the syntax of a logical system, then the points provide a semantics: each open denotes its extent. The system is automatically sound, and this spatiality result says that it is also complete.

Proposition 9.2.5 A topological space is spectral iff

- it is sober (localic),
- any finite intersection of compact open sets is still compact, and
- the compact open sets form a basis.

Note that the entire space must be compact, because this is the empty meet of compact opens.

Proof The compact opens are always closed under finite joins, so the second condition says that they form a distributive lattice. The third condition says that every open is the join of the compact opens less than it, and because these are closed under finite joins, they form a directed set. Thus the second two conditions say that the frame is the ideal completion of a distributive lattice.   ]

Spectral locales are spatial, and spectral spaces are localic, so there is no significant difference between the two concepts. The language of topological systems allows us to avoid committing ourselves to either. We shall usually refer to spectral *locales* because in practice (Chapter 10) we shall define them by presenting their frames.

Spectral is the customary adjective for spaces (these are precisely the spaces that arise as Zariski spectra of commutative rings), and we use it for locales on the principle that the language for locales should imitate that for spaces. It also helps to avoid confusion with some other uses of *coherent* in domain theory. However, Johnstone applies the word *coherent* to locales and spaces instead of *spectral,* and this usage is common in domain theory.

9.3 Spectral algebraic locales

Working in some spatial locale D, let us now investigate algebraicity on the points side. With respect to the specialization order on pt D, we know that a point x is compact iff $\uparrow x$ is Scott open. The topology ΩD is not necessarily as fine as the Scott topology (see, for instance, the Stone spaces of Section 9.5), but let us nonetheless seek opens a of the form $\uparrow x$. For all opens b, we should then have $a \leq b$ iff $x \vDash b$, so we require opens a for which the filter $\uparrow a$ is completely prime (corresponding to the point x): alternatively, we want completely prime filters with least elements. As a condition on a, this amounts to

$$\text{if } a \leq \bigvee S \text{ then } a \leq s \text{ for some } s \in S \tag{*}$$

Such an a is *completely coprime*. (*) includes two important cases: if it holds whenever S is directed, then a is simply a compact open, while if (*) holds whenever S is finite, then a is *coprime*.

BEWARE! The "co-" here means work in the opposite lattice: a is coprime in ΩD iff it is prime in $(\Omega D)^{op}$. This is a standard convention in category theory that governs the meanings of terms such as "colimit", "coproduct" and "codomain". Our word "coprime" is quite different from the one established in arithmetic, where some numbers are coprime iff they have no common factor other than 1. For us, some opens are coprime iff each one individually is coprime.

We make a series of easy observations. First, a is completely coprime iff it is both compact and coprime (in fact we shall usually refer to a as a compact, coprime open). Second, by an induction that we have seen before, to test coprimeness by (*) it suffices to take S of cardinality 0 or 2. Third, if D is spectral, then to test coprimeness of a it suffices to take S a set of compact opens. We summarize the combination of these:

Proposition 9.3.1 Let D be a spectral locale, and let a $\in$ ΩD. Then a is completely coprime iff

(i)   a is compact (a $\in$ KΩD),
(ii)   a $\neq$ **false**, and
(iii)   if a = b$\vee$c with b, c $\in$ KΩD, then either a = b or a = c.

Proof $\Rightarrow$ is clear, remembering that **false** is the empty join. For $\Leftarrow$, suppose that

$$a \leq \vee S = \vee^{\uparrow} \{\vee S': S' \subseteq K\Omega D, S' \text{ finite, and } \forall b \in S'. \exists c \in S. b \leq c\}$$

Because a is a compact open, we have a $\leq$ some $\vee$ S', so a = $\vee\{a\wedge b: b \in S'\}$ and by spectrality each a$\wedge$b is compact. By (ii), S' $\neq$ $\emptyset$, and so by iterating (iii) we find for some b $\in$ S', c $\in$ S with a $\leq$ b $\leq$ c.   ]

Just to summarize the argument so far,

Proposition 9.3.2 Let D be a spatial locale, and p a compact, coprime open.

(i) $\uparrow$p is a (completely prime filter representing a) compact point.
(ii)   If a is any open, then $\uparrow$p $\vDash$ a iff p $\leq$ a.
(iii)   If y is any point, then $\uparrow$p $\sqsubseteq$ y iff y $\vDash$ p.   ]

We can now express the idea that "there are enough compact points" in terms of coprime compact open sets.

Definition 9.3.3 A spectral locale D is a *spectral algebraic locale* iff every compact open can be expressed as a finite join of compact, coprime opens.

It follows that in a spectral locale every open a is a join (not necessarily finite) of compact coprimes; we call this a *coprime decomposition* of a. We can be rather more precise in expressing compact opens as joins of coprimes, by eliminating unnecessary disjuncts.

Definition 9.3.4 A join $\vee$S is *irredundant* iff for all a, b $\in$ S, if a $\leq$ b then a = b. (Otherwise a would be redundant.)

Proposition 9.3.5 Let D be a spectral locale. Then every compact open in D has a unique irredundant coprime decomposition, and it is finite.
Proof Let a $\in$ KΩD. First, a has a finite coprime decomposition, and we can clearly remove redundant elements until it is irredundant. Now let $\vee$P and $\vee$Q be two irredundant coprime decompositions of a. If p $\in$ P, then by coprimeness p $\leq$ q for some q $\in$ Q. In turn, q $\leq$ p' for some p' $\in$ P, by irredundancy p = p' = q, and so P $\subseteq$ Q. By symmetry, Q $\subseteq$ P, and so P = Q. This shows uniqueness.   ]

Note that if a and b have irredundant coprime decompositions $\bigvee P$ and $\bigvee Q$, then $a \leq b$ iff $\forall p \in P. \exists q \in Q. p \leq q$.

Lemma 9.3.6 Let D be a spectral algebraic locale. Then

(i)   pt D is an algebraic dcpo, and its compact points are in 1-1 order reversing correspondence with the compact, coprime opens.

(ii)   The compact points satisfy the *2/3 SFP condition:*
For each finite set S of compact points there is another such set M (a complete set of upper bounds for S) such that

- each $m \in M$ is an upper bound for S, and
- if m' is any compact upper bound for S, then $m' \sqsupseteq m$ for some $m \in M$.

(iii) ΩD is the Scott topology for pt D.

Proof (i) First, we show that if x is a point of D, then

$$x = \bigsqcup{}^{\uparrow} \{\uparrow p: p \text{ is a compact, coprime open and } x \vDash p\}$$

Every open a is a join $\bigvee Q$ of compact coprimes, so if $x \vDash a$ then $x \vDash q$ for some $q \in Q$ and $\uparrow q \vDash a$. Therefore x is a disjunction (and hence join) of these compact points $\uparrow p$.

To show the join is directed, suppose that $x \vDash p$ for $p \in P$, a finite set of compact coprimes. Then $x \vDash \bigwedge P = \bigvee Q$ (say), where Q is a finite set of compact coprimes. Now $x \vDash q$ for some $q \in Q$, and $q \leq p$ for all $p \in P$, so $\uparrow q$ is an upper bound for the $\uparrow p$'s.

If x is compact, then it must actually equal one of the $\uparrow p$'s, so we have shown that the compact points are precisely the points $\uparrow p$, and any point is the directed join of the compact points below it.

$$\uparrow p \sqsubseteq \uparrow q \Leftrightarrow \uparrow q \vDash p \Leftrightarrow q \leq p$$

(iii) In a locale, by Corollary 7.3.2, every open has Scott open extent. Now suppose that $U \subseteq$ pt D is Scott open. If $x \in U$ then $x \sqsupseteq \uparrow p \vDash U$ for some compact coprime p, and $p = \uparrow\uparrow p \leq U$. Therefore,

$$U = \bigcup \{p: \uparrow p \vDash U\} \in \Omega D.$$

(ii) This is a translation in terms of points of the statement that if P is a finite set of compact coprimes then $\bigwedge P$ has a finite coprime decomposition.   ]

Lemma 9.3.7 Let P be a poset satisfying the 2/3 SFP property of 9.3.6 (ii). Then Idl(P) with its Scott topology is a spectral algebraic space.

Proof Just from algebraicity of Idl(P), the sets $\uparrow x$ ($x \in P$) are a basis for the Scott topology, and the compact open sets are the finite joins of sets $\uparrow x$. $x \sqsubseteq y$ iff $\uparrow x \geq \uparrow y$. The 2/3 SFP property translates into closure under finite meets of the compact open sets.

It remains to show that the space is sober; we already know that it is T_0, so we just show that any point z is already in Idl(P). The set $I = \{x \in P: z \vDash \uparrow x\}$ is directed, for if S is a finite subset then let M be its complete set of minimal upper bounds.

$$z \vDash \bigwedge \{\uparrow x: x \in S\} = \bigvee \{\uparrow y: y \in M\},$$

so $z \vDash \uparrow y$ for some $y \in M$ and y is an upper bound for S in I. Thus z corresponds to an ideal I of P.   ]

Theorem 9.3.8 *Stone Duality for Spectral Algebraic Locales*
There is an equivalence between

- spectral algebraic locales (frames described as ideal completions of distributive lattices where every element is a join of coprimes), and
- algebraic dcpos with the 2/3 SFP property, under the Scott topology.

The correspondence applies not only to the topological systems involved, but also to the continuous maps: on the one hand we have frame homomorphisms in the reverse direction, while on the other are functions preserving directed joins.   ]

We use the phrase "Stone duality" for results that describe some class of spatial locales in two ways, in terms of the points and the opens. The prototype is Stone's Representation Theorem, 9.5.4.

Let us emphasize here that our dcpos are not required to have least (bottom) elements. These are important for fixpoint theory, but generally irrelevant for topology.

The next lemma is our key result for developing domain theory.

Lemma 9.3.9 *The Method of Quasicoprimes*
Let $\mathrm{Fr} \langle G \mid R \rangle$ be a coherent presentation for a frame, giving a locale D, and let $\mathbb{Q}$ be a set of finite subsets of G. As a temporary measure, we call the opens $\bigwedge Q$ for $Q \in \mathbb{Q}$ the *quasicoprime* opens. Suppose the following hold.

(i)   For each quasicoprime q, there is a point x such that the extent of q is $\uparrow x$.
(ii)   Every finite meet of generators is a join of quasicoprimes.

Then D is a spectral algebraic locale, and its compact coprime opens are precisely the quasicoprimes.

Proof Suppose q is a quasicoprime, with corresponding point x, and that $q \leq \bigvee S$ for some $S \subseteq \Omega D$. $x \vDash q$, so $x \vDash s$ for some $s \in S$, so the extent of q, $\uparrow x$, is contained in that of s. By Theorem 9.2.4 D is spatial, so $q \leq s$. This proves that q is completely coprime. Using hypothesis (ii), every open is a join of compact coprimes and so D is spectral algebraic. Finally, if q is a compact coprime, then it is a join of quasicoprimes, and by its join irreducibility it must be equal to one of them.   ]

Of course, this lemma is useful for showing that locales are spectral algebraic. But notice that we have also identified the compact coprimes (so, equivalently, the compact points). This turns out to be important in domain theory, particularly for function spaces. Two classes of domains important here, namely the Scott domains and the strongly algebraic (SFP) domains, are defined in terms of their compact coprimes, and so the method of the lemma extends easily to cover them.

Hypothesis (i) in the lemma is points side reasoning. To set it up, it is generally convenient to identify all the points of the locale, together with the specialization order. As noted before, these can be straightforwardly described in terms of the generators and relations, because a point is a homomorphism out of the frame, and these are described by the universal property of Definition 4.3.4. Hypothesis (ii) is frame side reasoning, set up by algebraic manipulation in the distributive lattice $K\Omega D$. Thus both hypotheses require more or less elementary reasoning. The lemma provides the crucial non-elementary part, namely the spatiality for spectral locales which we have proved using the axiom of choice in the form of Zorn's lemma.

9.4 Finiteness, 2nd countability and ω-algebraicity

Much of the theory is simpler if the locales are not too big. In this section we shall look at two simplifying assumptions of this kind, namely finiteness, and countability of some basis.

Proposition 9.4.1 Finite locales are spectral algebraic.
Proof By a finite locale, we mean one whose opens form a finite frame, in other words a finite distributive lattice, K (say). This is its own ideal completion, because every directed subset contains its join. Hence the locale is spectral.

To show algebraicity, suppose some open is not a join of coprimes, and choose a minimal such open, a. a is not itself coprime, nor is it **false** (the empty join), so a has the form $b \vee c$ for some $b < a$, $c < a$. But by minimality, b and c are joins of coprimes, so a is too – contradiction.]

Theorem 9.4.2 *Stone Duality for Finite Locales*

Finite locales and continuous maps between them are equivalent to finite posets and monotone functions.

Proof We use the duality Theorem 9.3.8 in the light of Proposition 9.4.1. For each finite locale, the points form a finite poset under the specialization order. Conversely, a finite poset is rather trivially an algebraic dcpo with the 2/3 SFP property, and its Scott open sets (its upper closed sets) form a finite distributive lattice. The Scott continuous maps are just the monotone functions.]

Definition 9.4.3 A topological system D satisfies the *second axiom of countability* (in brief: it is *second countable*) iff ΩD has a countable basis.

> There is a weaker property, *first countability*, which we shan't consider.

Our aim now is to show that when an algebraic dcpo is second countable (for its Scott topology), we don't need to consider general directed joins. ω-joins are sufficient for most purposes.

Definition 9.4.4 Let P be a poset. An *ω-chain* in P is a sequence $a = (a_i)$ $(i \in \omega)$ such that

$$a_0 \le a_1 \le a_2 \le \ldots$$

An *ω-join* is the join of an ω-chain.

For two ω-chains a and b, define

$a \le b$ iff for each i there exists j with $a_i \le b_j$.

If the joins $\bigvee_i a_i$ and $\bigvee_i b_i$ exist, then $a \le b$ is a sufficient condition for $\bigvee_i a_i \le \bigvee_i b_i$.

Define $a \equiv b$ iff $a \le b$ and $b \le a$; this is an equivalence relation.

Define ω-Idl(P) to be the set of equivalence classes of ω-chains modulo $\equiv$. It is the *ω-chain completion* of P.

Proposition 9.4.5 Let P be a poset.

(i) ω-Idl(P) is a poset containing a copy of P, with the same ordering, and every ω-chain in ω-Idl(P) has a join.

(ii)   If P is countable, then ω-Idl(P) $\cong$ Idl(P). Such an ideal completion is called an *ω-algebraic dcpo*.

(iii)   Let D be an ω-algebraic dcpo. Then every $x \in D$ is the join of an ω-chain of compact elements. $x \in D$ is compact iff whenever a is an ω-chain in D with $\bigvee a \ge x$, then some $a_i \ge x$.

Proof (i) Let us write [a] for the equivalence class of the ω-chain a. Then $[a] \le [b]$ in ω-Idl(P) iff $a \le b$ as chains, and this makes ω-Idl(P) a poset. P maps into it by

$x \mapsto [(x)]$ where (x) is the constant ω-chain in which every term is x, and $x \leq y$ iff $(x) \leq (y)$.

Let $(a^{(j)})$ be an ω-chain of ω-chains. We construct an ω-chain b such that b_n is a term from $a^{(n)}$ and is also an upper bound for $\{a^{(j)}_i : i, j \leq n\}$. Then $a^{(j)} \leq b$ for all j, because $a^{(j)}_n \leq b_n$ for all n. If c is some other upper bound of the $a^{(j)}$'s then for each n b_n, a term from $a^{(n)}$, is less than some term from c, so $b \leq c$. To construct b, suppose we are given b_n. $a^{(i)} \leq a^{(n+1)}$ $(i \leq n+1)$, so each $a^{(i)}_{n+1}$ is less than some term in $a^{(n+1)}$, as is also b_n. Take b_{n+1} to be the greatest of these terms in $a^{(n+1)}$.

(ii) If a is an ω-chain in P, then $\downarrow a = \downarrow \{a_i : i \in \omega\}$ is an ideal, and $a \leq b \Leftrightarrow \downarrow a \subseteq \downarrow b$. Thus ω-Idl(P) maps into Idl(P) – this doesn't rely on countability. Now suppose

$$P = \{x_1, x_2, x_3, \ldots\}$$

is an enumeration of P and I is an ideal. Define a chain a as follows. Let a_0 be an arbitrary element of I, and if $a_n \in I$ is defined, let

$$a_{n+1} = \begin{cases} a_n & \text{if } x_n \notin I \\ \text{an upper bound in } I \text{ for } \{a_n, x_n\} & \text{if } x_n \in I \end{cases}$$

Then $\downarrow a = I$, so the mapping of ω-Idl(P) to Idl(P) is an isomorphism.

(iii) As usual, every element is a directed join of compact elements. By (ii) this directed set is represented by an ω-chain of compact elements, and the element is the join of that chain. For the next part, the $\Rightarrow$ direction is *a fortiori,* and the $\Leftarrow$ direction follows from the fact that each element is an ω-join of compacts.]

Theorem 9.4.6 Let D be a spectral algebraic locale. Then D is second countable iff its points form an ω-algebraic dcpo.

We call D a *spectral ω-algebraic locale.*

Proof $\Rightarrow$: Any compact open is a finite join of basics, so if there is a countable basis then the usual basis of compact opens is also countable. Hence the compact points are countable.

$\Leftarrow$: The compact points are countable, so the compact coprime opens are too; but they form a basis.]

Note that the proof shows another result: that a spectral locale D is second countable iff $K\Omega D$ is countable.

ω-algebraic dcpos are computationally nicer than more general dcpos, because the ω-chains are much easier to describe than general directed sets. Fortunately, the countable basis condition is preserved by all the domain constructs that we describe.

9.5 Stone spaces

In this section we look at what may be seen as the origin of the localic approach, namely Stone's representation theorem for Boolean algebras. The particular spaces that arise, the *Boolean* or *Stone* spaces, are the spectral spaces that happen also to be Hausdorff, and so it is natural that they should have been the first spectral spaces to be investigated.

Definition 9.5.1 Let K be a distributive lattice.

If a, b $\in$ K, then b is a *complement* for a iff a$\wedge$b = **false**, a$\vee$b = **true**. When they exist, complements are unique: for if b and b' are two complements of a, then

$$b' = b'\wedge\textbf{true} = b'\wedge(a\vee b) = b'\wedge a \vee b'\wedge b = b'\wedge b = b \text{ (by symmetry)}$$

(Note that this relies on distributivity.)

K is a *Boolean algebra* iff all its elements have complements; we shall write a^c for the complement of a.

A spectral space D is a *Stone space,* or a *Boolean space,* iff KΩD is a Boolean algebra.

Proposition 9.5.2 Let D be a spectral space. Then D is Hausdorff iff it is a Stone space.

Proof $\Rightarrow$: Let a be a compact open. In a Hausdorff space, any compact set of points is closed (Lemma 8.3.3), so a is clopen, as is its set-theoretic complement a^c. In a compact space, any closed set of points is compact (Lemma 8.3.2), so a^c is compact open and hence a complement for a in KΩD.

$\Leftarrow$: Let x and y be distinct points. Without loss of generality, we can find an open a such that x $\vDash$ a, and y $\nvDash$ a; and since the compact opens form a basis, we can assume a is compact. Then a and a^c are disjoint open sets containing x and y respectively.   ]

Lemma 9.5.3 Let f: D $\rightarrow$ E be a continuous map between Stone spaces. Then Ωf maps compact opens to compact opens.

Proof The compact opens are precisely the clopens, and Ωf preserves clopens.   ]

In other words, if K and L are Boolean algebras, then a lattice homomorphism from K to Idl L in fact has its image in L and hence can be considered a homomorphism from K to L. This does not apply to arbitrary distributive lattices (see Exercise 8).

Theorem 9.5.4 *Stone's representation theorem for Boolean algebras, Stone Duality for Stone spaces*

Any Boolean algebra B is isomorphic to the lattice of clopens for the Stone space Spec B.

If B and C are Boolean algebras, then the homomorphisms from B to C are in 1-1 correspondence with the continuous maps from Spec C to Spec B.

Proof B is (isomorphic to) KΩSpec B, hence Spec B is a Stone space, hence B is its lattice of clopens. For the second part, use Lemma 9.5.3.   ]

As a consequence of the uniqueness of complements, although we have defined Boolean algebras as distributive lattices with a certain property, we can also define then algebraically as algebras with certain operators and laws: the operators of lattices and in addition the unary operator $-^c$, and the laws of distributive lattices with the defining equations for complements. We can now use the methods of Section 4.3 to construct Boolean algebras satisfying the following universal property.

Definition 9.5.5 Let K be a distributive lattice. The *Booleanization* of K is a Boolean algebra B, together with a lattice homomorphism f: K → B, such that if g: K → C is any other lattice homomorphism from K to a Boolean algebra C then there is a unique lattice homomorphism h: B → C such that f;h = g.

(Note that if B and C are Boolean algebras, and h: B → C is a lattice homomorphism, then it automatically preserves complements and hence is a Boolean algebra homomorphism.)

To construct the Booleanization, present a Boolean algebra using for generators the elements of K, and for relations the lattice relations already existing in K.

Categorically, Booleanization is a functor from **Distributive Lattices** to **Boolean Algebras**, left adjoint to the forgetful functor.

Definition 9.5.6 Let D be a spectral locale. Its *patch topology* patch D is the Stone space for which KΩpatch D is the Booleanization of KΩD.

The natural Booleanization homomorphism from KΩD to KΩpatch D gives a continuous map i: patch D → D.

Proposition 9.5.7 Let D be a spectral locale.

(i)   pt i is a bijection between points. Hence (using spatiality for spectral spaces) patch D can be thought of as a new, finer topology on the points of D.

(ii)   A subbasis for Ωpatch D is given by the compact opens of D and their set-theoretic complements.

Proof

(i) **2** is a Boolean algebra, so any point of D, as a lattice homomorphism from
KΩD to **2**, factors via the Booleanization KΩpatch D and hence is also a point of
patch D.

(ii)   Let L be the sublattice of ℘pt D generated by the compact opens for D and
their complements. L is clearly contained in KΩpatch D; but in fact from de
Morgan's laws it follows that L is itself a Boolean algebra, and we deduce that L =
KΩpatch D.   ]

Definition 9.5.8 Let P be a dcpo. The *Lawson* topology on P is given by a
subbasis comprising the Scott open sets and the complements of the sets $\uparrow$x, x ∈ P.

Theorem 9.5.9 Let D be a spectral algebraic locale. Then the Lawson and patch
topologies are the same. Hence, the Lawson topology makes pt D a Stone space.
Proof The Scott opens are just the opens for D (by Theorem 9.3.8), and these are
in Ωpatch D. Now suppose x ∈ pt D, x = $\sqcup^{\uparrow}$ Y where Y is a directed set of
compact points. Then $\uparrow$x = $\cap$ {$\uparrow$y: y ∈ Y}, and each $\uparrow$y is compact open, so pt
D\$\uparrow$x, equal to $\cup$ {pt D\$\uparrow$y: y ∈ Y}, is in Ωpatch D. Hence the Lawson topology is
contained in the patch.

Conversely, let a ∈ KΩD be expressed as a join $\vee$ {$\uparrow$x: x ∈ X}, where X is a
finite set of compact points. a is already Scott open, and its complement
$\cap$ {pt D\$\uparrow$x: x ∈ X} is Lawson open. Hence the patch topology is contained in the
Lawson.   ]

Finally, we note a connection with metric spaces.

Theorem 9.5.10 Let S be a second countable, spectral locale. Then S is a Stone
space iff its topology is given by an ultrametric on pt S.
Proof If the topology comes from an ultrametric, then it is Hausdorff (see remark
after Definition 5.5.2).

For the converse, let a_1, a_2, ... be an enumeration of KΩS. If x, y ∈ pt S,
define d(x, y) ∈ ℝ as follows.

If x = y, then d(x, y) = 0.

Otherwise, choose n = n(x, y) least such that one and only one of x and y satisfies a_n, and let d(x, y) = 2^{-n}. (If x = y, we shall conventionally write n(x, y) = ∞.)
We need to prove the ultrametric inequality,

$$d(x, z) \leq \max \{d(x, y), d(y, z)\}$$

This is clear if any two of x, y and z are equal; otherwise, it is equivalent to

$$n(x, z) \geq \min \{n(x, y), n(y, z)\} = m \text{ (say)}$$

which follows because if $i < m$ then $x \vdash a_i \Leftrightarrow y \vdash a_i \Leftrightarrow z \vdash a_i$.

Finally, we must show that the ultrametric describes the original topology. Consider first an open ball $B_\varepsilon(x) = \{y: d(x, y) < \varepsilon\}$, with $\varepsilon > 0$. For some n,

$$2^{-n-1} < \varepsilon \leq 2^{-n}$$

and then

$$d(x, y) < \varepsilon \Leftrightarrow d(x, y) < 2^{-n} \Leftrightarrow n(x, y) \geq n+1$$
$$\Leftrightarrow \forall i \leq n. (x \vdash a_i \leftrightarrow y \vdash a_i)$$
$$\Leftrightarrow y \vdash \bigwedge\{a_i: i \leq n, x \vdash a_i\} \wedge \bigwedge\{a_i{}^c: i \leq n, x \nvdash a_i\} = b \text{ (say)}$$

Hence $B_\varepsilon(x) = b$, which is open. Conversely, if $x \vdash a_n$, then with $\varepsilon = 2^{-n}$ we have $x \vdash B_\varepsilon(x) \leq a_n$, so that a_n is a join of open balls. **]**

Notes

Section 9.2: What I have called spectral spaces (or locales) are most commonly called *coherent,* and this shows signs of becoming standard. My main excuse for not conforming is that "coherent" has other meanings. Even within the close confines of domain theory one has the "coherence spaces" of Girard, quite different from coherent spaces.

Section 9.3: Theorem 9.3.8 is a special case of the *Stone duality* that relates the points side to the frame side for spatial locales, and is largely due to Plotkin [81] although he did not emphasize the spectral (2/3 SFP) context. Abramsky [87, 88], as well as filling in some details of the duality, explored a fundamental implication: whereas domain theory is generally treated as a study of certain dcpos, possibly with a topological gloss via the Scott topology, it can equivalently be treated as a study of certain distributive lattices (of compact open sets) and given a logical form. Abramsky's general method was to take domains as dcpos as understood, and to relate the logic to them. Here, and in Chapter 10, we have attempted to develop the domain theory directly from the topology and make the best possible use of the interplay between the points and the logic.

Section 9.5: Although we have arrived at Stone's theorem as a diversion from our main development, historically it was absolutely crucial to the mathematical ideas on which we rely. Johnstone [82] gives an interesting account of its influence.

Exercises

1. If P is a poset, then its Alexandrov topology – as a frame – is isomorphic to the Scott topology on Idl(P).

2. If D is a spectral locale, then its Scott open filters and points correspond to the filters and prime filters of $K\Omega D$.

3. Prove Theorem 9.4.2 (Stone duality for finite locales) directly, without using Theorem 9.3.8 (Stone duality for spectral algebraic locales).

4. Show that if a topological system has a countable subbasis (in algebraic terms, its frame is *countably generated*), then it is second countable.

5. Let D be a second countable spectral locale, defined by some given coherent presentation and an enumeration of the generators. Then one can derive an enumeration $\{c_1, c_2, c_3, \ldots\}$ of $K\Omega D$. If F is a Scott open filter in ΩD, and $a \in \Omega D$ with $F \nvdash a$, define an ascending sequence (a_n) by

$$a_0 \quad = a$$
$$a_{n+1} \quad = \begin{cases} a_n & \text{if } F \vdash a_n \vee c_{n+1} \\ a_n \vee c_{n+1} & \text{otherwise} \end{cases}$$

and let $p = \bigvee_n a_n$. Show that p is prime, and corresponds to a point in D that refines F but does not satisfy a. Use this to prove the Hofmann–Mislove Theorem for D without using the axiom of choice (Zorn's lemma, 8.2.1).

6. Let $\phi: A \to B$ be a frame homomorphism, and define its *right adjoint* $\psi: B \to A$ by

$$\psi(b) = \bigvee \{a: \phi(a) \le b\}$$

Show that $\phi(a) \le b \Leftrightarrow a \le \psi(b)$ (categorically, ψ is indeed the right adjoint to ϕ). Show that ψ preserves all meets, but need not preserve joins.

7. (Hofmann and Lawson [82]) If $f: D \to E$ is a continuous map between locales, we write $G(f): \Omega D \to \Omega E$ for the right adjoint of Ωf. f is *proper* iff $G(f)$ preserves directed joins, in other words it is continuous for the Scott topologies on the frames ΩD and ΩE.

Suppose that D and E are both spatial. Show that the following three conditions are equivalent:

(i)   f is proper.

(ii)   If F is a Scott open filter in ΩE, then $G(f)^{-1}(F) = \uparrow(\Omega f)(F)$ is a Scott open filter in ΩD.

(iii)   (a) If K is a compact saturated set of points in pt E, then $(\text{pt } f)^{-1}(K)$ is compact, and

(b) if C is a closed set in pt D, then $\downarrow(\text{pt } f)(C)$ is closed in pt E.

(Hint for (ii) $\Leftrightarrow$ (iii). If a is open in D, define $U = \text{pt } E \backslash \downarrow (\text{pt } f)(\text{pt } D \backslash a)$. Show that for any upper closed subset V of pt E, $(\text{pt } f)^{-1}(V) \subseteq a$ iff $V \subseteq U$. Deduce that if U is open then it is equal to $G(f)(a)$. Show also that if K is a compact saturated subset of pt E and x is a point in D, then $x \in (\text{pt } f)^{-1}(K) \Leftrightarrow x \vdash b$ for all $b \in G(f)^{-1}(\wedge K)$.)

8. Let $f: D \to E$ be a continuous map, with D and E spectral. f is *spectral* iff Ωf preserves compactness, i.e. it maps $K\Omega E$ into $K\Omega D$. Show that f is spectral iff it is proper. Give an example of a non-spectral continuous map between spectral spaces.

9. (Plotkin [81]) Let D be a spectral algebraic locale. Use the previous exercise to show that if $X \subseteq \text{pt } D$ is Lawson closed, then $\downarrow X$ is Scott closed and $\uparrow X$ is Scott compact, and hence $\downarrow X \cap \uparrow X$ is Lawson closed.

10. In any lattice, an element a is an *atom* iff $a \neq \textbf{false}$, and for all b, if $b \leq a$ then either $b = a$ or $b = \textbf{false}$. Show that in a Boolean algebra, the coprimes are precisely the atoms. Let D be a spectral algebraic Stone space. Show that D is finite and discrete. Deduce that any finite Boolean algebra is isomorphic to the power set of a finite set.

11. Let 2^ω be the subspace of $2^{*\omega}$ (the Kahn domain on $\{0, 1\}$) whose points are the infinite bitstreams. Show that 2^ω is a Stone space. Show that $K\Omega 2^\omega$ has no atoms at all.

12. Let X be a set, and let $X_\perp$ be the corresponding flat domain (see Section 3.7). Show that $X_\perp$ is spectral algebraic.

DOMAIN THEORY

In which we see how certain parts of domain theory can be done topologically.

10.1 Why domain theory?

In most computer programming languages, each item of data is given a *type* to determine the operations that can be done on it. There will usually be primitive types, such as those for integers and floating point numbers, and many languages also provide constructors for building user-defined types. Given types S and T, some examples are –

- A record type S×T . Each element of it is a record with two components, one of type S and the other of type T.
- A union type S+T. Each element can be either of type S or of type T.
- A higher-order function type [S→T]. Its elements are the functions that take an argument of type S and give a result of type T.

We can now define the set of possible elements for each type in two stages. First, for each primitive type, we say directly what its elements are. Next, for each constructor, we say how it makes new elements out of the old ones: so the record type uses pairs, the function type uses functions, and so on.

However, in building up new types, we want to be able not only to combine already defined types, but also to define new ones recursively. For instance the type List(A) of lists of elements of type A (*atoms*) can be defined by

List(A) = {**nil**} + A×List(A)

This says that every list is either **nil** – the empty list –, or is constructed from an atom (the head) and another list (the tail).

These recursive definitions lead very quickly to contradictions if we are not careful. Take, for instance, the types defined here by mutual recursion:

state   = [location→storable value]
storable value = ... +procedure+ ...
procedure   = [state→state]

This models the idea that the state of a computer is given by saying what value is stored at each location, that in particular procedures can be stored, and that a procedure is given by saying how it transforms the state of the computer (this is for procedures that have no arguments and deliver no results, like GOSUB routines in BASIC). Suppose now that there are n possible states. Then

number of possible procedures	$= n^n$,
number of possible storable values	$\geq n^n$,
number of possible states	$\geq n^n > n$.

We have a contradiction, and in fact, by Cantor's diagonal argument, it remains *even if n is infinite.*

The problem here is with the function type, which is where the cardinality blows up. The solution is that we don't actually need all the functions that, set-theoretically, are supposed to exist; all the functions follow routines stored in the computer, and hence must be *computable*. These are far fewer than the general functions, few enough in fact to resolve the contradiction for us.

Now we see that our "sets of possible values" for the types must have more than just their set structure, so that we can determine which functions to admit. We don't really need to investigate in detail what computability is, as long as the extra structure allows us to omit enough uncomputable functions. Speaking rather broadly, we might call a *domain* a set with this extra structure, whatever it is.

The basic idea we shall exploit here is to take the extra structure to be topological, so that a domain is a topological system and the admissible functions are the continuous maps. In fact, the domains used in actual computer science are highly specialized topological systems, but we can see at least the topological workings by looking at spectral algebraic locales and investigating various type constructors on them.

Thinking of a spectral algebraic locale as representing a type, we think of the points of the locale as representing the elements of the type. The reasoning at the end of Section 7.3 suggests that computable functions between types ought to be Scott continuous, and so (in the light of Theorem 9.3.8) continuous maps between the locales. Moreover, if the frames are presented by generators and relations, then these continuous maps can be described on the frame side by saying how their frame parts act on the generators.

We now systematically work through the type constructors. For each one, we show how it combines spectral algebraic domains, and we present the new frame using generators and relations. We then want to prove that it is a spectral algebraic locale, and for this we use the method of quasicoprimes, Lemma 9.3.9. Sometimes (notably for function spaces) this requires extra assumptions on the domains we are combining.

The methods of this chapter and the next are derived from part of those described in Abramsky [87] and [88], which give complete syntactical descriptions in the cases of the so-called *Scott domains* and *SFP domains*.

10.2 Bottoms and lifting

Definition 10.2.1 A dcpo is called a *cpo* iff it has a least element (called *bottom*, or $\perp$).

More generally, a *topological system with bottom* is a topological system equipped with a point $\perp$ such that $\perp \vDash a$ iff $a = \textbf{true}$.

A continuous map f between two topological systems with bottom is *strict* iff pt $f(\perp) = \perp$.

In a topological system with bottom, $\perp$ is a least point in the specialization order. Hence if a system is T_0 (a locale, for instance) there is at most one way of choosing a bottom.

A cpo is also sometimes called an *ipo* (inductive partial order). These terms are also often used for posets with bottom in which every ω-chain has a join; confusion is usually avoided by considering only ω-algebraic dcpos, where any directed set contains an ω-chain with the same join.

Bottoms are vital because of their relation to recursive definitions, using a trick of finding *fixpoints*.

Proposition 10.2.2 Let D be a cpo, and let f: $D \to D$ be Scott continuous. Then there is a point $x = Fix\,f \in D$ satisfying

(i) $f(x) = x$ (x is a *fixpoint* of f), and
(ii) $\forall y \in D. (f(y) \sqsubseteq y \to x \sqsubseteq y)$ (so x is the *least fixpoint* of f).

Proof Consider the sequence

$$\perp \sqsubseteq f(\perp) \sqsubseteq f^2(\perp) \sqsubseteq f^3(\perp) \sqsubseteq \ldots$$

This is indeed an ascending sequence; for $\perp \sqsubseteq f(\perp)$ by definition of bottom, and if $f^i(\perp) \sqsubseteq f^{i+1}(\perp)$, then $f^{i+1}(\perp) \sqsubseteq f^{i+2}(\perp)$ by monotonicity. Therefore its terms form a directed set, and have a join x, say. Now by continuity

$$f(x) = f(\bigsqcup_i^{\uparrow} f^i(\perp)) = \bigsqcup_i^{\uparrow} f^{i+1}(\perp) = x$$

If $f(y) \sqsubseteq y$, then $\perp \sqsubseteq y$, and if $f^i(\perp) \sqsubseteq y$ then $f^{i+1}(\perp) \sqsubseteq f(y) \sqsubseteq y$, so by induction $f^i(\perp) \sqsubseteq y$ for all i and $x \sqsubseteq y$.   ]

Exercise – What happens if there is no bottom?

Now suppose that we want to define a function recursively, by

f(x) = expression involving x and also f (in recursive calls)

If x and f(x) have types S and T, then f is to have type [S→T]. If g is any other function of type [S→T], then we can imagine substituting it for f in the body of the definition: this gives a new function F(g) of x, still of type [S→T]. Thus F, transforming one function g into another F(g) (we call it a *functional*), is a function of type [[S→T]→[S→T]]. Suppose now that T has a bottom, $\perp_T$: then so does [S→T] – its bottom is the function that takes every element of S to the $\perp_T$. The f that we want satisfies f = F(f), and so we take it to be Fix F.

As an example, suppose that **nat** is the type of natural numbers, and we want to define the function factorial, of type [**nat**→**nat**], by

factorial(n) = if n=0 then 1 else n*factorial(n–1) fi

The functional F is defined by

F(g)(n) = if n=0 then 1 else n*g(n–1) fi

If we represent the type **nat** by the flat domain $\mathbb{N}_\perp$, with the understanding that an arithmetic expression containing $\perp$ evaluates to $\perp$, then

$$F^i(\lambda x.\ \perp)(n) \quad = \begin{cases} n! & \text{if } n < i \\ \perp & \text{otherwise} \end{cases}$$
$$(\text{Fix } F)(n) \quad = n! \text{ for all } n \in \mathbb{N}$$

This shows how to use fixpoints to do recursion, and it makes bottoms a desirable feature of domains. Fortunately, they are easy to put in.

Proposition 10.2.3 Let D be a spectral algebraic locale. Then pt D has a bottom iff **true** is coprime.
Proof Using the 2/3 SFP property, the empty set of points has a finite complete set of minimal upper bound, i.e. minimal points, and these correspond to the decomposition of **true** into a join of coprimes. pt D has a bottom iff there is a unique minimal point, i.e. there is a unique maximal coprime, i.e. **true** itself is coprime.]

Definition 10.2.4 Let D be a topological system. Then its *lifting*, lift D, or $D_\perp$, is the topological system with bottom defined as follows. It has points **up** x (x ∈ pt D) together with a new bottom $\perp$, and opens **lift** a (for each a in ΩD) in the same order as for ΩD, together with a new **true**. These opens form a frame; all meets and joins of predicates **lift** a, excepting the empty meet **true**, are calculated as in ΩD. For satisfaction, **up** x ⊨ **lift** a iff x ⊨ a, **up** x ⊨ **true** for all x, and $\perp$ ⊨ **true**.

Proposition 10.2.5 Let D be a topological system. If D localic, spectral, or spectral algebraic, then so is $D_\perp$.

Proof Suppose D is localic. A locale point of $D_\perp$ is a function from ΩD to **2** that preserves all joins and finite *non-empty* meets. If it maps **lift true** to **true**, then it is already a point of D; otherwise it maps all opens **lift a** to **false**. This second possibility is the new bottom.

For the rest, observe that **lift a** is compact or coprime compact iff a is, and the new **true** is coprime compact.]

10.3 Products

We have already seen how to define topological products, but we still need to check that they preserve spectral algebraicity.

Theorem 10.3.1 Let D and E be spectral algebraic locales. Then the product D×E is a spectral algebraic locale, presented by

$$\Omega(D\times E) = \text{Fr} \langle\ a\otimes\textbf{true}, \textbf{true}\otimes b : a \in K\Omega D, b \in K\Omega E\ |$$
$$(\bigvee S)\otimes\textbf{true} = \bigvee\{a\otimes\textbf{true}: a \in S\} \qquad (S \subseteq K\Omega D, \text{S finite})$$
$$(\bigwedge S)\otimes\textbf{true} = \bigwedge\{a\otimes\textbf{true}: a \in S\} \qquad (S \subseteq K\Omega D, \text{S finite})$$
$$\textbf{true}\otimes(\bigvee T) = \bigvee\{\textbf{true}\otimes b: b \in T\} \qquad (T \subseteq K\Omega E, \text{T finite})$$
$$\textbf{true}\otimes(\bigwedge T) = \bigwedge\{\textbf{true}\otimes b: b \in T\} \qquad (T \subseteq K\Omega E, \text{T finite}) \quad \rangle$$

Its compact coprime opens are those of the form $p\otimes\textbf{true} \wedge \textbf{true}\otimes q$ (i.e. $p\otimes q$ in our other notation) where p and q are coprimes in $K\Omega D$ and $K\Omega E$.

Proof We already know that $\Omega(D\times E)$ can be presented by "putting presentations for ΩD and ΩE side by side with no interaction" (Exercise 10 of Chapter 6). This is what we have done here, using spectrality to tell us that presentations for $K\Omega D$ and $K\Omega E$ as distributive lattices also present ΩD and ΩE as frames (Theorem 9.2.2). This shows, regardless of algebraicity, that for spectral locales the given presentation presents the product locale (by Proposition 6.4.6 this is the product topological system). We could also use local compactness – Theorems 9.2.4 and 8.5.8 – to show that this product is spatial.

Next, we must show algebraicity, and we use Lemma 9.3.9. Temporarily, we define as *quasicoprime* any open of the form $p\otimes\textbf{true} \wedge \textbf{true}\otimes q$ as in the statement.

First, note that the points of the product locale are the pairs $\langle x, y \rangle$ where x and y are points from D and E. We know this already by Proposition 6.4.6 (i), but let us verify it directly. A point is a function from the generators to **2** that respects the relations, so it gives functions from $K\Omega D$ to **2** (defined by the action on the generators $a\otimes\textbf{true}$) and from $K\Omega E$ to **2**, and respecting the relations says precisely that these are distributive lattice homomorphisms, and hence points of D and E. From this we have

$$\langle x, y \rangle \vDash a \otimes \textbf{true} \qquad \text{iff } x \vDash a$$
$$\langle x, y \rangle \vDash \textbf{true} \otimes b \qquad \text{iff } y \vDash b$$

and we can deduce that $\langle x, y \rangle \sqsubseteq \langle x', y' \rangle$ iff $x \sqsubseteq x'$ and $y \sqsubseteq y'$.

Now let $p \otimes \textbf{true} \wedge \textbf{true} \otimes q$ be a quasicoprime: then p and q correspond to points $\uparrow p$ and $\uparrow q$ of D and E. $\langle x, y \rangle \sqsupseteq \langle \uparrow p, \uparrow q \rangle$ iff $\langle x, y \rangle \vDash p \otimes \textbf{true} \wedge \textbf{true} \otimes q$, which proves condition (i) of the Quasicoprimes Lemma.

Finally, any meet of generators can be written in the form $a \otimes \textbf{true} \wedge \textbf{true} \otimes b$. We can write $a = \bigvee P$ and $b = \bigvee Q$, where P and Q are sets of coprimes from $K\Omega D$ and $K\Omega E$ respectively, and then by distributivity

$$a \otimes \textbf{true} \wedge \textbf{true} \otimes b = \bigvee \{ p \otimes \textbf{true} \wedge \textbf{true} \otimes q : p \in P, q \in Q \}$$

This proves condition (ii) of the Quasicoprimes Lemma.   ]

Proposition 10.3.2 If locales D and E have bottoms, then so does D×E.
Proof The bottom is $\langle \bot, \bot \rangle$.   ]

We can also define continuous maps in terms of this presentation. For instance, for the projection

$$p_1 : D \times E \to D, \qquad \text{pt } p_1(\langle x, y \rangle) = x$$

we first define $\Omega p_1 : K\Omega D \to \Omega(D \times E)$ by

$$\Omega p_1(a) = a \otimes \textbf{true}$$

(use the relations in $\Omega(D \times E)$ to verify that this preserves finite meets and joins) and extend this to the whole of ΩD by Proposition 9.1.5. Then $\langle x, y \rangle \vDash \Omega p_1(a) \Leftrightarrow x \vDash a$ for compact a by definition of Ωp_1, and hence by spectrality for all a, and this is enough to show that Ωp_1 is the frame part of the projection pt p_1.

10.4 Sums

For a disjoint (topological) sum D+E we know already from Section 6.3 that $\Omega(D+E)$ is $\Omega D \times \Omega E$; the opens $\langle a, \textbf{false} \rangle$ and $\langle \textbf{false}, b \rangle$ form a subbasis and we use them as generators.

Theorem 10.4.1 Let D and E be spectral algebraic locales. Then the disjoint sum D+E is a spectral algebraic locale, presented by

$$\Omega(D+E) = \text{Fr} \langle\; \langle a, \textbf{false}\rangle, \langle \textbf{false}, b\rangle : a \in K\Omega D, b \in K\Omega E \;|$$

$$\langle \bigvee S, \textbf{false}\rangle = \bigvee\{\langle a, \textbf{false}\rangle : a \in S\} \qquad (S \subseteq K\Omega D, S \text{ finite})$$

$$\langle \bigwedge S, \textbf{false}\rangle = \bigwedge\{\langle a, \textbf{false}\rangle : a \in S\} \qquad (\emptyset \neq S \subseteq K\Omega D, S \text{ finite})$$

$$\langle \textbf{false}, \bigvee T\rangle = \bigvee\{\langle \textbf{false}, b\rangle : b \in T\} \qquad (T \subseteq K\Omega E, T \text{ finite})$$

$$\langle \textbf{false}, \bigwedge T\rangle = \bigwedge\{\langle \textbf{false}, b\rangle : b \in T\} \qquad (\emptyset \neq T \subseteq K\Omega E, T \text{ finite})$$

$$\langle \textbf{true}, \textbf{false}\rangle \vee \langle \textbf{false}, \textbf{true}\rangle = \textbf{true}$$

$$\langle \textbf{true}, \textbf{false}\rangle \wedge \langle \textbf{false}, \textbf{true}\rangle = \textbf{false} \qquad \rangle$$

Its compact coprime opens are those of the form $\langle p, \textbf{false}\rangle$ or $\langle \textbf{false}, q\rangle$ where p and q are coprimes in $K\Omega D$ and $K\Omega E$.

Proof Note here that the expressions $\langle a, \textbf{false}\rangle$ and $\langle \textbf{false}, b\rangle$ are formal expressions made out of a and b, so for $a = \textbf{false}_D$ and $b = \textbf{false}_E$ there are two different expressions $\langle \textbf{false}_D, \textbf{false}\rangle$ and $\langle \textbf{false}, \textbf{false}_E\rangle$. The first and third relations tell us that these are both equal to **false**, so no harm is done if we write them as $\langle \textbf{false}, \textbf{false}\rangle$.

First, we investigate the points of the spectral locale (F, say) that we have presented. A point gives a pair of functions $x: K\Omega D \to \mathbf{2}$ and $y: K\Omega E \to \mathbf{2}$, and the first four schemes of relations tell us that x and y preserve finite joins and finite non-empty meets. From the fifth and sixth relations, one of x(**true**) and y(**true**) is **true** and the other is **false**. If x(**true**) is **true** then x is a point and y(b) = **false** for all b; otherwise x(a) is always **false** and y is a point. Every such pair gives a point of our frame, so the points form a disjoint union pt D+pt E.

If $x \in$ pt D and $y \in$ pt E, then x and y are incomparable under the specialization order in our new locale. For instance, x satisfies $\langle \textbf{true}, \textbf{false}\rangle$ but y doesn't, so x does not approximate y. On the other hand, points in the same summand have the same specialization relation in F as they did in the summand.

As before, we call *quasicoprime* any open of the form that we wish to prove coprime. If p is coprime in $K\Omega D$, then the extent of $\langle p, \textbf{false}\rangle$ is $\uparrow p$ in pt F, which proves that $\langle p, \textbf{false}\rangle$ is coprime; similarly, the other quasicoprimes are coprime.

Meets of generators can be written in the form **true**, $\langle a, \textbf{false}\rangle$, $\langle \textbf{false}, b\rangle$ or **false**. **false** is already the empty join of coprimes. For $\langle a, \textbf{false}\rangle$, if $a = \bigvee P$ where P is a finite set of coprimes in $K\Omega D$, then $\bigvee\{\langle p, \textbf{false}\rangle : p \in P\}$ is a coprime decomposition for $\langle a, \textbf{false}\rangle$; $\langle \textbf{false}, b\rangle$ is similar. Next, if $\textbf{true}_D$ and $\textbf{true}_E$ have coprime decompositions $\bigvee P$ and $\bigvee Q$, then

$$\textbf{true}_F = \langle \textbf{true}_D, \textbf{false}\rangle \vee \langle \textbf{false}, \textbf{true}_E\rangle$$

$$= \bigvee\{\langle p, \textbf{false}\rangle : p \in P\} \vee \bigvee\{\langle \textbf{false}, q\rangle : q \in Q\}$$

is a coprime decomposition for **true**$_F$.

Finally, we show that this locale is the sum defined in Chapter 6. We know from Theorem 9.3.8 that ΩF is the Scott topology on pt D+pt E. But any directed subset of pt D+pt E must lie entirely within either pt D or pt E, and we deduce that the Scott topology for the sum is $\Omega D \times \Omega E$.]

Again, we can use the presentation to define continuous maps. For instance the injection i_1: D $\rightarrow$ D+E has inverse image part Ωi_1: Ω(D+E) $\rightarrow$ ΩD defined by

$$\Omega i_1(\langle a, \textbf{false} \rangle) = a, \qquad \Omega i_1(\langle \textbf{false}, b \rangle) = \textbf{false}$$

It is easy to check that this preserves the relations, and that it does indeed give the injection on the points.

A persistent nuisance in domain theory is that D+E will not have a bottom: bottoms from D and E will be two incomparable minimal elements in the sum. In fact some rather general arguments (Huwig and Poigné [87]) show that the requirement of fixpoints (which is why we wanted bottoms) is incompatible with a true sum with the universal property of Theorem 6.3.2.

There are two ways of forcing a bottom. The *separated* sum is $(D+E)_\perp$, so we already know how this works. In the *coalesced* sum (which we write D$\oplus$E), given that D and E already had bottoms, we merge them.

topological
(disjoint) sum   separated sum   coalesced sum

Theorem 10.4.2 Let D and E be spectral algebraic locales with bottoms. Then the coalesced sum D$\oplus$E is a spectral algebraic locale with bottom, presented by

Ω(D$\oplus$E) = Fr $\langle$ $\langle$a, **false**$\rangle$, $\langle$**false**, b$\rangle$: a $\in$ KΩD, b $\in$ KΩE $|$
   $\langle \bigvee S, \textbf{false} \rangle = \bigvee \{\langle a, \textbf{false}\rangle : a \in S\}$ (S $\subseteq$ KΩD, S finite)
   $\langle \bigwedge S, \textbf{false} \rangle = \bigwedge \{\langle a, \textbf{false}\rangle : a \in S\}$ (S $\subseteq$ KΩD, S finite)
   $\langle \textbf{false}, \bigvee T \rangle = \bigvee \{\langle \textbf{false}, b\rangle : b \in T\}$ (T $\subseteq$ KΩE, T finite)
   $\langle \textbf{false}, \bigwedge T \rangle = \bigwedge \{\langle \textbf{false}, b\rangle : b \in T\}$ (T $\subseteq$ KΩE, T finite)
   $\langle a, \textbf{false} \rangle \wedge \langle \textbf{false}, b \rangle = \textbf{false}$ if a $\neq$ **true**, b $\neq$ **true** $\rangle$

Its compact coprime opens are those of the form $\langle$p, **false**$\rangle$ or $\langle$**false**, q$\rangle$ where p and q are coprimes in KΩD and KΩE.

Proof Let F be the locale presented above. From the first four relation schemes, a point gives a pair $\langle$x, y$\rangle$ of points from D and E. Suppose x $\neq$ $\perp$. Then x(a) = **true** for some a $\neq$ **true**, so y(b) = **false** for all b $\neq$ **true**: y = $\perp$. We deduce that the points are pairs $\langle x, y \rangle$ for which at least one of x and y is $\bot$. They can be categorized as $\langle x, \bot \rangle$ $(x \neq \bot)$, $\langle \bot, y \rangle$ $(y \neq \bot)$ and $\bot = \langle \bot, \bot \rangle$.

To complete the proof using Lemma 9.3.9 (exercise), one shows

(i)   the specialization order is $\langle x, y \rangle \sqsubseteq \langle x', y' \rangle$ iff $x \sqsubseteq x'$ and $y \sqsubseteq y'$;

(ii)   If p and q are coprimes in KΩD and KΩE, then

$$\langle x, y \rangle \vDash \langle p, \textbf{false} \rangle \text{ iff } \langle x, y \rangle \sqsupseteq \langle \uparrow p, \bot \rangle \text{ and}$$
$$\langle x, y \rangle \vDash \langle \textbf{false}, q \rangle \text{ iff } \langle x, y \rangle \sqsupseteq \langle \bot, \uparrow p \rangle$$

(iii)   every meet of generators is a join of opens $\langle p, \textbf{false} \rangle$ or $\langle \textbf{false}, q \rangle$ where p or q is coprime;

Note the difference between this and the disjoint sum: here

$$\langle \textbf{true}, \textbf{false} \rangle = \langle \textbf{false}, \textbf{true} \rangle = \textbf{true}. \qquad]$$

10.5 Function spaces and Scott domains

We saw in Section 10.1 that function types were desirable and also a source of difficulty. They were a prime reason for including topological structure in domains, and we want the points of a function domain [D→E] to be the continuous maps – specifically, the Scott continuous maps – from D to E. We show first that [D→E] is readily made into a cpo, comprising the points of a spectral locale. However, it will not in general be algebraic, and we shall introduce the class of *Scott domains* to remedy this.

Proposition 10.5.1 Let D and E be dcpos, considered as topological spaces, with their Scott topologies. Let the function space [D→E] be given its pointwise topology.

(i)   The specialization order is the *pointwise* order:

$$f \sqsubseteq g \Leftrightarrow \forall x \in D.\ f(x) \sqsubseteq g(x) \Leftrightarrow \forall b \in \Omega E.\ \Omega f(b) \leq \Omega g(b)$$

(ii)   pt [D→E] is a dcpo, with

$$(\text{pt } \sqcup^{\uparrow} S)(x) = \sqcup^{\uparrow} \{f(x) : f \in S\})$$
$$(\Omega \sqcup^{\uparrow} S)(b) = \vee^{\uparrow} \{\Omega f(b) : f \in S\})$$

(iii)   If E has a bottom $\bot$, then so does [D→E]:

$$\text{pt } \bot(x) = \bot$$
$$\Omega\bot(b) = \begin{cases} \textbf{true} & \text{if } b = \textbf{true} \\ \textbf{false} & \text{otherwise} \end{cases}$$

Proof

(i) $f \sqsubseteq g \Leftrightarrow \forall x \in D, b \in \Omega E. (f \vDash [x \rightarrow b] \rightarrow g \vDash [x \rightarrow b])$

$\Leftrightarrow \forall x \in D, b \in \Omega E. (f(x) \vDash b \rightarrow g(x) \vDash b)$

$\Leftrightarrow \forall x \in D. f(x) \sqsubseteq g(x)$

$\Leftrightarrow \forall b \in \Omega E, x \in D. (x \vDash \Omega f(b) \rightarrow x \vDash \Omega g(b))$

$\Leftrightarrow \forall b \in \Omega E. \Omega f(b) \leq \Omega g(b)$ (by spatiality)

(ii) The points part defined here for $\bigsqcup^{\uparrow} S$ is continuous, it then must be the join, and its inverse image $\Omega \bigsqcup^{\uparrow} S$ is as defined (using the fact that we have Scott topologies).

(iii) – easy.]

This can be seen as the order theoretic view of function spaces, constructing a dcpo $[D \rightarrow E]$ out of dcpos D and E, and this in itself is all that is needed to perform the fixpoint trick of Section 10.2 and hence give a semantics to recursion.

Example 10.5.2 In Example 5.2.2, we recursively defined a function to complement the bits of a bit stream. Using functionals, this would appear as

F(g)(b::s) = (if b=0 then 1 else 0)::g(s) (tacitly, $F(g)(\perp) = \perp$)
complement = Fix F

Exercise – show that F is Scott continuous.

To compute complement(s), we take the join of

$\perp(s) \sqsubseteq F(\perp)(s) \sqsubseteq F^2(\perp)(s) \sqsubseteq F^3(\perp)(s) \sqsubseteq \ldots$
$\perp(x) = \perp$ for all x
$F(\perp)(0::x) = 1::\perp, F(\perp)(1::x) = 0::\perp$
$F^2(\perp)(0::0::x) = 1::1::\perp, F^2(\perp)(0::1::x) = 1::0::\perp$, etc.

dcpos are too general to give a good theory, so as before, we go to spectral algebraic locales. As a sample pathology, Johnstone [81] gives an example of a dcpo whose Scott topology is not sober.

Theorem 10.5.3 Let D and E be spectral algebraic locales. Then the pointwise and compact-open topologies on $[D \rightarrow E]$ coincide, giving a spectral space presentable by

$\Omega[D \rightarrow E] = \text{Fr} \langle [x \rightarrow b] : x \in \text{Kpt } D, b \in K\Omega E \mid$
$[x \rightarrow b] \leq [y \rightarrow b]$ if $x \sqsubseteq y$
$[x \rightarrow \bigvee S] = \bigvee \{[x \rightarrow b]: b \in S\}$ $(S \subseteq K\Omega E, S$ finite)
$[x \rightarrow \bigwedge S] = \bigwedge \{[x \rightarrow b]: b \in S\}$ $(S \subseteq K\Omega E, S$ finite) $\rangle$

Proof The points of the locale $[D \rightarrow E]$ presented here are the functions θ from Kpt D×KΩE to **2** such that for each x, $\theta(x, -)$ is a point of E (by the last two relation schemes), and if x ⊑ y then θ(x, -) ⊑ θ(y, -). In other words, they are the monotone functions from Kpt D to pt E, i.e. (by Proposition 9.1.2) the Scott continuous functions f from pt D to pt E, with f(x) ⊨ b iff f ⊨ [x→b]. By spectrality the locale is spatial, so it presents a topology on the function space. Its subbasics [x→b] are all open for the pointwise topology, so it suffices to show that they form a subbasis for the compact-open topology.

Let K ∈ QD, and suppose f ⊨ [K→b], i.e. K ⊨ Ωf(b). By spectrality of D we can find a compact open a such that K ⊨ a ≤ Ωf(b); by algebraicity, let ⋁P be a coprime decomposition for a. Then f ⊨ ⋀{[↑p→b]: p ∈ P} ≤ [K→b].   ]

In order to prove algebraicity, we need to know when a basic open ⋀$_i$ [x$_i$→b$_i$] is coprime, in other words when it defines a function. Using the second relation scheme, the b$_i$s must be coprimes ↑y$_i$. The function would then have to be the least f such that f(x$_i$) ⊒ y$_i$ for all i.

If E has a bottom, then for a single subbasic [x→↑y] the function f is easy to define as a *step* function:

$$f(z) = \begin{cases} y & \text{if } z \sqsupseteq x \\ \bot & \text{otherwise} \end{cases}$$

(Exercise – show that this is continuous.) However, even for basics [x→↑y]∧[x→↑y'] there is no general way of finding prime decompositions. The first solution we give is to work in domains where if the conjunction is not **false**, then y and y' have a least upper bound y" so that the conjunction is [x→↑y"].

Theorem 10.5.4 *Stone Duality for Scott Domains*
The following two kinds of topological system are equivalent under the duality of Theorem 9.3.8.

(i)   An algebraic dcpo in which every subset bounded above has a least upper bound (a *bounded complete* algebraic dcpo), with its Scott topology.

(ii)   A spectral algebraic locale in which any finite meet of compact coprimes is either coprime or **false**.

Proof (i) → (ii): The condition implies the 2/3 SFP condition of Lemma 9.3.6: every finite set of compact points has either no upper bounds at all, or a unique minimal one, necessarily compact. Therefore with its Scott topology it forms a spectral algebraic locale. Given a finite set of compact coprimes, their meet is either coprime or **false** according as the corresponding compact points have a least upper bound or not.

(ii) → (i): Reversing the argument above shows that every bounded finite set of compact points has a least upper bound, and algebraicity enables us to extend this to arbitrary bounded sets of arbitrary points.]

Definition 10.5.5 A spectral algebraic locale as in Theorem 10.5.4 – i.e. a bounded complete algebraic dcpo – is a *Scott domain*.

A Scott domain may be empty (the trivial topological system $(\varnothing, \mathbb{1})$). However, it is usual to exclude this. A non-empty Scott domain must have a bottom, for **true** is a meet (the empty one) of coprimes and so is either coprime or **false**. The latter case is the trivial system, and the former gives a bottom.

For Scott domains, we can modify Lemma 9.3.9 so that we only need coprime decompositions for generators, and not their meets.

Lemma 10.5.6 *The Method of Quasicoprimes for Scott Domains*
Let Fr $\langle G \mid R \rangle$ be a coherent presentation for a frame, giving a locale D, and let $\mathbb{Q}$ be a set of finite subsets of G. As a temporary measure, we call the opens $\bigwedge Q$ for $Q \in \mathbb{Q}$ the *quasicoprime* opens. Suppose that

(i)   for each quasicoprime q, there is a point x such that the extent of q is $\uparrow x$,
(ii)   every generator is a join of quasicoprimes, and
(iii)   every finite meet of quasicoprimes is either quasicoprime or **false**.

Then D is a Scott domain, and its compact coprime opens are precisely the quasicoprimes.
Proof Let G' be a finite set of generators. For each $g \in G'$, we have a finite set P_g of quasicoprimes such that $g = \bigvee P_g$. Then $\bigwedge G' = \bigwedge_{g \in G'} \bigvee P_g$. By distributivity, this can be rewritten as a join of meets of quasicoprimes; and by (iii) this is a join of quasicoprimes. We have now proved condition (ii) of Lemma 9.3.9, and we deduce that D is spectral algebraic and that its coprimes are the quasicoprimes. Then (iii) tells us that D is a Scott domain.]

Theorem 10.5.7 If D and E are Scott domains, then so is the function space [D→E], presented in Theorem 10.5.3.
Its compact coprimes are the opens of the form $\bigwedge \{[x \to p]: \langle x, p \rangle \in S\}$, where S is a finite subset of Kpt D × {coprimes of KΩE}, and S satisfies the following *consistency* property:

For every $I \subseteq S$, if $\{x: \exists p.\langle x, p \rangle \in I\}$ is bounded above,
    then $\bigwedge \{p: \exists x.\langle x, p \rangle \in I\} \neq$ **false** (so it is coprime).

Proof If S is a consistent set, define a function f_0 from pt D to pt E by

$$f_0(y) = \uparrow \bigwedge \{p: \exists x.\langle x, p \rangle \in S \text{ and } x \subseteq y\}$$

Consistency of S implies that this meet is coprime and hence defines a point. f_0 is continuous, and

$$f \sqsupseteq f_0 \Leftrightarrow \forall y \in \text{pt } D, \langle x, p \rangle \in S. (y \sqsupseteq x \to f(y) \vDash p)$$
$$\Leftrightarrow \forall \langle x, p \rangle \in S. f(x) \vDash p$$
$$\Leftrightarrow f \vDash \bigwedge \{[x \to p]: \langle x, p \rangle \in S\}$$

Therefore $\bigwedge \{[x \to p]: \langle x, p \rangle \in S\} = \uparrow f_0$ is coprime (condition (i) for Lemma 10.5.6).

For each generator $[x \to b]$, a coprime decomposition of b enables us to write $[x \to b]$ as a join of elements of the form $[x \to p]$, p coprime. We show that $S = \{\langle x, p \rangle\}$ is consistent. The consistency property is obvious for $I = S$; for $I = \emptyset$, the empty set is bounded above in pt D (by x), and the empty meet **true** $\geq p \neq$ **false**. (This is just ruling out the empty domain.) Thus $[x \to b]$ is a join of quasicoprimes.

Finally, suppose some $S \subseteq \text{Kpt } D \times \{\text{coprimes of } K\Omega E\}$ is inconsistent, with $I \subseteq S$ such that $\{x: \exists p.\langle x, p \rangle \in I\}$ is bounded above by y (say), and $\bigwedge \{p: \exists x.\langle x, p \rangle \in I\}$ is **false**. Then

$$\bigwedge \{[x \to p]: \langle x, p \rangle \in S\} \leq \bigwedge \{[x \to p]: \langle x, p \rangle \in I\}$$
$$\leq \bigwedge \{[y \to p]: \exists x.\langle x, p \rangle \in I\}$$
$$= [y, \bigwedge \{p: \exists x.\langle x, p \rangle \in I\}] = \textbf{false}$$

Therefore a meet of quasicoprimes is either again quasicoprime or **false**. The result follows from Lemma 10.5.6. ▪

In the Scott domains, we have found a class of spectral algebraic locales that is closed under the formation of function spaces. Fortunately, they are also closed under most other domain constructs. If closure for spectral algebraic locales is shown using Lemma 9.3.9, it is usually easy to upgrade this by proving condition (iii) of Lemma 10.5.6. Scott domains are closed under –

- products
- separated or coalesced sums (not disjoint sums, because of the problem with bottoms)
- function spaces
- Smyth and Hoare power domains (see next chapter), but not Plotkin power domains

Moreover, although we have not studied the recursive definition of domains in detail, if the definition involves just the constructs listed above, then the solution is a Scott domain (Exercise 11). This makes them a useful category of domains for computing uses: a program can generally be found a meaning in a Scott domain.

10.6 Strongly algebraic locales (SFP)

In Section 10.5, we wanted a class of spectral algebraic locales for which $[D\to E]$ was algebraic (we knew that it was spectral) whenever D and E were in the class, and we found that this worked for the Scott domains. We now try to do this in greater generality and look for as big a class as possible. If D is in it, then $[D\to D]$ must be algebraic, and we present a theorem of Smyth [83'] showing that this suffices to define a class closed under function spaces, the *strongly algebraic locales*.

Let us then fix, for the time being, a spectral algebraic locale D.

If $[D\to D]$ is algebraic, then Id_D is the directed join of its compact approximants. We therefore start by investigating $\downarrow Id_D$. Suppose $f \sqsubseteq Id_D$. If x is a minimal point (one of the minimal upper bounds of the empty set) then $f(x) = x$: x is a fixpoint of f. More generally, suppose T is a finite set of compact fixpoints, and x (necessarily compact) is a minimal upper bound of T. If $t \in T$, then $f(x) \sqsupseteq f(t) = t$, so $f(x)$ is an upper bound of T less than x and so x is also a fixpoint. The set of compact fixpoints of f is therefore MUB-closed:

Definition 10.6.1 A subset M of Kpt D is *MUB-closed* iff whenever T is a finite subset of M then the minimal upper bounds of T are all in M.

The intersection of any family of MUB-closed sets is still MUB-closed, and so any subset S of Kpt D generates a *MUB-closure*, the intersection of the MUB-closed sets containing it.

We can be more concrete about the MUB-closure. Let $S_0 = S$, and once S_i is defined, define

$$S_{i+1} = \{\text{minimal upper bounds of finite subsets of } S_i\}.$$

Then $S_0 \subseteq S_1 \subseteq S_2 \subseteq \dots$, and their union is the MUB-closure of S.

The MUB-closed sets are important because they enable us to define some functions in $[D\to D]$ and hence to approach the question of algebraicity of $[D\to D]$. Since for the time being we shall be working mostly on the points side, we shall generally follow the convention mentioned after Definition 5.2.1 and omit 'pt' when referring to the points part of a continuous map.

Lemma 10.6.2 Let $S \subseteq$ Kpt D, and let M be its MUB-closure.

(i)   There is a continuous function e_S in $\downarrow Id$, defined by

$$e_S(x) = \bigsqcup{}^{\uparrow} \{s \in M : s \sqsubseteq x\}$$

It is the least function in $\downarrow Id$ fixing all the points in S.

(ii)   The compact fixpoints of e_S are the elements of M.

(iii) e_S is idempotent (i.e. $e_S ; e_S = e_S$).

(iv)   If M is a finite set, then e_S is a compact function.

(v)   If S is a finite set and $[D\to D]$ is algebraic, then e_S is a compact function.

(vi)   If S and S' are MUB-closed subsets of Kpt D, then $e_S \sqsubseteq e_{S'} \Leftrightarrow S \subseteq S'$.

Proof (i) By MUB-closure of M the join is directed, so e_S is well-defined, and it is clearly monotone and less than Id. If $s \in M$ and $s \subseteq \bigsqcup^{\uparrow} X$, then by compactness $s \subseteq$ some $x \in X$, so $s \subseteq e_S(x)$. Therefore $e_S(\bigsqcup^{\uparrow} X) \subseteq \bigsqcup^{\uparrow} \{e_S(x): x \in X\}$ and e_S is continuous. Also e_S fixes every $s \in M$.

Now suppose that $g \subseteq$ Id and g fixes every $s \in S$. Then by induction on i, g fixes every element of every S_i, and hence every element of M. For suppose $s \in S_{i+1}$: s is a minimal upper bound for some finite $T \subseteq S_i$. If $t \in T$ then $s \sqsupseteq t$, so $g(s) \sqsupseteq g(t) = t$ (by induction). Therefore $g(s)$ is an upper bound for T, less than the minimal upper bound s, so $g(s) = s$. Now for all x,

$$g(x) \sqsupseteq \bigsqcup^{\uparrow} \{g(s) : s \in M, s \subseteq x\} = \bigsqcup^{\uparrow} \{s \in M: s \subseteq x\} = e_S(x),$$

so $g \sqsupseteq e_S$.

(ii) If x is a compact fixpoint of e_S then $x = e_S(x) = \bigsqcup^{\uparrow} \{s \in M: s \subseteq x\}$, so by compactness x is equal to one of the s's.

(iii) $e_S \subseteq$ Id $\Rightarrow e_S;e_S \subseteq e_S$, and $e_S;e_S$ fixes all the points in S, so $e_S;e_S \sqsupseteq e_S$.

(iv) $e_S(x) \in M$ for all x. If $e_S \subseteq \bigsqcup^{\uparrow} G$, then for each $s \in M$ there is some $g_s \in G$ such that $s = e_S(s) \subseteq g_s(s)$, and if g is an upper bound in G for $\{g_s: s \in M\}$ then for all $s \in M$, $s \subseteq g(s)$. Then for any x, $e_S(x) \subseteq g(e_S(x)) \subseteq g(x)$ and so $e_S \subseteq g$.

(v) e_S is the directed join $\bigsqcup^{\uparrow} F$, say, of its compact approximants. For each $s \in S$,

$$s = e_S(s) = \bigsqcup^{\uparrow} \{f(s): f \in F\},$$

so for some $f_s \in F$, we have $f_s(s) = s$. Let f be a compact upper bound for the f_s's in $\downarrow e_S$. Then f fixes every $s \in S$, so $f \sqsupseteq e_S$ and hence $e_S = f$ is compact.

(vi) $e_S \subseteq e_{S'} \Leftrightarrow e_{S'}$ fixes all the elements of $S \Leftrightarrow S \subseteq S'$.]

Proposition 10.6.3 *A special case of Smyth's Theorem [83']*
Let D be a spectral algebraic locale for which $[D \rightarrow D]$ is algebraic. Then every finite set of compact points has finite MUB-closure.

Proof Let S be a finite set of compact points, and M its MUB-closure. We proceed via two lemmas.

Lemma 10.6.3.1 Any directed subset of M already contains its join.
Proof Let $Y \subseteq M$ be directed, with join m, and define a function g by

$$g(x) = \begin{cases} e_S(x) & \text{if } x \subseteq m \\ e_S(m) = m & \text{otherwise} \end{cases}$$

This is easily checked to be continuous. If $s \in S \cap \downarrow m$, then s is fixed by g and hence by some compact approximant f_s to g. Let f be a compact upper bound for $\{f_s: s \in S \cap \downarrow m\}$ in $\downarrow g$; f fixes every s in $S_0 \cap \downarrow m$. By induction on i, much as in 10.6.2 (i), f fixes every $s \in S_i \cap \downarrow m$ for every i. Hence if $s \in M \cap \downarrow m$, and in particular if $s \in Y$, then $f(s) = s$, so $f(m) = m$.

Now for each z, let Kz be the constant function for z: K$z(x) = z$. Then

$$f \subseteq g \subseteq Km = \bigsqcup^{\uparrow} \{Ky: y \in Y\}$$

and so $f \sqsubseteq Ky$ for some $y \in Y$. Then $m = f(m) \sqsubseteq Ky(m) = y$, so Y already contains its join. ⌉

Lemma 10.6.3.2 M is finite.

Proof Define a *chain* in M to be a sequence $s_1 \sqsubseteq s_2 \sqsubseteq \ldots \sqsubseteq s_l$ such that $s_1 \in S_1$ and $s_{i+1} \in S_{i+1} \backslash S_i$ for all i. Suppose $x \in M$. If $x \in S_1$, then x on its own forms a chain. Otherwise, $x \in S_{j+1} \backslash S_j$ for some j and there is some finite $T \subseteq S_j$ for which x is a minimal upper bound; T is non-empty (otherwise $x \in S_1$). If $j = 1$ then we can choose $y \in T$, and then $y \sqsubseteq x$ is a chain; if $j \geq 2$, then for some $y \in T$ we have $x \sqsupseteq y \in S_j \backslash S_{j-1}$. By continuing this process, we eventually get a chain ending with x: every element of M is the end of a chain.

Next, we use the argument of *König's Lemma* to show that the chains have bounded length. For otherwise, we can build up an infinite chain, contradicting Lemma 10.6.3.1. Suppose for this, that we already have a finite chain of length l with arbitrarily long prolongations. Then since S_{l+1} is finite, there is some s_{l+1} extending the chain so that the new chain also has arbitrarily long prolongations. There is nothing to stop us doing this to infinity.

Now we know the length of chains is bounded by some l, and we deduce that $M = S_l$, finite. ⌉

This concludes the proof of the Proposition. ⌉⌉

Definition 10.6.4 A spectral algebraic locale is a *strongly algebraic locale* iff every finite set of compact points has finite MUB-closure.

Generally, the term *strongly algebraic domain,* or *SFP domain,* is taken to mean a strongly algebraic locale in our sense that also has a bottom and is ω-algebraic.

It is now relatively easy to prove our original goal, algebraicity of the function spaces, by showing that if D and E are strongly algebraic locales, and if f: D → E is continuous, then

$$f = \bigsqcup^{\uparrow} \{e_T \circ f \circ e_S \colon S, T \text{ finite MUB-closed sets in } D, E\},$$

and each $e_T \circ f \circ e_S$ is compact. However, we shall instead present the ideas of Abramsky [88], where he extends the methods we have already seen to cover strongly algebraic locales. This has the advantage of proving directly that [D→E] is strongly algebraic.

First, we must transform Definition 10.6.4 into a statement about opens. If S is a finite set of compact points of D, then its minimal upper bounds correspond to the coprimes in the irredundant coprime decomposition of $\bigwedge \{\uparrow s \colon s \in S\}$. It follows that S is MUB-closed iff the lattice generated in $K\Omega D$ by $\{\uparrow s \colon s \in S\}$ contains all the coprimes in the irredundant coprime decompositions of its elements – we shall call such a sublattice of $K\Omega D$ *ICD-closed.*

Proposition 10.6.5 Let D be a spectral algebraic locale. Then D is strongly algebraic iff every finite subset of $K\Omega D$ generates a finite ICD-closed sublattice. ⌉

Lemma 10.6.6 *The Method of Quasicoprimes for Strongly Algebraic Locales.*

Let E_i ($1 \leq i \leq n$) be a set of strongly algebraic locales, let the locale D have a coherent presentation

$$\Omega D = Fr \langle G \mid R \rangle$$

in which $G \subseteq \prod_i K\Omega E_i$, and let $\mathcal{Q}$ be a set of finite subsets of G.

As a temporary measure, we call the opens $\wedge Q$ for $Q \in \mathcal{Q}$ the *quasicoprime* opens. Also, for any $S \subseteq \prod_i K\Omega E_i$ we write S_j for $\{s_j : s \in S\}$.

Suppose that the following two conditions hold.

(i)   For each quasicoprime q, there is a point x of D such that the extent of q is $\uparrow x$.

(ii)   Let S be a finite subset of G, and for each j let M_j be the ICD-closed sublattice of $K\Omega E_j$
           generated by S_j. Then $\wedge S$ is a join of quasicoprimes, each a meet of generators from
           $\prod_i M_i$.

Then D is a strongly algebraic locale, and its compact coprime opens are precisely the quasicoprimes.
Proof By Lemma 9.3.9, D is spectral algebraic. It now suffices to show that any finite set T of generators generates a finite ICD-closed sublattice in $K\Omega D$. For $1 \le j \le n$, let M_j be the ICD-closed sublattice of $K\Omega E_j$ generated by T_j, and let T' be the set of joins of coprimes, each of which is a meet of generators from $\prod_i M_i$. T' is finite, and is closed under finite joins, irredundant coprime decompositions and (by condition (ii)) meets.   ]

Theorem 10.6.7 (Abramsky [88]) If D and E are strongly algebraic locales, then so is $[D \to E]$. It is presented by

$$\Omega[D \to E] = Fr \langle [a, b] : a \in K\Omega D, b \in K\Omega E \mid$$

$\quad [\vee S, b] = \wedge \{[a, b] : a \in S\}$ $\qquad$ $(S \subseteq K\Omega D,$ S finite$)$

$\quad [p, \vee T] = \vee \{[p, b] : b \in T\}$ $\qquad$ $(p$ coprime, $T \subseteq K\Omega E,$ T finite$)$

$\quad [a, \wedge T] = \wedge \{[a, b] : b \in T\}$ $\qquad$ $(T \subseteq K\Omega E,$ T finite$)$ $\quad \rangle$

with $f \vdash [a, b]$ iff $a \le \Omega f(b)$.

The coprimes are meets of the form $\wedge \{[p, f(p)] : p \in M\}$ where M is a finite set of coprimes in $K\Omega D$ for which the set of corresponding points is MUB-closed, and $f: M \to K\Omega E$ is a monotone function such that each $f(p)$ is coprime.
Proof We use a different presentation from that in Theorem 10.5.3 in order to fit Lemma 10.6.6, but the two locales are homeomorphic with frame isomorphisms given by

$\quad [x \to b] \mapsto [\uparrow x, b]$

$\quad [a, b] \mapsto \wedge \{[\uparrow p \to b] : p \in P\}$ $\quad$ where $\vee P$ is the irredundant coprime decomposition of a

Let a quasicoprime $\wedge \{[p, f(p)] : p \in M\}$ be given, and define a map g by

$$\Omega g(b) = \vee \{p \in M : f(p) \le b\}$$

This preserves joins because the $f(p)$'s are all coprimes. As for meets, the difficult direction is $\wedge \{\Omega g(b) : b \in T\} \le \Omega g(\wedge T)$ (T a finite subset of $K\Omega E$). The left-hand side is

$$\wedge \{\vee \{p \in M : f(p) \le b\} : b \in T\} = \vee \{\wedge \{p_b : b \in T\} : p_b \in M, f(p_b) \le b\}$$

By MUB-closure of M, $\wedge \{p_b: b \in T\} = \vee Q$ with $Q \subseteq M$. Then by monotonicity of f, if $q \in Q$ then $f(q) \leq f(p_b) \leq b$ for all $b \in T$, so $f(q) \leq \wedge T$, and it follows that $\vee Q \leq \Omega g(\wedge T)$.

If h is any other continuous map, then

$$h \vdash \wedge \{[p, f(p)]: p \in M\} \Leftrightarrow \forall p \in M. \; p \leq \Omega h(f(p))$$
$$\Leftrightarrow \forall p \in M, \forall b \in K\Omega E. \; (f(p) \leq b \rightarrow p \leq \Omega h(b))$$
$$\Leftrightarrow \forall b \in K\Omega E. \; (\Omega g(b) \leq \Omega h(b))$$
$$\Leftrightarrow g \sqsubseteq h$$

Thus the extent of $\wedge \{[p, f(p)]: p \in M\}$ is $\uparrow g$.

Next, we show how to decompose meets of generators into joins of coprimes. To apply Lemma 10.6.6, we identify each generator [a, b] with the pair $\langle a, b \rangle$ in $K\Omega D \times K\Omega E$. It should be born in mind that there are now two notions of equality between generators, depending on whether they are considered elements of $\Omega[D \rightarrow E]$ or $K\Omega D \times K\Omega E$. There should not be any confusion in practice.

Let X be a finite set of generators, and let M_1 and M_2 be the ICD-closed sublattices generated by the sets

$$X_1 = \{a: \exists b. \, [a, b] \in X\}, \qquad X_2 = \{b: \exists a. \, [a, b] \in X\}$$

We are going to make various reductions to get $\wedge X$ as a join of coprimes, and at no stage do we use any generators outside $M_1 \times M_2$. This requires checking, but is not difficult.

First, by taking coprime decompositions of a and b, any generator [a, b] can be reduced by the first two relations to a join of meets of generators [p, q], where p and q are coprimes. Thus any meet of generators can be reduced to such a join. Moreover, using the third relation, we can assume that in each of these meets, the p's are distinct. Thus $\wedge X$ is a join of meets $\wedge \{[p, f(p)]: p \in S\}$ where the p's and f(p)'s are coprimes.

Next, we extend S to its MUB-closure M. Suppose S is not already MUB-closed. Then its has some finite subset T such that some coprime p' in the irredundant coprime decomposition of $\wedge T$ is not in S. Then

$$\wedge \{[p, f(p)]: p \in T\} \leq \wedge \{[p', f(p)]: p \in T\} = [p', \wedge \{f(p): p \in T\}]$$
$$\wedge \{[p, f(p)]: p \in S\} = \wedge \{[p, f(p)]: p \in S\} \wedge [p', \wedge \{f(p): p \in T\}]$$

By taking a coprime decomposition of $\wedge \{f(p): p \in T\}$, we can reduce $\wedge \{[p, f(p)]: p \in S\}$ to a join of meets $\wedge \{[p, f(p)]: p \in S \cup \{p'\}\}$, and by iterating this we can assume that S = M is MUB-closed.

Finally, we must make f monotone. Call $p \in M$ *good* iff f is monotone on $\uparrow p \cap M$. If all M's elements are good then f is monotone and we are done; otherwise, let q be a maximal bad element. Then if $q \leq r$ we have $[r, f(r)] \leq [q, f(r)]$, so

$$\wedge \{[p, f(p)]: p \in M\} = \wedge \{[p, f(p)]: q \neq p \in M\} \wedge [q, \wedge \{f(r): q \leq r\}]$$

By taking a coprime decomposition of $\wedge \{f(r): q \leq r\}$, we can reduce the original meet to a join of meets $\wedge \{[p, f'(p)]: p \in M\}$, where each f' agrees with f everywhere except at q. If p is good for f, then f' agrees with f on ↑p and p is good for f. But q is also good for f', for by maximality of q, f is monotone on {r ∈ M: r > q}, and f' agrees with it there, while if q ≤ r then f'(q) ≤ f'(r) by construction. Each f' therefore has strictly more good elements than f. When this process stops, we have the coprime form as stated.   ]

The same proof in fact proves another result: if D and E are spectral algebraic locales, and D is strongly algebraic, then [D→E] is algebraic.

We have now proved –

Theorem 10.6.8 Let D be a spectral algebraic locale. Then D is strongly algebraic iff [D→D] is algebraic.   ]

10.7 Domain equations

We conclude with a look at the problem with which we introduced domains, namely recursive definitions of them. Unfortunately we have not the space to go into this in detail, but a few examples will give the general flavour. Further details are contained in Exercises 7 to 14.

Bit streams, 2*ω

The points are the finite and infinite lists of bits, ordered by the prefix ordering, and every list is either bottom, or a bit followed by another list. We express this by the *domain equation*

$$D = (2 \times D)_\perp$$

Here 2 is the discrete topological space {0, 1}, and × is the ordinary topological product: so for *any* spectral algebraic locale D we can construct $(2 \times D)_\perp$. We are looking for a D that solves the equation. Actually, it is too much to expect D and $(2 \times D)_\perp$ to be equal, but as long as they are homeomorphic we are happy. We therefore want mutually inverse continuous maps

unfold: $D \to (2 \times D)_\perp$ and   fold: $(2 \times D)_\perp \to D$

Unfold shows how to analyse each point in D in terms of the structure of $(2 \times D)_\perp$: to say whether it is ⊥ or a bit followed by a list, and if the latter, which bit and which list. Thus

unfold (empty list)   = ⊥
unfold (b::x)   = ⟨b, x⟩

Fold, on the other hand, shows how to synthesize points of D out of the pieces that make up $(2 \times D)_\perp$:

fold ($\perp$) = empty list
fold ($\langle b, x \rangle$) = b::x

Given that we have already put a lot of work into understanding the structure of this domain, it all looks rather trivial. However, there are general techniques for constructing domains out of domain equations, and we can demonstrate them in D. They rely on the idea that if D is a solution, and it is a domain, then it contains the trivial domain $\{\perp\}$. Therefore $D \cong (2 \times D)_\perp$ ought to contain $(2 \times \{\perp\})_\perp$ and hence also $(2 \times (2 \times \{\perp\})_\perp)_\perp$, $(2 \times (2 \times (2 \times \{\perp\})_\perp)_\perp)_\perp$, and so on. If for brevity (and also to hint at the general case) we write F(E) for the expression $(2 \times E)_\perp$, then these are $\{\perp\}$, $F(\{\perp\})$, $F^2(\{\perp\})$, $F^3(\{\perp\})$ and so on. Pictorially, they are –

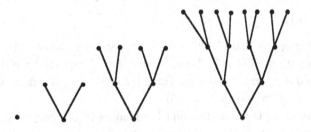

It should be clear that in some sense D is the limit of these finite approximations to it. To make this precise we need a concept that we haven't stressed, namely the *functoriality* of our domain constructors. This says that we can define the constructors not only on the locales, but also on the continuous maps between them. For instance, if f: $E \rightarrow E'$ is a continuous map, then it induces a continuous map F(f) from F(E) to F(E') – it just takes $\perp$ to $\perp$, and $\langle b, x \rangle$ to $\langle b, f(x) \rangle$. Moreover, this action on maps preserves composition (including the nullary composition: when applied to the identity map, it gives an identity map). Categorically speaking, F is a *functor*.

There are now two ways of seeing D as a limit. First, F(E) has a bottom for every E, and so there is a map from $\{\perp\}$ to F(E) ($\perp \mapsto \perp$). In particular, there is a map f from $\{\perp\}$ to $F(\{\perp\})$. This gives us $F^i(f): F^i(\{\perp\}) \rightarrow F^{i+1}(\{\perp\})$ for all i.

$$\{\perp\} \underset{f}{\rightarrow} F(\{\perp\}) \underset{F(f)}{\rightarrow} F^2(\{\perp\}) \underset{F^2(f)}{\rightarrow} F^3(\{\perp\}) \underset{F^3(f)}{\rightarrow} \dots \tag{\dagger}$$

In fact these are all 1-1, so we can think of $F^{i+1}(\{\perp\})$ as having the points of $F^i(\{\perp\})$ (the image of $F^i(f)$) together with some more. Taking the "union" gives us the compact points of D, and of course we obtain D by ideal completion. Categorically speaking, D is a colimit of the diagram ($\dagger$).

Second, there is a unique continuous map from any locale to $\{\bot\}$, and in particular there is a map g: $F(\{\bot\}) \to \{\bot\}$ and hence $F^i(g)$: $F^{i+1}(\{\bot\}) \to F^i(\{\bot\})$

$$\{\bot\} \;\overset{}{\leftarrow}\; F(\{\bot\}) \;\overset{}{\leftarrow}\; F^2(\{\bot\}) \;\overset{}{\leftarrow}\; F^3(\{\bot\}) \;\leftarrow\; \dots \qquad (\ddagger)$$
$$\quad\;\; g \qquad\qquad F(g) \qquad\qquad F^2(g) \qquad\qquad F^3(g)$$

It is an easy exercise to check that the action of $F^i(g)$ is to leave unchanged the lists of length $\le i$, and to *truncate* those of length $i+1$ by omitting the final term. Let us introduce a notation for this (which makes sense even for infinite lists),

$$s|i = \begin{cases} s & \text{if s has length} \le i \\ s \text{ truncated to i terms} & \text{if s is longer} \end{cases}$$

so that $F^i(g)(s) = s|i$. Any list s in D is completely specified by its finite truncations

$$t^{(i)} = s|i \in F^i(\{\bot\}),$$

and these have the property that $t^{(i+1)}|i = t^{(i)}$. Moreover, any sequence $(t^{(i)})$ with this property comes from a list in D, for if we ever have length $t^{(n)} < n$ then $t^{(j)} = t^{(n)}$ for all $j \ge n$, and $(t^{(i)})$ comes from the finite list $t^{(n)}$, while if length $t^{(i)} = i$ for all i then the $t^{(i)}$'s build up into an infinite list.

We can thus construct D as the domain of sequences $(t^{(i)})$ where $t^{(i)} \in F^i(\{\bot\})$ and $t^{(i+1)}|i = t^{(i)}$. Categorically speaking, D is the limit of the diagram (‡).

It may seem from this that the second method, the *limit* method, is better because it is more general: the map g always exists, whereas the map f depends on having a bottom in $F(\{\bot\})$. However, we shall see later (in the example on function spaces) that the full power comes from using both methods together – as we can here.

Now let us turn to the open sets of D. Again, these can be built up using the domain equation: this is really applying the colimit method to the diagram of finite frames

$$K\Omega\{\bot\} \to K\Omega F(\{\bot\}) \to \;\; K\Omega F^2(\{\bot\}) \to \;\;\;\; K\Omega F^3(\{\bot\}) \to \dots$$
$$\quad\; \Omega g \qquad\qquad \Omega F(g) \qquad\qquad \Omega F^2(g) \qquad\qquad \Omega F^3(g) \qquad (\ddagger*)$$

Let us write **true, false, 0** $(= \{0\})$ and **1** $(\{1\})$ for the open sets of 2. If a is any open set for D, then we can construct some opens for $2\times D$:

$0\otimes a$, $1\otimes a$ and **true**$\otimes a = 0\otimes a \vee 1\otimes a$ (and **false**$\otimes a = $ **false**).

In addition for lift($2\times D$) we have a new **true**. For instance,

$0\otimes$**starts** $l = $ **starts**$(0::l)$
$1\otimes$**starts** $l = $ **starts**$(1::l)$

This shows how to build up the generators for ΩD recursively, starting just with the opens **true** and **false**, and the relations are those derived from the constructs that make up F. Just from the data in ($\ddagger$*), we can show that this describes a spectral locale that solves the domain equation. However, to show algebraicity we need a sensible description of the coprimes and we'd really like the homomorphisms $\Omega F^i(g)$ to preserve coprimes. This is something that the existence of f enables us to prove. Further details about these issues can be found in Abramsky [87], and in Exercises 7 to 16.

Function spaces and the untyped λ-calculus
In the untyped λ-calculus (the classic reference is Barendregt [84]; a useful introduction is Hindley and Seldin [86]) everything is supposed to be a function. Any element can be applied to any other, including itself. This is thus clearly related to the domain equation

$$D = [D \rightarrow D]$$

From the cardinality argument at the beginning of this chapter, if we try to work in set theory and take $[D \rightarrow D]$ to mean the set of all functions from D to D, there is only a trivial solution to this: D must be a singleton. This originally made the untyped λ-calculus suspect, because it seemed to have no interesting models, but Scott showed that in domain theory, where we reinterpret $[D \rightarrow D]$, there are non-trivial solutions.

If we use the methods we saw for bit streams, we cannot expect to reach Scott's solutions: the methods always give the simplest solution, which is just $\{\perp\}$. However, we get something more interesting if we try to solve

$$D = [D \rightarrow D]_\perp$$

This has been studied by Abramsky [87, 90], and also, following him, by Ong [88], in connection with the *lazy λ-calculus*. The effect of the lifting is to make a distinction between $\perp$, a completely divergent object, and $\lambda x.\perp$, which is known to be a function but which diverges whenever it is applied to an argument. Computationally, this corresponds to not trying to evaluate a function beyond the λ until application time, and is the way things are generally done in practice.

Writing now F(D) for $[D \rightarrow D]_\perp$, our immediate problem is that *F is not a functor*. The methods of the previous example therefore break down very quickly. This is a persistent problem with anything involving function spaces. We break the problem down into parts and consider $[D \rightarrow E]$.

First, if we have a map g: $E \rightarrow E'$, then there is a map

$$[D{\to}g]: [D{\to}E] \to [D{\to}E'], \qquad f \mapsto f;g.$$

For fixed D, $[D{\to}E]$ is a functor of E.

On the other hand, a map h: $D \to D'$ gives a map

$$[h{\to}E]: [D'{\to}E] \to [D{\to}E], \qquad f \mapsto h;f.$$

For fixed E, $[D{\to}E]$ is not a functor of D, because $[h{\to}E]$ goes in the wrong direction. Such reversed functors are called *contravariant functors* (the true functors are then called *covariant*). This contravariance destroys our limit constructions, and, more seriously, it means that $[D{\to}D]$ is neither a covariant nor a contravariant functor of D – it is simply not defined on maps.

The solution here is to use the two limit constructions simultaneously. If we are given two maps i: $D \to D'$ and p: $D' \to D$, then we can also define two maps between $[D{\to}D]$ and $[D'{\to}D']$:

$$[p{\to}i]: [D{\to}D] \to [D'{\to}D'] \quad f \mapsto p;f;i$$
$$[i{\to}p]: [D'{\to}D'] \to [D{\to}D] \quad g \mapsto i;g;p$$

The lifting is functorial, so now we can start off with the obvious pair of maps between $\{\bot\}$ and $F(\{\bot\}) = [\{\bot\}{\to}\{\bot\}]_\bot$ and define pairs of maps between $F^i(\{\bot\})$ and $F^{i+1}(\{\bot\})$ for all i. From this we can construct a solution to the domain equation using either the colimit method or the limit method (and they give isomorphic answers). This is called the *bilimit* solution to the domain equation.

Notes

It should be repeated that our working idea of domain, namely the spectral algebraic locale, excludes two standard features: bottoms, and 2nd countability (ω-algebraicity). 2nd countability is needed to give effective constructions of domains, and bottoms are needed to get fixpoints (for the usual semantics of recursive definitions) and bilimit solutions (see Exercise 15) of domain equations. From a topological point of view, however, these features are unimportant and we have taken pains not to assume them except where necessary.

The standard reference for domain theory is the excellent and comprehensive lecture notes of Plotkin [81], which, unfortunately, have never appeared in book form. A good (though now slightly old-fashioned) account of domain theory as a tool for denotational semantics is Stoy [77].

Section 10.1 – Domain Theory is traditionally seen as a theory of cpos – Manes and Arbib [86] is a good exposition of this kind of approach. This order theoretic account usually works well in describing the points of constructed domains and their order, but is less natural in saying which points are compact (look at function spaces, for example).

To get the best of both worlds, our method of quasicoprimes is hybrid: it treats a domain rather as a cpo in determining the points, but as a locale in determining the compact ones. This is a reason for using the non-committal context of topological systems. It would be interesting to carry through a purely localic program, showing directly that each localic construction (presenting a frame by generators and relations) satisfies some universal property.

Sections 10.2-10.5 – The basic work of the domain theory is due to Dana Scott. He formalized the notion of Scott domain, and showed that this class of domains was closed under the various constructions. In his original papers (e.g. Scott [70], Scott and Strachey [71]), Scott domains as we now know them were made into complete lattices by adjoining a top, "overdefined" element, and this method is followed in Stoy [77]. However, it seems that – along with others – he was aware of the alternative possibility of using cpos without top, and over the years their greater usefulness has become apparent. Of course, once one goes into SFP domains it is no longer the case that adjoining a top converts the domain into a lattice.

Plotkin and Smyth together seem to have developed the idea that topological notions are computationally useful, and in [83] Smyth addressed the Stone duality between functions and their inverse image maps. This was already known to computer science in a very restricted context, as the theory of predicate transformers, but Smyth showed how much deeper this went. He also pointed out that it implied links between domain theory and Dijkstra's axiomatic semantics, and this led Abramsky [87, 88] to the idea of formalizing – roughly speaking – the Stone dual of domain theory. Our presentation of domain theory is derived from his work.

Section 10.6 – Strongly algebraic domains were first described by Plotkin [76] in the context of ω-algebraic cpos (with ⊥), and called by him SFP (Sequence of Finite Posets) domains. He gave, roughly speaking, the definition we have in 10.6.4, and showed that they can be equivalently characterized as bilimits of sequences of finite locales connected by embedding-projection pairs, hence the name (see Exercises 7 to 12). A corollary of this is that SFP is closed under all decent domain constructs (including function spaces), because the class of finite domains is.

His definition of SFP for an ω-algebraic cpo had three clauses: that every finite set of compact points has a finite set of minimal upper bounds, that it is a complete set of minimal upper bounds (i.e. every upper bound is greater than one of them), and that finitely generated MUB-closures are finite. For this reason the spectral algebraic domains, which satisfy the first two clauses (the second characterization of Theorem 9.3.8), are often called 2/3 SFP domains.

Plotkin also conjectured that for any ω-algebraic cpo D, algebraicity of [D→D] implied that D was SFP, and this was proved by Smyth [83']. Our proof is essentially a reworking of Smyth's (assisted by Taylor's exposition in [86]), but it is considerably simpler because we have started out from the assumption that D is a spectral algebraic locale – we have assumed the 2/3 SFP condition that Smyth manages to prove. Taylor suggests out that Smyth's proof relies on ω-algebraicity for the 2/3 SFP part, but not for the final third. This allows us to avoid mention of ω-algebraicity. We have also adapted the proof to cover locales without bottom, in which form the result was stated by Gunter [85] but not proved in detail.

The main part of Theorem 10.6.7, that if D and E are strongly algebraic then so is [D→E], was proved by Plotkin in his original paper [76]. Abramsky [88] gave the characterization of the coprimes (using a result of Gunter [85]), and also the algorithm by which one reduces compact opens to joins of coprimes (our Theorem 10.6.7). He points out that the algorithm can be executed for arbitrary spectral algebraic locales; the role of strong algebraicity is to ensure that it terminates. Abramsky's proof is somewhat more complicated by the care he has taken to ensure that his axiom system is constructive. Our generalization – mentioned after the Theorem – to the case where D is strongly algebraic but E is merely spectral algebraic is apparently new, and relies on an induction step (the discussion of "good" elements) slightly more refined than Abramsky's.

Section 10.7 – As mentioned in Section 10.1, the idea of solving domain equations is one reason for the existence of domain theory. The presentation given here is slightly unusual in that we allow locales without bottom to appear in the domain equation D = F(D). This is acceptable as long as the final expression F(D) has a bottom. Thus for the Kahn domain $A^{*\omega}$ on an alphabet A, we accept A as a discrete space and solve $D = (A \times D)_\perp$. The traditional method takes A as a flat domain (lifted discrete space) and solves $D = A \otimes D$, where for the nonce $\otimes$ represents a "left-strict product" in which $\langle \perp, x \rangle = \perp \neq \langle a, \perp \rangle$. Similarly, we can often use the categorically natural disjoint sum rather than choosing between the coalesced and separated sums. The presentation here shows that the absence of bottoms does not make spectral algebraic locales (2/3 SFP domains) or strongly algebraic locales (SFP domains) any less well behaved topologically.

It is convenient to use domain equations to create user-defined types in a computer programming language. Whatever syntax one uses for "the [canonical] solution of D = F(D)" – Abramsky [87] writes "μD.F(D)" –, this should be syntactically guaranteed to be meaningful. To use the bilimit method – the sensible one, given that we want to allow contravariant constructions such as function spaces – F(D) must have a bottom whenever D does. When the purpose is to get a purely syntactic system, such as Abramsky's, it is therefore reasonable to consider only constructions that operate on domains with bottom to produce another domain with bottom: lifting, products, the *coalesced* sum, function spaces, power domains (as in the next Chapter) and combinations of these.

Exercises

1. If D is a spectral locale, then the frame for $D_\perp$ is presented by

$$\Omega(D_\perp) = \text{Fr} \langle \text{ lift } a : a \in K\Omega D \mid$$
$$\text{lift } (\vee S) = \vee \{\text{lift } a: a \in S\} \qquad (S \subseteq K\Omega D, S \text{ finite})$$
$$\text{lift } (\wedge S) = \wedge \{\text{lift } a: a \in S\} \qquad (\emptyset \neq S \subseteq K\Omega D, S \text{ finite}) \quad \rangle$$

2. (Universal characterization of lifting.) Let D be a topological system. Define a continuous map up: $D \to D_\perp$ such that pt up $(x) = \textbf{up } x$ as in Definition 10.2.4.

Show that if E is a topological system with bottom, and f: $D \to E$ is a continuous map, then there is a unique strict continuous map g: $D_\perp \to E$ such that $f = \text{up};g$.

Categorically, we have a category $TS_\perp$ of topological systems with bottom and strict continuous maps. $(-)_\perp$ is a functor left adjoint to the forgetful functor from $TS_\perp$ to **Topological Systems**.

2. Let A and B be arbitrary frames. Show that $A \times B$ can be presented as

$$A \times B = \text{Fr} \langle \langle a, \textbf{false} \rangle, \langle \textbf{false}, b \rangle : a \in A, b \in B \mid$$
$$\langle \vee S, \textbf{false} \rangle = \vee \{\langle a, \textbf{false} \rangle: a \in S\} \qquad (S \subseteq A)$$
$$\langle \wedge S, \textbf{false} \rangle = \wedge \{\langle a, \textbf{false} \rangle: a \in S\} \qquad (\emptyset \neq S \subseteq A, S \text{ finite})$$
$$\langle \textbf{false}, \vee T \rangle = \vee \{\langle \textbf{false}, b \rangle: b \in T\} \qquad (T \subseteq B)$$
$$\langle \textbf{false}, \wedge T \rangle = \wedge \{\langle \textbf{false}, b \rangle: b \in T\} \qquad (\emptyset \neq T \subseteq B, T \text{ finite})$$
$$\langle \textbf{true}, \textbf{false} \rangle \vee \langle \textbf{false}, \textbf{true} \rangle = \textbf{true}$$
$$\langle \textbf{true}, \textbf{false} \rangle \wedge \langle \textbf{false}, \textbf{true} \rangle = \textbf{false} \qquad \rangle$$

3. Show that any Scott domain is SFP.

4. Show that the following two diagrams represent a spectral algebraic locale that is not SFP, and an SFP domain that is not a Scott domain.

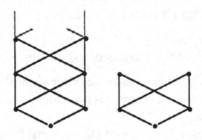

5. Let D be a spectral algebraic domain with bottom. The MUB-closure of $\emptyset$ is $\{\bot\}$ and $e_\emptyset$ is $K\bot$, the constant $\bot$ function, which is bottom in $[D{\to}D]$. If $s \in$ Kpt D then the MUB-closure of $\{s\}$ is $\{s, \bot\}$, and $e_{\{s\}}$ is the *step function* $[s{\Rightarrow}s]$, defined by

$$[s{\Rightarrow}s]\,(x) = \begin{cases} s & \text{if } x \sqsupseteq s \\ \bot & \text{otherwise} \end{cases}$$

Id is the join of these, and if $S \subseteq$ Kpt D then e_S is the join in $\downarrow$Id of $\{[s{\Rightarrow}s]: s \in S\}$.

6. Verify that the class of Scott domains is closed under products and separated and coalesced sums; and that the class of strongly algebraic locales is closed under these constructions and disjoint sums.

7. Let D and E be topological systems. An *embedding-projection pair* between D and E is a pair (i, p) of continuous maps, i: D $\to$ E and p: E $\to$ D, such that i;p = Id_D and p;i $\sqsubseteq \text{Id}_E$ (see Exercise 4 of Chapter 8). Show that pt i and Ωp are 1-1, and pt p and Ωi are onto. Show that

$$\forall x{\in} \text{pt D}, \forall y{\in} \text{pt E}. \ (\text{pt } i(x) \sqsubseteq y \leftrightarrow x \sqsubseteq \text{pt } p(y))$$
$$\forall a{\in} \Omega D, \forall b{\in} \Omega E. \ (\Omega p(a) \leq b \leftrightarrow a \leq \Omega i(b))$$

(categorically, pt i and Ωp are left adjoint to pt p and Ωi) and deduce that if D and E are T_0 then each of i and p is determined by the other. Show that pt i and Ωp both preserve compactness, and that if E is spatial or localic, then D is too.

An embedding i for which such a p exists is called a *reflective* embedding, and p is its *reflector*. In domain theory, reflective embeddings are often just called *embeddings;* but there is an obvious conflict with the standard topological term.

Show that identity maps are reflective embeddings, and that a composition of reflective embeddings is again a reflective embedding.

8. Let D, D', E and E' be spatial locales and let i: D $\to$ E and i': D' $\to$ E' be reflective embeddings, with reflectors p and p'. Define j from $[D{\to}D']$ to $[E{\to}E']$ by (on the points side) $f \mapsto p;f;i'$. Show that this is a reflective embedding. Define similar reflective embeddings for sums and products.

Exercises 9 to 16 show how to solve domain equations using the *bilimit* construction. A full account is given in Smyth and Plotkin [82].

9. ω^{op}-*limits*. Let (D_n) $(n \in \omega)$ be a sequence of topological systems, and for each n suppose that p_n: $D_{n+1} \to D_n$ is a continuous map. Show that a topological system D can be defined as follows.

A point of D is a sequence (x_n), $x_n \in$ pt D_n, such that for each n, $x_n = $ pt $p_n(x_{n+1})$.

The opens of D are presented by

$$\Omega D = Fr \langle \Omega q_n(a) : a \in \Omega D_n |$$
$$\Omega q_n(\vee S) = \vee \{\Omega q_n(a): a \in S\} \qquad (S \subseteq \Omega D_n)$$
$$\Omega q_n(\wedge S) = \wedge \{\Omega q_n(a): a \in S\} \qquad (S \subseteq \Omega D_n, S \text{ finite})$$
$$\Omega q_n(a) = \Omega q_{n+1}(\Omega p_n(a)) \qquad (a \in \Omega D_n) \rangle$$

$(x_n) \vDash \Omega q_m(a)$ iff $x_m \vDash a$.

Define also continuous maps $q_n: D \to D_n$ such that Ωq_n agrees with the formal notation above, and pt $q_m((x_n)) = x_m$. Show that $q_{n+1};p_n = q_n$.

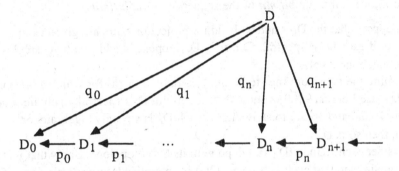

Show that this diagram satisfies the following two universal properties.

(i)   If E is any other topological system, with continuous maps $r_n: E \to D_n$ such that $r_{n+1};p_n = r_n$, then there is a unique continuous map r: E $\to$ D such that $r;q_n = r_n$ for all n.

(ii)   If E is any other topological system, and r and r' are any continuous maps from E to D, then $r \sqsubseteq r'$ iff $r;q_n \sqsubseteq r';q_n$ for all n.

(i) says that D is the *limit* – also known as the *inverse limit* – of the sequence of D_n's and p_n's in the category of topological systems. Because it is the limit of a sequence indexed by the natural numbers, we may call it an ω^{op}-*limit*. This is indeed the limit in the category of topological systems; the general construction has been seen already in Exercise 13 of Chapter 6.

Show that if each D_n is a locale, or second countable, then D is too.

10.   *ω-bilimits.* Suppose in Exercise 9 that each D_n is a locale, and that each p_n is the reflector of a reflective embedding $i_n: D_n \to D_{n+1}$. Use the universal properties to show that for each n, q_n is the reflector of a reflective embedding $j_n: D_n \to D$, and that $j_n = i_n;j_{n+1}$.

Show that $Id_D = \bigsqcup^{\uparrow}_n q_n;j_n$ and deduce that for any continuous maps k and k' from D to a topological system E, we have $k \sqsubseteq k'$ iff for all n, $j_n;k \sqsubseteq j_n;k'$.

Show that the diagram satisfies the following universal properties.

(i)   If E is any locale, with continuous maps $k_n: D_n \to E$ such that $i_n; k_{n+1} = k_n$,
then there is a unique continuous map $k: D \to E$ such that $j_n; k = k_n$ for all
n. (Hint – use $\bigsqcup^{\uparrow}_n q_n; k_n$.)

(ii)   If, in (i), each k_n is a reflective embedding, then so is k.

(i) says that D is the *colimit* (an ω-*colimit*) of the sequence of D_n's and i_n's in the
category of locales (and continuous maps); (ii) says that it is a colimit in the
category of locales and reflective embeddings. Because it is also a limit (using the
reflectors), we call it the *bilimit* of the sequence (an ω-*bilimit*).

11.   Suppose that the D_n's and embedding-projection pairs are given as in 10.
Show that if each D_n is spectral, then so is D. Suppose in addition that each D_n is a
spectral algebraic locale.

Defining the quasicoprimes to be the generators $\Omega q_n(a)$ for which a is coprime
in $K\Omega D_n$, use Lemma 9.3.9 to show that the bilimit D is spectral algebraic. Use
Lemmas 10.6.6 and 10.5.6 to show that if each D_n is strongly algebraic, or a Scott
domain, then so is D.

Consider each frame ΩD_n as a dcpo with its Scott topology. Show that it is a
Scott domain, and that each pair $(\Omega p_n, \Omega i_n)$ is an embedding-projection pair. Show
that ΩD (again with its Scott topology) is the bilimit of this system.

12.   Let D be a strongly ω-algebraic locale. Let $(x_n: n \in \omega)$ be an enumeration of
the compact points, let M_n be the MUB-closure of $\{x_i: 0 \leq i \leq n\}$, and let e_n be the
corresponding idempotent map e_{M_n}. Show that each e_n corresponds to a reflective
embedding of a finite locale into D, and that D is the bilimit of this system. Hence a
spectral algebraic locale is strongly ω-algebraic iff it is a bilimit of a sequence of
finite locales. (This is one of the main theorems of Plotkin [76], and explains the
title SFP – sequence of finite posets – domain.)

13.   (This requires a little more knowledge of category theory.) The methods
above relate to bilimits of sequences of topological systems, i.e. diagrams over the
poset ω. Show that they also work for diagrams over any directed poset – giving
directed bilimits –, or, more generally, over any filtered category – giving filtered
bilimits. A category C is *filtered* iff, to use the expression of Definition 7.2.1, "the
finite colimits have already been dealt with." More precisely:

- C is non-empty ("the empty coproduct has been dealt with").
- If a and b are objects in C, then C contains an object c and morphisms f: a $\to$
c and g: b $\to$ c ("binary coproducts have been dealt with").

- If f and g are morphisms from a to b, then there is an object c and a
  morphism h: b → c such that f;h = g;h ("coequalizers have already been dealt
  with").

A spectral algebraic locale is strongly algebraic iff it is a directed bilimit of
finite locales.

14.   We adapt Exercises 9 and 10 to the category of dcpos. Suppose in Exercise 9
that each D_n is a dcpo with its Scott topology. Show that pt D is also a dcpo, with

$$(x_n) \sqsubseteq (y_n) \quad \text{iff } x_n \sqsubseteq y_n \text{ for all } n$$

Let D' be the topological space of pt D with its Scott topology, let f: D' → D be the
unique continuous map with pt f = $\text{Id}_{\text{pt } D}$, and let $q_n' = f;q_n$. Show that properties
analogous to (i) and (ii) in Exercise 9 hold, with D replaced by D', q_n replaced by
q_n', and E replaced by any dcpo. This says that D' is the limit of the sequence in the
category of dcpos (with their Scott topologies).
      Now suppose, as in Exercise 10, that each p_n is the reflector of a reflective
embedding i_n. Show that the constructions there can be carried through, with D
replaced by D' and locales replaced by dcpos. Thus D' is the bilimit of the sequence
in the category of dcpos and reflective embeddings.
      The point of this Exercise is to do the easy, order theoretic constructions on
dcpos, without worrying too much about the topology: we simply impose the Scott
topology on everything. Exercises 9 and 10 contain more careful topological
analyses, and we are happiest when – as in Exercise 11 – the two give the same
result: the topological bilimit has the Scott topology.

15.   Let F be a *continuous functor* on the category of dcpos (considered as
topological spaces with their Scott topologies) and reflective embeddings. In other
words,

(i)   For each dcpo D, F(D) is another.
(ii)   For each reflective embedding i: D → E of dcpos, there is a reflective
         embedding F(i): F(D) → F(E).
(iii) $F(\text{Id}_D) = \text{Id}_{F(D)}$
(iv) $F(i;j) = F(i);F(j)$

(This much says that F is a functor.)

(v)   F preserves ω-bilimits.

Suppose also that F(D) has a bottom for all D. Show that there is a unique
reflective embedding i from the one-point dcpo 1 to F(1). Define an ω-diagram by
$D_n = F^n(1)$ and $i_n = F^n(i)$. Show that its bilimit D satisfies $D \cong F(D)$, and for any

$E \cong F(E)$ there is a unique continuous map – actually a reflective embedding – f from D to E such that $f; \cong = \cong; F(f)$. Categorically, D is an initial solution to the domain equation $D \cong F(D)$.

Suppose in addition that whenever E is finite, so is F(E). Show that D is strongly algebraic (actually an SFP domain). Finally, suppose in addition that whenever E is a Scott domain then so is F(E). Show that D is a Scott domain.

16.   Let i: D $\rightarrow$ E be a reflective embedding, and suppose that E is a dcpo with its Scott topology. Show that D is too.

There is a 1-1 correspondence between reflective subspaces of E and *idempotent subidentity maps* on E, continuous maps e: E $\rightarrow$ E such that $e^2 = e \sqsubseteq \mathrm{Id}_E$. Let us write IdSub(E) for the set of idempotent subidentity maps; show that it is closed under directed joins in [E$\rightarrow$E].

Suppose that F is a functor as in Exercise 15, satisfying the conditions (i) to (iv). For each E, F gives a function from IdSub(E) to IdSub(F(E)); show that F is continuous (satisfies (v)) iff for every E this function preserves directed joins.

Deduce that F(D) = [D$\rightarrow$D] is a continuous functor on dcpos and reflective embeddings.

CHAPTER ELEVEN

POWER DOMAINS

In which we investigate domains of subsets of a given domain.

11.1 Non-determinism and sets

In a non-deterministic computation, the result is not completely determined by the argument. There are various reasons why this may be so, but in any case the theoretical result is going to be a *set* of possible actual results. We must therefore ask how we might make a domain out of the set of sets of points of a domain: how we might form a *power domain*. We must first define an approximation ordering on the sets of points.

It is helpful to think of approximate elements as being bad. An approximate bit stream is one that quickly stops emitting bits, but it doesn't tell us that – it just leaves us in suspense. The more refined it is, the longer it can go on emitting bits, the better we like it. This obviously extends to sets:

(*)   *If you refine the elements of a set, then you refine the set.*

Formalizing this, we arrive at the *Egli-Milner* preorder $\sqsubseteq_{EM}$ on sets: $X \sqsubseteq_{EM} Y$ iff

- for all $x \in X$ there is some $y \in Y$ with $x \sqsubseteq y$, and
- for all $y \in Y$ there is some $x \in X$ with $x \sqsubseteq y$.

Whenever we define an ordering $\sqsubseteq$ on sets, it will include the Egli-Milner ordering: if $X \sqsubseteq_{EM} Y$, then $X \sqsubseteq Y$. However, the two parts of the definition correspond to more general ways of refining a set.

The first corresponds to *demonic* non-determinism in which non-determinism is bad. A big set corresponds to many different possibilities to take into account. A typical example is where the non-determinism arises because some implementation feature of a computer language is not defined in the report, but left up to the implementer – for instance, the order of evaluation of function arguments. In reasoning about a program, you must allow for all possible evaluation orders, because you don't know which one will actually be used. This is a rudimentary example of a profound difficulty in concurrency, where one often doesn't know in which order some actions will take place.

For demonic non-determinism, if you drop elements from a set then you refine the set.

Combining this with the first principle (*), we can formalize an ordering $\sqsubseteq_U$ on sets, the *Smyth* or *upper* preorder:

$X \sqsubseteq_U Y$ iff for all $y \in Y$ there is some $x \in X$ with $x \sqsubseteq y$.

The second possibility is *angelic* non-determinism in which the non-determinism is good. A big set corresponds to many different possibilities for you to choose from, as in situations where the non-determinism arises from input from you to the computer.

For angelic non-determinism, if you add elements to a set then you refine the set.

Formally, we get the *Hoare* or *lower* ordering $\sqsubseteq_L$ on sets:

$X \sqsubseteq_L Y$ iff for all $x \in X$ there is some $y \in Y$ with $x \sqsubseteq y$.

Proposition 11.1.1 Let X and Y be subsets of a poset.

(i) $X \sqsubseteq_U Y \Leftrightarrow \mathord{\uparrow}X \supseteq \mathord{\uparrow}Y$
(ii) $X \sqsubseteq_L Y \Leftrightarrow \mathord{\downarrow}X \subseteq \mathord{\downarrow}Y$
(iii) $X \sqsubseteq_{EM} Y \Leftrightarrow X \sqsubseteq_U Y$ and $X \sqsubseteq_L Y$]

It is clear from this that we should not normally expect these to be partial orders, although they are preorders. They can therefore make different subsets equivalent. For instance with the upper order, X and Y are equivalent (write $X \equiv_U Y$) iff $X \sqsubseteq_U Y$ and $Y \sqsubseteq_U X$, i.e. iff $\mathord{\uparrow}X = \mathord{\uparrow}Y$.

These are the basic ideas; however, in all three cases, we shall see that the best approach is not to take *all* sets of points under the chosen order. This will be discussed in each case.

11.2 The Smyth power domain

This is the power domain appropriate to demonic non-determinism. The upper preorder $\sqsubseteq_U$ is the same as the one defined in Lemma 8.2.3, and here too it turns out best to restrict ourselves to compact subsets. Then by the Hofmann–Mislove Theorem 8.2.5 we can identify the demonic non-deterministic sets in D (by which we mean the equivalence classes of compact sets under $\equiv_U$) with the Scott open filters in ΩD.

Definition 11.2.1 Let D be a locale. $P_S D$, the *Smyth, or upper power locale* of D, is defined by

$\Omega P_S D = \mathrm{Fr} \langle\, \Box a : a \in \Omega D \,|$

$$\square(\wedge S) = \wedge \{\square a: a \in S\} \qquad\qquad (S \subseteq \Omega D, S \text{ finite})$$
$$\square(\vee^{\uparrow} S) = \vee^{\uparrow} \{\square a: a \in S\} \qquad (S \subseteq \Omega D, S \text{ directed}) \quad \rangle$$

A point of $P_S D$ is a function from ΩD to **2** that preserves finite meets and directed joins, in other words a Scott open filter of ΩD. Hence pt $P_S D$ can be identified with QD.

This "Smyth power domain" is not the standard one. It is usual to impose an extra relation $\square$ **false** = **false**, which excludes the empty compact set from the points. (See note after Proposition 11.2.4, and also Exercise 3.)

Theorem 11.2.2 Let D be a spectral locale. Then $P_S D$ is a Scott domain, presented by

$$\Omega P_S D = \text{Fr} \langle \ \square a : a \in K\Omega D \ |$$
$$\square(\wedge S) = \wedge \{\square a: a \in S\} \qquad (S \subseteq K\Omega D, S \text{ finite}) \ \rangle$$

Its compact coprime opens are the generators $\square a$.

Proof Let A be the coherent frame presented in the statement. Then the obvious homomorphism from A to $\Omega P_S D$ is an isomorphism, with inverse is defined by $\square a \mapsto \vee \{\square b: b \in K\Omega D, b \leq a\}$ (one must check, of course, that this respects the relations).

If $a \in K\Omega D$, then $\uparrow a$ is a Scott open filter, and for any Scott open filter G,

$$G \vDash \square a \Leftrightarrow \uparrow a \subseteq G$$

Thus the generators $\square a$ are coprimes. Finally, any meet of generators is still a generator. We can now apply Lemma 10.5.6.   ]

Proposition 11.2.3 Let D be a spectral locale. Then pt $P_S D$ (i.e. QD) is a coherent frame, $\text{Idl}((K\Omega D)^{op})$.

Proof From Theorem 11.2.2, the compact points are the Scott open filters $\uparrow a$ for a in $K\Omega D$.

$$\uparrow a \subseteq \uparrow b \Leftrightarrow \uparrow b \vDash a \Leftrightarrow b \leq a$$

so Kpt $P_S D \cong (K\Omega D)^{op}$ and by algebraicity pt $P_S D \cong \text{Idl}(K\Omega D^{op})$. Since $K\Omega D^{op}$ is a distributive lattice, pt $P_S D$ is a frame.]

We know from the Hofmann–Mislove Theorem that pt $P_s D$ can be constructed by taking the compact subsets of pt D, ordering them with $\subseteq_U$ and taking equivalence classes under $\equiv_U$. For a spectral algebraic locale we can do better than this, describing pt $P_S D$ in terms of *finite* sets, rather than general compact ones.

Proposition 11.2.4 Let D be a spectral algebraic locale. Then the points of P_S D can be constructed as follows:

1.   Take the set $\wp_{fin}$ (Kpt D) of finite subsets of compact points of D.
2.   Preorder it using $\sqsubseteq_U$.
3.   Take equivalence classes $\wp_{fin}$ (Kpt D)/$\equiv_U$.
4.   Take the ideal completion.

The compact points, equivalence classes [X] where $X \in \wp_{fin}$ (K pt D), have a distributive lattice structure represented by

top, $\top$ $= [\emptyset]$
$[X] \sqcap [Y]$ $= [X \cup Y]$
bottom, $\bot$ $= [\{$minimal points of D$\}]$
$[X] \sqcup [Y]$ $= [\bigcup \{\{$minimal upper bounds of $\{x, y\}\}: x \in X, y \in Y\}]$

Proof The compact points of D correspond 1-1, but in reverse order, with the coprimes of KΩD. If X is a finite subset of Kpt D, then $\uparrow$X is compact and open, and hence in KΩD. Moreover, the irredundant coprime decompositions enable us to get any compact coprime open into this form. Since $\uparrow$X $\leq$ $\uparrow$Y $\Leftrightarrow$ X $\sqsupseteq_U$Y, we deduce that $\wp_{fin}$ (Kpt D)/$\equiv_U$ is isomorphic to KΩD^{op}, and we can now use Proposition 11.2.3. The description of the lattice structure is easily checked.   ]

Note – it is usual to omit the empty set [$\emptyset$] from the Smyth power domain, but there is no mathematical reason for doing this and there are applications (for instance, Vickers [86]) where [$\emptyset$] plays a natural part. Therefore the omission ought really to be justified on computational grounds in each case. A *historical* reason for the omission is that the Smyth power domain was originally described in relation to the Plotkin power domain, where $\emptyset$ is a nuisance. Of course, without [$\emptyset$], the points of P_S D no longer form a frame.

Finally, we can formalize a *Smyth non-deterministic map* from one locale D to another, E, as –

        a continuous map from D to P_S E,
i.e.   a frame homomorphism from ΩP_S E to ΩD,
i.e.   a function from ΩE to ΩD that preserves finite meets and directed joins.

Proposition 11.2.5 Let D and E be spectral locales. Then the following are equivalent:

(i)   A Smyth non-deterministic map from D to E.
(ii)   A function from ΩE to ΩD that preserves finite meets and directed joins.
(iii)   A function from QD to QE that preserves finite meets and directed joins.

Proof We have already seen that (i) and (ii) are equivalent for locales. By Theorem 9.1.5, a function as in (ii) is equivalent to a function f: $K\Omega E \to \Omega D$ that preserves finite meets. Define

$$S = \{(b, a) \in K\Omega E \times K\Omega D: a \le f(b)\}$$

This determines f by $f(b) = \bigvee \{a: (b, a) \in S\}$. S satisfies –

- if $b' \ge b$, $a \ge a'$ and $(b, a) \in S$, then $(b', a') \in S$,
- if $(b, a_i) \in S$ $(1 \le i \le n)$ then $(b, \bigvee_i a_i) \in S$, and
- if $(b_i, a) \in S$ $(1 \le i \le n)$ then $(\bigwedge_i b_i, a) \in S$ (by preservation of meets).

These three conditions are sufficient to ensure that S defines such a function f. Now let

$$S' = \{(a, b) \in K\Omega D^{op} \times K\Omega E^{op}: (b, a) \in S\}$$

S' satisfies the same three conditions, and so defines a function

$$g: K\Omega D^{op} \to Idl(K\Omega E^{op})$$

that preserves finite meets, and hence a function

$$QD = Idl(K\Omega D^{op}) \to QE = Idl(K\Omega E^{op})$$

that preserves finite meets and directed joins as in (iii). The argument reverses.]

11.3 Closed sets and the Hoare power domain

We think of the opens in a topological system D as being affirmative assertions: they may possibly be definitively observed. Their negations, on the other hand, are refutative. These can often be thought of as *manufacturers' guarantees*. The manufacturer (or programmer) puts his head on the block by guaranteeing that some open will never be observed. If it is, then we take the system back for repairs. For an open a, we write a^c for this refutative assertion – as opposed to the Heyting negation $\neg a$ of Section 3.10.

If the system is a topological space, we can identify a^c with a *closed* set, $\{x: x \nvDash a\}$ (the set of points consistent with the guarantee), which is just the complement of a. Then $a^c \subseteq b^c \Leftrightarrow a \ge b$, so in general we think of the refutative assertions as being the elements of $(\Omega D)^{op}$.

A guarantee a^c is compatible with an observation b so long as $b \nleq a$ – spatially, some point in b is not in a. We can therefore define a corresponding "compatibility function" $\hat{a}$ from ΩD to **2**,

$$\hat{a}(b) = \begin{cases} \textbf{true} & \text{if } b \not\leq a \\ \textbf{false} & \text{if } b \leq a \end{cases}$$

Such a function preserves all joins, but not meets in general (for instance, $\widehat{\textbf{true}}$ doesn't preserve the empty meet). Conversely, if $\theta: \Omega D \to \textbf{2}$ is a function preserving all joins, then

$$\theta = \hat{a} \text{ where } a = \bigvee \{b: \theta(b) = \textbf{false}\},$$

so we can identify the refutative assertions with such functions.

$$a^c \leq b^c \Leftrightarrow \text{for all } c, \hat{a}(c) \leq \hat{b}(c)$$

Note also that in a dcpo D, a subset X is closed in the Scott topology iff it is lower closed, and whenever S is a directed subset of X then $\bigvee^{\uparrow} S \in X$.

Definition 11.3.1 Let D be a locale. $P_H D$, its *Hoare*, or *lower power locale*, is defined by

$$\Omega P_H D = Fr \langle \diamond a : a \in \Omega D \mid$$
$$\diamond \bigvee S = \bigvee \{\diamond a: a \in S\} \ (S \subseteq \Omega D) \rangle$$

Our discussion above showed that pt $P_H D$ is isomorphic to $(\Omega D)^{op}$.

Again, this "Hoare power domain" is not the standard one. It is usual to impose an extra relation $\diamond \textbf{true} = \textbf{true}$, which excludes the empty closed set from the points. (See Exercise 3.)

Theorem 11.3.2 Let D be a spectral algebraic locale. Then $P_H D$ is a Scott domain, presented by

$$\Omega P_H D = Fr \langle \diamond a : a \in K\Omega D \mid$$
$$\diamond(\bigvee S) = \bigvee \{\diamond a: a \in S\} \qquad (S \subseteq K\Omega D, S \text{ finite}) \ \rangle$$

Its compact coprime opens are the finite meets of generators $\diamond p$, p coprime in $K\Omega D$.

Proof First, it is easy to show that for any spectral D, the presentation given here in the statement gives a frame isomorphic to that of Definition 11.3.1.

Next, suppose P is a finite set of coprimes in $K\Omega D$. For any point x, $\downarrow x$ is closed, so for the points $\uparrow p$ ($p \in P$) we see that $\downarrow \{\uparrow p: p \in P\}$ is closed. Now for any closed set a^c,

$$a^c \vDash \bigwedge \{\diamond p: p \in P\}$$
$$\Leftrightarrow \text{for all } p \in P, p \not\leq a, \text{ i.e. } \uparrow p \in a^c$$
$$\Leftrightarrow \text{for all } p \in P, \downarrow \uparrow p \subseteq a^c$$
$$\Leftrightarrow \downarrow \{\uparrow p: p \in P\} \subseteq a^c$$

Hence $\bigwedge \{\diamond p: p \in P\}$ is coprime, with corresponding point $\downarrow \{\uparrow p: p \in P\}$.

If $\bigvee Q$ is a coprime decomposition of a, then $\Diamond a = \bigvee \{\Diamond q: q \in Q\}$, and we now appeal to Lemma 10.5.6.]

Proposition 11.3.3 Let D be a spectral algebraic locale. Then pt P_H D is a frame.

Proof As we know, pt P_H D is isomorphic to ΩD^{op}, whose elements can, by spatiality, be identified with the closed sets. This is a complete lattice, but we still need to show the frame distributivity law. For closed sets, meet is intersection, but the join of a family of closed sets is the closure of its union.

Let F be closed, and let S be a family of closed sets. We wish to show that

$$F \cap Cl(\bigcup S) \subseteq Cl(\bigcup \{F \cap G: G \in S\}) = H \text{ (say)}$$

Suppose $x \in F \cap Cl(\bigcup S)$, $x = \bigsqcup^{\uparrow} Y$ where Y is a directed set of compact points. Now if $y \in Y$ then $\uparrow y$ is Scott open, so pt $D \backslash \uparrow y$ is Scott closed and does not contain $Cl(\bigcup S)$, so for some $G \in S$, it does not contain G. Therefore $y \in G$, so $y \in F \cap G \subseteq H$, which is closed under directed joins, so $x \in H$.

Note that by 11.3.2 pt P_H D is an algebraic dcpo, but it's not necessarily a coherent frame – its compact elements need not form a sublattice. (The problem is closure under intersection; see Exercise 4.)]

Proposition 11.3.4 Let D be a spectral algebraic locale. Then pt P_H D is isomorphic to $Idl(\wp_{fin}(Kpt\ D)/\equiv_L)$ (c.f. Proposition 11.2.4).

Proof The compact points of P_H D are the downward closures of finite sets of compact points; using Proposition 11.1.1 (ii), these are the equivalence classes in $\wp_{fin}(Kpt\ D)/\equiv_L$.]

11.4 The Plotkin power domain

For the Hoare and Smyth power domains, we topologized certain families of sets of points using subbasic open sets $\Box a$ and $\Diamond a$, with

$$X \vDash \Box a \quad \text{iff} \quad X \subseteq a$$
$$X \vDash \Diamond a \quad \text{iff} \quad X \cap a \neq \emptyset$$

For the Plotkin power domain, we take both kinds of subbasic simultaneously. As with the previous power domains, our definition is non-standard in including the empty set among the points.

Definition 11.4.1 Let D be a spectral algebraic locale. The *Plotkin power locale* P_P D is defined by

$\Omega P_P\, D = Fr \langle\; \Box a, \Diamond a : a \in K\Omega D \;|$

(1) $\Box (\bigwedge S) = \bigwedge \{\Box a: a \in S\}$ $(S \subseteq K\Omega D,\ S\ \text{finite})$

(2) $\Diamond (\bigvee S) = \bigvee \{\Diamond a: a \in S\}$ $(S \subseteq K\Omega D,\ S\ \text{finite})$

(3) $\Box (a\vee b) \le \Box a \vee \Diamond b$

(4) $\Box a \wedge \Diamond b \le \Diamond (a\wedge b)$ $\rangle$

This is also known as the *Vietoris locale* of D (see Exercise 1).

Definition 11.4.2 Let D be a spectral algebraic locale. A subset X of pt D is a *Plotkin* set iff it is compact, and $X = {\uparrow}X \cap Cl(X)$.

Smyth [83] calls these *compact convex* sets, but there is a risk of confusion with another established use of the term "convex" to describe sets X such that $X = {\uparrow}X \cap {\downarrow}X$.

Theorem 11.4.3 Let D be a spectral algebraic locale. Then the points of P_P D can be identified with the Plotkin sets, with

$X \vDash \Box a$ iff $X \subseteq a$,
$X \vDash \Diamond a$ iff $X \cap a \ne \emptyset$.
$X \sqsubseteq Y$ iff ${\uparrow}X \supseteq {\uparrow}Y$ and $Cl(X) \subseteq Cl(Y)$.

Proof P_P D is a sublocale of $P_S\, D \times P_H\, D$, so a point gives a pair (C, f^c) where C is a compact, saturated subset of pt D and f^c is a closed subset:

$(C, f^c) \vDash \Box a$ iff $C \vDash \Box a$ (i.e. $C \subseteq a$)
$(C, f^c) \vDash \Diamond a$ iff $f^c \vDash \Diamond a$ (i.e. $a \not\le f$, i.e. $f^c \cap a \ne \emptyset$, i.e. f^c meets a)

By Lemma 8.3.2, $X = C \cap f^c$ is compact. Also,

$${\uparrow}X \cap Cl(X) \subseteq {\uparrow}C \cap Cl(f^c) = C \cap f^c = X,$$

so X is a Plotkin set. We show that

$(C, f^c) \vDash \Box a$ iff $X \subseteq a$, and $(C, f^c) \vDash \Diamond a$ iff X meets a.

If $X \subseteq a$, then $C \subseteq a\cup f$, so by compactness $C \subseteq a\cup f'$ for some compact $f' \le f$. Therefore

$(C, f^c) \vDash \Box (a\vee f') \le \Box a \vee \Diamond f'.$

But (C, f^c) doesn't satisfy $\Diamond f'$, so it must satisfy $\Box a$.

Now suppose $(C, f^c) \vDash \Diamond a$, and let

$F' = \{d \in K\Omega D: \text{for some } c \in K\Omega D, C \subseteq c \text{ and } d \ge c\wedge a\}$

F' is a filter in $K\Omega D$, and hence (by Theorem 9.1.5) defines a Scott open filter F of ΩD. If $d \in F'$, then for some c

$$(C, f^c) \vdash \Box c \wedge \Diamond a \le \Diamond(c \wedge a) \le \Diamond d$$

We deduce that $f \notin F$. By the Hofmann–Mislove Theorem, there is a point x satisfying every open set in F – these include a and all the open sets containing C – but not f. Thus $x \in C \cap f^c \cap a$ and X meets a.

We now have that for all $a \in K\Omega D$,

$$C \vdash \Box a \Leftrightarrow X \subseteq a \Leftrightarrow \uparrow X \vdash \Box a, \text{ and}$$
$$f^c \vdash \Diamond a \Leftrightarrow X \text{ meets } a \Leftrightarrow Cl(X) \vdash \Diamond a,$$

so $C = \uparrow X$ and $f^c = Cl(X)$.

Now *any* $X \subseteq pt\ D$ defines a point of $P_P\ D$, by the satisfaction relation defined at the start of this section. If X is compact, then this point is given by $(\uparrow X, Cl(X))$, and if X is a Plotkin set, then we recover X from this point.

The specialization order is clear.]

Theorem 11.4.4 Let D be a spectral algebraic locale. Then so is $P_P\ D$. Its compact coprime opens are those of the form

$$\Box(\bigvee P) \wedge \bigwedge\{\Diamond p : p \in P\}$$

where P is a finite set of coprimes from $K\Omega D$.

Proof Let $e = \Box(\bigvee P) \wedge \bigwedge\{\Diamond p : p \in P\}$ be a quasicoprime, and let $X = \{\uparrow p : p \in P\}$ be the corresponding set of compact points. Then $Y = \uparrow X \cap Cl(X)$ is a Plotkin set with $\uparrow Y = \uparrow X$ and $Cl(Y) = Cl(X) = \downarrow X$. Now for any Plotkin set Z,

$$Z \sqsupseteq Y \Leftrightarrow \uparrow Z \subseteq \uparrow Y = \uparrow X \text{ and } Cl(Z) \supseteq Cl(Y) = Cl(X) = \downarrow X$$

The first part of this says that $Z \subseteq \uparrow X$, i.e. $Z \vdash \Box(\bigvee P)$. The second says that each point $\uparrow p$ is in $Cl(Z)$, i.e. $Cl(Z)$ meets each p, i.e. $Z \vdash \bigwedge\{\Diamond p : p \in P\}$.

Therefore $Z \sqsupseteq Y \Leftrightarrow Z \vdash e$, and it follows that e is indeed coprime.

We now wish to show that every meet of generators is a join of coprimes. First, by using relation schemas (1) and (2), irredundant coprime decompositions and distributivity, we can reduce any meet of generators to a join of compact opens of the form $e = \Box(\bigvee P) \wedge \bigwedge\{\Diamond q : q \in Q\}$, where P and Q are finite sets of coprimes. Our aim is to reduce e to a join of similar forms in which P and Q are equal.

Next, we show that without loss of generality we can assume that $P \sqsupseteq_U Q$ (as subsets of $K\Omega D$). Our proof is by induction on the number n of elements of P that are not greater than any element of Q. For $n = 0$ we are already done. For $n \ge 1$, take p in P not minorized in Q, and let $P' = P\backslash\{p\}$, $Q' = Q \cup \{p\}$. Then

$$\Box(\bigvee P) = \Box(\bigvee P' \vee p) \le \Box(\bigvee P') \vee \Diamond p,$$

so

$$\square(\vee P) \wedge \wedge\{\diamond q: q \in Q\}$$
$$= (\square(\vee P') \wedge \wedge\{\diamond q: q \in Q\}) \vee (\square(\vee P) \wedge \wedge\{\diamond q: q \in Q'\})$$

and we can use the induction hypothesis on both disjuncts.

Next, we show that without loss of generality we can assume that $P \sqsupseteq_{EM} Q$, the proof being by induction on the number n of elements of Q that are not majorized in P. For n = 0 we are already done. For $n \geq 1$, take $q \in Q$ not majorized in P, and let Q' be $Q\backslash\{q\}$ (note that we still have $P \sqsupseteq_U Q'$). Then

$$\square(\vee P) \wedge \diamond q \leq \diamond(\vee \{p \wedge q: p \in P\}) = \vee \{\diamond(p \wedge q): p \in P\},$$

so

$$e = \square(\vee P) \wedge \wedge\{\diamond q: q \in Q\}$$
$$= \vee \{\square(\vee P) \wedge \diamond(p \wedge q) \wedge \wedge\{\diamond q: q \in Q'\}: p \in P\}$$

Now for each p, let $\vee R_p$ be a coprime decomposition of $p \wedge q$. Then

$$e = \vee \{\square(\vee P) \wedge \wedge\{\diamond q: q \in Q' \cup \{r\}\}: p \in P, r \in R_p\}$$

We have $P \sqsupseteq_U Q' \cup \{r\}$, and $Q' \cup \{r\}$ has only $n-1$ elements not majorized in P, so we can use the induction hypothesis on all the disjuncts.

Finally, we can replace both sets P and Q by their union to get disjuncts in the required form. This completes the proof of the hypotheses of Lemma 9.3.9.　　　]

Theorem 11.4.5 Let D be a spectral algebraic locale. Then

$$\text{pt } P_P D \cong \text{Idl}(\wp_{\text{fin}}(\text{Kpt } D)/\equiv_{EM}).$$

Proof The compact points of $P_P D$ are the Plotkin closures of finite sets of compact points. Given X and Y in $\wp_{\text{fin}}(\text{Kpt } D)$, with Plotkin closures X' and Y', we have

$$X' \subseteq Y' \text{ iff } \uparrow X \supseteq \uparrow Y \text{ and } \downarrow X \subseteq \downarrow Y, \text{ i.e. iff } X \subseteq_{EM} Y.　　　]$$

The empty set represents a rather special point in $P_P D$, because $\{\emptyset\}$ is open; in fact it is $\square$**false**.

Proposition 11.4.6 Let $P_P^+ D$ be the locale whose frame has the same presentation as for $P_P D$ with an extra relation $\diamond$**true** = **true** (or, alternatively, $\square$**false** = **false**). Then

$$P_P D \cong \{\emptyset\} + P_P^+ D$$

where $\{\emptyset\}$ is the one point space.

Proof
$\square$**false** and $\diamond$**true** are complements: for

□ **false** ∧ ◇ **true** ≤ ◇ (**false** ∧ **true**) = ◇ **false** = **false**, and
true = □ **true** = □ (**false** ∨ **true**) ≤ □ **false** ∨ ◇ **true**.

It follows from Proposition 6.3.4 that $P_P D \cong E + P_P^+ D$, where the frame for E has the presentation for $\Omega P_P D$ subject to an extra relation □ **false** = **true**. But in ΩE we have

◇ a = □ **false** ∧ ◇ a ≤ ◇ (**false** ∧ a) = ◇ **false** = **false**, and
true = □ **false** ≤ □ a.

Therefore ΩE is **2** and E is a one-point space. We write it as {Ø} because the frame homomorphism from $\Omega P_P D$ to ΩE corresponding to the injection is the point Ø.]

It follows that $P_P D$ almost certainly has no bottom, and for domain theory it is common to refer to $P_P^+ D$ as the Plotkin power domain. Its points are the non-empty Plotkin sets, and if D has a bottom ⊥ then {⊥} is bottom in $P_P^+ D$.

We next examine the meets and joins in pt $P_P D$. We saw how set-theoretic union gave well-defined binary operations in the Smyth and Hoare power domains, respectively a meet and a join. For the Plotkin power domain we still have the binary operation, but it is neither a meet nor a join *for the specialization order*. In fact it allows us to define a completely different order on the power domain.

Definition 11.4.7 Let D be a spectral algebraic domain. We already have an order ⊑ on its Plotkin sets, namely the specialization order in pt $P_P D$. Define X ≤ Y iff X ⊆ Y as sets, and define

X∨Y = the Plotkin closure of X∪Y, i.e. ↑(X∪Y) ∩ Cl(X∪Y)

Then ∨ is the binary join for pt $P_P D$ under ≤; Ø is the nullary join.

Proposition 11.4.8 As a function from pt $P_P D$ × pt $P_P D$ to pt $P_P D$, ∨ is the point part of a continuous map.
Proof Define the inverse image function $\Omega\vee$ by

$$\Omega\vee (□a) = □a \otimes □a, \quad \Omega\vee (◇a) = ◇a \otimes \mathbf{true} \vee \mathbf{true} \otimes ◇a$$

It is a routine matter to show that this respects the relations; then

⟨X, Y⟩ ⊨ $\Omega\vee$ (□a) ⟺ X ⊨ □a and Y ⊨ □a
 ⟺ X ⊆ a and Y ⊆ a
 ⟺ X∪Y ⊆ a
 ⟺ X∨Y ⊨ □a

⟨X, Y⟩ ⊨ $\Omega\vee$ (◇a) ⟺ X ⊨ ◇a or Y ⊨ ◇a

⇔ X meets a or Y meets a

⇔ X∪Y meets a

⇔ X∨Y ⊢ ◇a   ]

Example 11.4.9 Let D be a finite discrete space, X = pt D. Then P_P D is also discrete,

pt P_P D = $\wp$X

Ω P_P D = $\wp$ $\wp$X

⊑ is the discrete order, ≤ is ⊆, and ∨ is ∪.

Example 11.4.10 Let D be the three point domain {t, f, ⊥}. We give a poset diagram for both orders on pt P_P D: the solid lines represent the specialization order ⊑, with lesser elements near the bottom of the page as usual, while the dotted lines represent the inclusion order ≤, with lesser elements to the left.

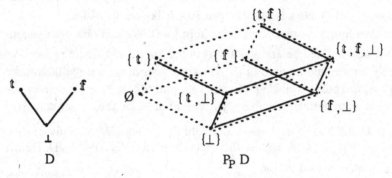

As it happens, in this case all subsets of pt D are Plotkin sets.

11.5 Sets implemented as lists

Lists are so readily implemented on computers that it is often convenient to use them even though the structure natural to the application may be different. The natural structure may, for instance, ignore order and multiplicities among the elements of the list, so that it really uses sets as an abstract data type, implemented concretely as lists. Jones [80] discusses some aspects of this.

To compute on a set, we must analyse it in terms of its elements. It is natural to do this with a function EltOf: Sets → Elements×Sets; EltOf(S) = (x, S') where x is an element of S and S' is S with x removed. S may be empty, in which case EltOf returns an exceptional value **empty**. The set as a set has no structure to determine which element x should be returned, so EltOf must be non-deterministic. On the other hand, if S is implemented as a list, then it is natural to choose its head. The non-determinism thus arises from the historical accident of how S was put together as a list. It is also natural to use the tail for S'; notice that this means that we do not guarantee that x ∉ S': we have only removed one occurrence of x in S.

What properties can we observe of a set S? They must be independent of order and multiplicities. We shan't attempt a complete description, but at least if a is a property of elements, then we have recursive algorithms that amount to observing □a and ◇a for sets:

S ⊨ □a iff either S is **empty**, or for some (x, S') = EltOf(S), x ⊨ a and S' ⊨ □a
S ⊨ ◇a iff for some (x, S') = EltOf(S), either x ⊨ a or S' ⊨ ◇a

We now formalize this. Let A be any spectral algebraic locale, the type of the elements, and let D = List(A) be the bilimit solution to the domain equation

$$D = (\{\mathbf{nil}\} + A \times D)_\bot$$

A list here (a point of List(A)) is either ⊥, **nil**, or a pair (x, l), the "cons" x::l. Notice the difference between ⊥ and **nil**. **nil** is empty and is prepared to say so, whereas ⊥ is created divergently, so no properties are ever going to be established for it. It has no elements, but we shall never discover this. Overall, the points of List(A) are terminated finite lists (when the elements are removed, **nil** is left), unterminated finite lists (when the elements are removed, ⊥ is left) and infinite lists. Although the unterminated finite lists are a nuisance, they are a physical reality, corresponding on the points side to divergent lists, and on the frame side to partial states of information.

Opens of List(A) are built up using ↑**nil** (the list is empty) and a⊗γ (the head satisfies a and the tail satisfies γ, where a ∈ ΩA and γ ∈ ΩList(A)).

Now let a be an open for A. We define functions F_a, G_a: ΩList(A) → ΩList(A) by

$$F_a(\gamma) = {\uparrow}\mathbf{nil} \vee a{\otimes}\gamma \qquad G_a(\gamma) = a{\otimes}\mathbf{true} \vee \mathbf{true}{\otimes}\gamma$$

These are both Scott continuous maps on the frames – in other words, they preserve directed joins –, so they have least fixpoints in ΩList(A)

$$\Box a = \text{Fix } F_a = \bigvee{}^{\uparrow} \{F_a{}^n(\mathbf{false}): n \in \omega\}$$
$$\Diamond a = \text{Fix } G_a = \bigvee{}^{\uparrow} \{G_a{}^n(\mathbf{false}): n \in \omega\}$$

Note by Proposition 10.2.2 that for all γ, if $F_a(\gamma) \le \gamma$ then $\Box a \le \gamma$, and if $G_a(\gamma) \le \gamma$ then $\Diamond a \le \gamma$.

□a is the strongest property of lists such that **nil** ⊨ □a, and if x ⊨ a and l ⊨ □a then x::l ⊨ □a. A list satisfies □a iff all its elements satisfy a, provided that it is a terminated finite list. For other kinds of list we never know that we have seen all the elements, so we never get to assert $\square a$. Note that $\square \mathbf{true}$ means the list is terminated finite, and $\square \mathbf{false}$ means it is **nil**.

$\lozenge a$ is the strongest property of lists such that if $x \vDash a$ or $l \vDash \lozenge a$ then $x{::}l \vDash \lozenge a$. A list satisfies $\lozenge a$ iff one of its elements satisfies a. Note that $\lozenge \mathbf{true}$ means the list is inhabited (it has an element, i.e. it is neither $\bot$ nor **nil**).

Proposition 11.5.1 For $a \in K\Omega A$, the opens $\square a$ and $\lozenge a$ of List(A) satisfy all the relations of the Plotkin power domain (Definition 11.4.1) *except* $\square \mathbf{true} = \mathbf{true}$.

Proof First, if $a \le b$ then for all γ, $F_a(\gamma) \le F_b(\gamma)$ and $G_a(\gamma) \le G_b(\gamma)$, and it follows that $\square a \le \square b$ and $\lozenge a \le \lozenge b$. Also, $G_{\mathbf{false}}(\mathbf{false}) = \mathbf{false}$, so that $\lozenge \mathbf{false} = \mathbf{false}$. For the remainder, we note the following:

$$F_a(\gamma) \wedge F_b(\delta) = F_{a \wedge b}(\gamma \wedge \delta)$$
$$G_a(\gamma) \vee G_b(\delta) = G_{a \vee b}(\gamma \curlyvee \delta)$$
$$F_a(\gamma) \wedge G_b(\delta) = (a \wedge b) \otimes \gamma \vee a \otimes (\gamma \wedge \delta) \le G_{a \wedge b}(\gamma \wedge \delta)$$
$$F_a(\gamma) \vee G_b(\delta) = \uparrow\!\mathbf{nil} \vee a \otimes \gamma \vee b \otimes \mathbf{true} \vee \mathbf{true} \otimes \delta$$
$$\ge \uparrow\!\mathbf{nil} \vee a \otimes \gamma \vee b \otimes \gamma \vee (a \vee b) \otimes \delta = F_{a \vee b}(\gamma \curlyvee \delta)$$

Now for the non-trivial directions in the four relations in 11.4.1,

$$F_a(\square b \to \square(a \wedge b)) \wedge \square b = F_a(\square b \to \square(a \wedge b)) \wedge F_b(\square b)$$
$$= F_{a \wedge b}((\square b \to \square(a \wedge b)) \wedge \square b) \le F_{a \wedge b}(\square(a \wedge b)) = \square(a \wedge b)$$
$$\therefore\ F_a(\square b \to \square(a \wedge b)) \le \square b \to \square(a \wedge b)$$
$$\therefore\ \square a \le \square b \to \square(a \wedge b)$$
$$\therefore\ \square a \wedge \square b \le \square(a \wedge b) \qquad \text{– (1) for binary meets}$$

$$G_{a \vee b}(\lozenge a \vee \lozenge b) = G_a(\lozenge a) \vee G_b(\lozenge b) = \lozenge a \vee \lozenge b$$
$$\therefore\ \lozenge(a \vee b) \le \lozenge a \vee \lozenge b \qquad \text{– (2) for binary joins}$$

$$F_{a \vee b}(\square a \vee \lozenge b) \le F_a(\square a) \vee G_b(\lozenge b) = \square a \vee \lozenge b$$
$$\therefore\ \square(a \vee b) \le \square a \vee \lozenge b \qquad (3)$$

$$F_a(\lozenge b \to \lozenge(a \wedge b)) \wedge \lozenge b = F_a(\lozenge b \to \lozenge(a \wedge b)) \wedge G_b(\lozenge b)$$
$$\le G_{a \wedge b}((\lozenge b \to \lozenge(a \wedge b)) \wedge \lozenge b) \le G_{a \wedge b}(\lozenge(a \wedge b)) = \lozenge(a \wedge b)$$
$$\therefore\ F_a(\lozenge b \to \lozenge(a \wedge b)) \le \lozenge b \to \lozenge(a \wedge b)$$
$$\therefore\ \square a \le \lozenge b \to \lozenge(a \wedge b)$$
$$\therefore\ \square a \wedge \lozenge b \le \lozenge(a \wedge b) \qquad (4)$$

We have already argued that $\bot$ does not satisfy $\square \mathbf{true}$, so in List(A) $\square \mathbf{true}$ is not equal to **true**.]

Given the spectral algebraic locale A, let us now define the locale $P_{PH} A$ by the relations of 11.5.1, that is to say all the relations of the Plotkin (Vietoris) power locale except $\square \mathbf{true} = \mathbf{true}$. It is easy to see that the points satisfying $\square \mathbf{true}$ are points of Pp A, hence Plotkin sets in pt A, while those not satisfying $\Box$ **true** do not satisfy $\Box$ a for any a, and can be considered points of P$_H$ A, closed sets in pt A. The closed sets are also Plotkin sets, and hence appear twice; but they are subject in Pp A to the Egli-Milner ordering, while in P$_H$ A to the lower ordering. Each Plotkin copy refines the corresponding closed copy.

It is now easy to use the method of quasicoprimes to show that PpH A is spectral algebraic, with coprimes of the forms described for Pp A and P$_H$ A. Alternatively, one can prove that PpH A is homeomorphic to $1_\bot \oplus P_p^+(A_\bot)$, where $\oplus$ is the coalesced sum (Exercise).

Notes

The first power domain to appear in computer science was Plotkin's, introduced by him in [76] to provide a semantics for non-determinism. (He gives a much more thorough account in [81].) Smyth later [78] described the Smyth power domain, and in [83] gave a topological description of all three power domains, describing the representatives as we have done here, and related them to an older construction of spaces of subsets due to Vietoris. The localic theory is due to Johnstone ([82] and [82']). He gives the construction of Exercise 1 below, calling it the Vietoris locale. Independently, Winskel [83] introduced $\Box$ and $\Diamond$ in a modal logic for power domains, and Robinson [86] completed the connections between these different ideas.

The main results of Section 11.4, Theorems 3 and 4, are adapted from Abramsky [87] and extended to cover spectral algebraic locales without bottom. Robinson [86] also proves the result analogous to 11.4.3 for algebraic cpos (again, with bottom).

Although without doubt Plotkin and Smyth gave to computer science the power domains named after them, the Hoare power domain appears to have arisen as folklore. Hoare's name was attached to it as a suggestion that it might be an appropriate formalism for his work on partial correctness. One reason for continuing the nomenclature is that otherwise one must refer to the upper or lower power domains, and it is difficult to remember which is which (upper = Smyth, because the canonical representatives are *upper*-closed). Carl Gunter suggests a notation using the musical symbols for flat, sharp and natural to distinguish the lower/Hoare, upper/Smyth and Egli-Milner/Plotkin notions.

Our PpH construction in Section 11.5 is intended as an illustration of localic reasoning rather than a serious proposal for a new power domain. However, it is worth pointing out that where in [87, 90] Abramsky studies synchronization trees and bisimulation, his domain equation is a generalization of $D = P_{PH} D$.

Exercises

1. For an arbitrary locale D, define a locale V(D) by

$$\Omega V(D) = Fr \langle\ \Box a,\ \Diamond a : a \in \Omega D\ |$$
$$\Diamond\bigvee S = \bigvee \{\Diamond a: a \in S\}\ \ (S \subseteq \Omega D),$$
$$\Box\bigwedge S = \bigwedge \{\Box a: a \in S\}\ \ (S \subseteq A,\ S\ \text{finite}),$$
$$\Box\bigvee^{\uparrow} S = \bigvee^{\uparrow} \{\Box a: a \in S\}\ \ (S \subseteq A,\ S\ \text{directed}),$$
$$\Box(a\vee b) \le \Box a \vee \Diamond b$$
$$\Box a \wedge \Diamond b \le \Diamond(a\wedge b)\ \ \rangle$$

Show that if D is spectral, then V(D) is homeomorphic to our P_P D.

In this general case, the points of V(D) are best expressed as *sublocales* of D. For details, see Johnstone [82'].

2. Define a domain D as an Alexandrov topology by taking as points those subsets of $\{0, 1, 2, 3\}$ with cardinality at most 2, excluding $\{0, 2\}$ and $\{1, 3\}$. They are to be ordered by the subset ordering. Show that D is a Scott domain, but that P_P^+ D is not.

3. Show that to exclude the empty set from the Hoare and Smyth power domains, you add relations $\Diamond$**true** = **true** ("every set has an element") and $\Box$**false** = **false** ("no set can be empty") respectively.

4. Define a domain D as an Alexandrov topology by taking points

$$pt\ D = \{\bot\}\cup\omega\cup\{T_1, T_2\}$$

ordered by

$$\bot \sqsubseteq x \qquad\qquad \text{for all x}$$
$$n \sqsubseteq T_1, n \sqsubseteq T_2 \qquad \text{for all } n \in \omega$$

Show that D is spectral algebraic, but that $(\Omega D)^{op}$ is not a coherent frame.

CHAPTER TWELVE

SPECTRA OF RINGS

In which we see some old examples of spectral locales.

This chapter is included mainly for the benefit of interested mathematicians, and so can be considered to be all in small print. All the same, the notion of *quantale* discussed here has already appeared in connection with computer science, and it may become more widely used.

It has been known since the '40s that it is possible to construct topological spaces, *spectra,* out of rings, and these have been used to give representations of the rings in sheaves. The idea is to associate another, usually simpler, ring with each point of the space so that in some sense this assignment of rings to points is "continuous". This is a *sheaf of rings* over the space and gives ways of building up complicated rings from simpler ones.

We do not have space to go into the sheaf theory; Johnstone [82] has a concise discussion of sheaves, and presents in greater detail most of the material here. However, since the spaces arising are generally spectral locales, it is interesting to see how the localic viewpoint can help us. In particular, we shall see that the *Zariski spectrum* of a commutative ring is obtained by formally forcing the product of ideals to coincide with the intersection.

To remove all doubts about our subject matter, we state

Definition 12.0.1 A *ring* is a set R equipped with operations $+$, $-$, 0, $\times$ and 1 such that

- R is an Abelian group under $+$, $-$ and 0,
- $\times$ is associative with unit 1, and
- $\times$ distributes over $+$ on both sides.

We usually write $a \times b$ as ab. We do not assume that $\times$ is always commutative. However, spectra of non-commutative rings are much more complicated and at present not very well understood. We shall discuss the example of Cohn's *field spectrum* for non-commutative rings, a generalization of the Zariski spectrum.

12.1 The Pierce spectrum

The first example uses the idea that multiplication in a ring R is something like a conjunction, but too unconstrained to actually be one. In particular, multiplication does not in general satisfy the idempotence law $r^2 = r$. We therefore look at the set

E(R) of *central idempotents* in R, i.e. those elements e satisfying $e^2 = e$ and $er = re$ for all r. E(R) is closed under products, and so it is a semilattice under multiplication.

Note the special case when R is commutative: all idempotents are central.

Proposition 12.1.1 E(R) is a Boolean algebra whose meet is given by multiplication in R.

Proof We have already an order $\leq$, defined by $e \leq f$ iff $ef = e$. The bottom element **false** is 0, and binary join is defined by

$$e \vee f = e + f - ef$$

For $e(e \vee f) = e^2 + ef - e^2 f = e$, so $e \leq e \vee f$ and by symmetry $f \leq e \vee f$; and if $e \leq g$ and $f \leq g$ then

$$(e \vee f)g = eg + fg - efg = e + f - ef = e \vee f,$$

so $e \vee f \leq g$. To prove that E(R) is a distributive lattice,

$$e(f \vee g) = ef + eg - efg = ef + eg - efeg = ef \vee eg.$$

Finally, each e has a complement $e^c = 1 - e$. For this is again a central idempotent, $e \cdot e^c = 0$, and $e \vee e^c = 1$.   ]

Since E(R) is a Boolean algebra, its spectrum is a Stone locale. This is the *Pierce spectrum* of R. Central idempotents correspond to decompositions of R as a direct product, and the Pierce spectrum is related to a representation of R in terms of indecomposable rings.

12.2 Quantales and the Zariski spectrum

We assume in this section that R is a *commutative* ring, and develop its *Zariski spectrum,* which turns out to be a spectral locale. In fact Hochster [69] has shown that all spectral locales can be obtained this way, hence the name.

Let A be the set of ideals of R: $a \subseteq R$ is an ideal iff it is a subgroup with respect to addition, and if $r \in R$ and $x \in a$ then $rx \in a$ ("Ra $\subseteq$ a"). As is well-known, if A is considered as a poset under inclusion, then any set S of ideals has a join

$$\Sigma S = \{\text{finite sums of elements from } \cup S\}$$

Hence A is a complete lattice; in fact a meet of ideals is just the intersection. However, A is not necessarily distributive, so in general it is not a frame. On the other hand, the *product* of ideals, defined by ab = {finite sums of products xy where x ∈ a, y ∈ b}

does distribute over joins. To get a distributive meet, and hence a frame, we make products coincide with intersections. We abstract these ideas, following some of the methods of Joyal and Tierney [84] and Mulvey [86].

Definition 12.2.1 A *quantale* is a complete lattice A, equipped with an associative binary product · (often elided) that distributes on both sides over all joins, and a nullary product 1 that is a unit for ·.

If A and B are quantales, then a function f: A → B is a *quantale homomorphism* iff it preserves all joins and finite products (· and 1).

Proposition 12.2.2
(i)   In a quantale A, if $a \leq b$ then $ca \leq cb$ and $ac \leq bc$ for all c.
(ii)   [Joyal and Tierney] A quantale A is a frame, with products as meets, iff 1 is its greatest element and multiplication is idempotent.

Proof (i) ca ∨ cb = c(a∨b) = cb, so $ca \leq cb$. The other inequality is similar.
(ii) The ⇒ direction is trivial. For the other way, $ab \leq a1 = a$ and $ab \leq 1b = b$. If c is a lower bound of a and b, then $c = c^2 \leq ab$.   ]

Because frames are just quantales satisfying extra axioms, universal algebra tells us that we can find for each quantale A a quantale congruence $\equiv_{Fr}$ such that $A/\equiv_{Fr}$ is a *universal frame* over A: in other words, $A/\equiv_{Fr}$ is a frame, and any other quantale homomorphism from A to a frame factors uniquely via $A/\equiv_{Fr}$ (it makes congruent elements equal). $\equiv_{Fr}$ is the intersection of all the congruences ≡ for which $A/\equiv$ is a frame.

(As usual, a congruence is an equivalence relation ≡ that respects the operations:

if $a_i \equiv b_i$ for all indices i, then $\bigvee_i a_i \equiv \bigvee_i b_i$, and

if $a \equiv a'$ and $b \equiv b'$ then $a \cdot b \equiv a' \cdot b'$.

Its equivalence classes [a] again form a quantale $A/\equiv$, a homomorphic image of the original one. Proposition 12.2.2 tells us that $A/\equiv$ is a frame iff for all a, $a \vee 1 \equiv 1$ and $a \cdot a \equiv a$.)

We use the phrase "modulo frames" to describe properties of equivalence classes for $\equiv_{Fr}$. For instance, if a, b ∈ A, then $a \leq b$ *modulo frames* iff $[a] \leq [b]$ in $A/\equiv_{Fr}$.

We now know how to construct locales out of quantales.

Definition 12.2.3 Let R be a commutative ring. Then the *Zariski spectrum* of R is the locale corresponding to the universal frame over the quantale of ideals of R.

To get more information about the Zariski spectrum, we must examine these universal frames more closely. In particular, we want to prove spectrality, and we use an analogue of the Hofmann-Mislove Theorem to deduce it from a corresponding property of quantales.

Definition 12.2.4 Let A be a quantale. An element $p \in A$ is *prime* iff

$$\textstyle\prod_{i=1}^{n} a_i \leq p \Leftrightarrow a_i \leq p \text{ for some } i$$

As usual, the crucial cases are when $n = 0$ (saying $1 \nleq p$) and $n = 2$.

Proposition 12.2.5 Let A be a quantale.

(i)   The following data are equivalent:

- a prime element p of A
- a quantale homomorphism from A to **2**
- a point of the locale of $A/\equiv_{Fr}$ (by abuse of language, we call this a *point* of A)

(ii) (The Hofmann-Mislove Theorem for quantales)
        Let F: $A \to$ **2** be a function that preserves products and directed joins, and let

$$C = \{x: x \text{ is a point of A, and } F \sqsubseteq x\}$$

where we write $F \sqsubseteq x$ iff for all $a \in A$, if $F(a) = $ **true** then $x(a) = $ **true**. Then $F(a) = $ **true** iff for all $x \in C$, $x(a) = $ **true**.

(iii)   The functions from A to **2** that preserve products and directed joins correspond to the Scott open filters of $A/\equiv_{Fr}$.

Proof (i) The argument is much the same as for frames. Since **2** is a frame, any quantale homomorphism from A to it factors via $A/\equiv_{Fr}$.

(ii) The $\Leftarrow$ direction is the problem, but the proof is just like that of Lemma 8.2.2.

Suppose $F(c) = $ **false**. What we want (by (i)) is a prime $p \geq c$ with $F(p) = $ **false**. As before, the set $\{a \geq c: F(a) = $ **false**$\}$ has a maximal element p. Let us write T (for *top*) for $\bigvee A$. Then $F(TpT) = $ **false**, so by maximality $TpT = p$, i.e. $apb \leq p$ for all a, b. The $\Leftarrow$ part of Definition 12.2.4 follows, and also $p \nleq 1$. Now suppose $ab \leq p$. Then

$$F(a \vee p) \wedge F(b \vee p) = F((a \vee p)(b \vee p)) = F(ab \vee ap \vee pb \vee p^2) \leq F(p) = \textbf{false}$$

One of $F(a \vee p)$ and $F(b \vee p)$ is **false**, so by maximality of p either $a \leq p$ or $b \leq p$. Hence p is a prime as required.

(iii) This follows from (ii).   ]

Definition 12.2.6 A quantale A is *coherent* iff

- every $a \in A$ is a join of compact elements

- compact elements are preserved under products (including the nullary product: 1 is compact)

Theorem 12.2.7 Let A be a coherent quantale in which 1 is the greatest element.

(i)   Suppose b, c $\in$ A with b compact. Then b $\leq$ c modulo frames iff $b^r \leq c$ for some r $\geq$ 0.

(ii)   a $\in$ A is compact modulo frames iff a $\equiv_{Fr}$ a' for some compact a'.

(iii)   A/$\equiv_{Fr}$ gives a spectral locale.

Proof (i) $\Leftarrow$: Modulo frames, b^r = 1 (**true**, if r = 0) or b, so b $\leq b^r$.

$\Rightarrow$: Define F: A $\rightarrow$ **2** by F(a) = **true** iff some $b^r \leq$ a. F clearly preserves products, and it preserves directed joins because all the powers b^r are compact. Define C as in Proposition 12.2.5 (ii). F(b) = **true**, so if x $\in$ C then x(b) = **true**; hence, because x is a quantale homomorphism to a frame, x(c) = **true**. We deduce from the Proposition that F(c) = **true**.

(ii) $\Rightarrow$: This actually holds for arbitrary congruences. a is a directed join of compact elements, and this still holds modulo the congruence. Therefore modulo the congruence a must be equal to one of the compact elements.

$\Leftarrow$: Take b $\in$ A compact. We show that it is compact modulo frames. If b $\leq \vee^\uparrow$ S modulo frames, then by (i) $b^r \leq \vee^\uparrow$ S for some r $\geq$ 0. b^r is still compact, so $b^r \leq$ c for some c $\in$ S and b $\leq$ c modulo frames.

(iii) This follows from (ii).   **]**

Theorem 12.2.8 Let R be a commutative ring. Then its Zariski spectrum has as points the prime ideals of R. Its closed sets are those of the form V(a) = {p : p $\supseteq$ a} for a an ideal of R. It is a spectral locale.

Proof Let A be the set of ideals of R. A is a commutative quantale, and its greatest element R is the unit for multiplication. Every ideal is the sum of its cyclic subideals (those generated by a single element), and from this we can deduce that the compact elements are precisely the finitely generated ideals. It is easy to calculate that a product of finitely generated ideals is finitely generated. Hence A is a coherent quantale and we can use Theorem 12.2.7.

The prime elements of A are the prime ideals of R. The open sets are the extents of the elements [a] of A/$\equiv_{Fr}$, and the corresponding closed set is {p : p $\not\vDash$ [a]} = V(a). **]**

12.3 Cohn's field spectrum

We now drop our assumption that rings are commutative, and describe Cohn's non-commutative generalization of the Zariski spectrum. This is described fully in Cohn

[71], and parts of its development are difficult pieces of ring theory that we do not wish to go into. What is of interest for us is that again the spectrum is given by a universal frame over a coherent quantale. This time it is not the quantale of ideals, but that of *matrix ideals* according to a definition of Cohn's.

Cohn shows that each *prime* matrix ideal of R corresponds to a homomorphism f from R to a field k (not necessarily commutative) generated by the image of f. The matrix ideal is then the set of square matrices over R that become singular (non-invertible) over k. Although there seems to be no similar interpretation for the general matrix ideals, it is helpful to realize that the operations used in defining them have direct consequences for singularity of matrices over fields.

Definition 12.3.1 Let R be a ring.

An n×n matrix X over R is *non-full* iff it can be written as a product YZ, where Y and Z are matrices over R of orders n×m and m×n and m < n.

A *row determinantal sum* $X \nabla Y$ of two square matrices of the same order can be calculated if they differ in at most one row, and then the determinantal sum takes the sum of these two differing rows and agrees on all the rest. For instance, if $X_{ij} = Y_{ij}$ for $i \neq k$ (they may differ on the kth row) then

$$(X \nabla Y)_{ij} = \begin{cases} X_{ij}+Y_{ij} & \text{if } i = k \\ X_{ij} = Y_{ij} & \text{if } i \neq k \end{cases}$$

Column determinantal sums are defined similarly.

The *diagonal sum* $X \oplus Y$ of two square matrices is the partitioned matrix $\begin{pmatrix} X & 0 \\ 0 & Y \end{pmatrix}$.

A *matrix ideal* over R is a set a of square matrices over R satisfying

- every non-full matrix over R is in a,
- a is closed under determinantal sums whenever they exist,
- if $X \in$ a and Y is any other square matrix, then $X \oplus Y \in$ a, and
- if a contains a matrix $X \oplus I$ (where I is an identity matrix), then a also contains X.

The intersection of any family of matrix ideals is still a matrix ideal, so for any set S of square matrices we can define MI⟨S⟩, the matrix ideal *generated* by S, as the intersection of all the matrix ideals containing S.

Lemma 12.3.2 If $X \in$ MI⟨S⟩, then $X \in$ MI⟨S'⟩ for some finite $S' \subseteq S$.
Proof In other words, MI⟨S⟩ = $\cup$ { MI⟨S'⟩: $S' \subseteq S$, S' finite } = a' (say). It suffices to show that a' is a matrix ideal, for we know that it contains S. The least straightforward part is the determinantal sums. If some $X \nabla Y$ is defined with $X \in$ MI⟨S'⟩ and $Y \in$ MI⟨S''⟩, then $X \nabla Y \in$ MI⟨S'∪S''⟩.]

Lemma 12.3.3 Let a be a matrix ideal over R and let U, V, W, X and Y be square matrices. Then

$$U \oplus V \oplus W \oplus X \oplus Y \in a \iff U \oplus X \oplus W \oplus V \oplus Y \in a$$

Proof This is easily deduced from lemmas in Cohn [71].]

Theorem 12.3.4 The set A of matrix ideals of a ring R is a coherent quantale.
Proof First, because the intersection of any family of matrix ideals is still a matrix ideal, A is a complete lattice. The join in A of a family of matrix ideals is its *sum*, the matrix ideal generated by the union.

The product a·b of two matrix ideals a and b is generated by all matrices $X \oplus Y$ with X in a and Y in b. The unit for this multiplication is generated by the unique 0×0 matrix. It contains all square matrices.

Let us also define for any matrix ideal a and set of matrices B,

$$a/B = \{X: X \oplus Y \in a \text{ for all } Y \in B\}$$

Using Lemma 12.3.3, we can see that this is a matrix ideal.

BEWARE! We use this notation because it is exactly the same trick as in Theorem 4.4.2. Cohn, however, writes a/B for $\{X: X \oplus Y \in a \text{ for } some \ Y \in B\}$.

Lemma 12.3.4.1 $MI\langle S \rangle \cdot MI\langle T \rangle$ is generated by the matrices $X \oplus Y$ with X in S and Y in T.
Proof Let c be the matrix ideal generated by these matrices $X \oplus Y$. Clearly $MI\langle S \rangle \cdot MI\langle T \rangle$ contains c. For the converse, $S \subseteq c/T$, so $MI\langle S \rangle \leq c/T$, $T \subseteq c/MI\langle S \rangle$, $MI\langle T \rangle \leq c/MI\langle S \rangle$ and $MI\langle S \rangle \cdot MI\langle T \rangle \leq c$.]

We use this lemma to show that both (a·b)·c and a·(b·c) are generated by the matrices $X \oplus Y \oplus Z$ (X ∈ a, Y ∈ b, Z ∈ c), and we deduce that multiplication is associative.

For distributivity, if $S \subseteq A$ and a ∈ A, then b ≤ {b·a: b ∈ S}/a for all b ∈ S, hence $S \leq \{b·a: b \in S\}/a$ and (S)·a ≤ {b·a: b ∈ S}.

Although the diagonal sum $X \oplus Y$ is not in itself commutative, Lemma 12.3.3 shows that the multiplication on matrix ideals *is* commutative, so the opposite distributivity law requires no further proof.

Finally, the compact elements of A are the finitely generated matrix ideals, Lemma 12.3.2 shows that every element is a join of them, and Lemma 12.3.4.1 shows that they are closed under multiplication.]

We can now apply Theorem 12.2.7 to deduce the existence for each ring R of a spectral locale whose points are the prime matrix ideals. This is Cohn's *field spectrum*.

Notes

A general reference for quantales is Rosenthal [90].

Quantales have been invented more than once, and these notes summarize some areas where the ideas have been used. (I am indebted to Harold Simmons and Samson Abramsky for pointing some of these out to me.) The reasoning in Chapter 2 leads to quantales if one allows for the idea that observations may affect the things being observed (if a and b are observations, then ab is the composite, a followed by b): then the order and multiplicity of conjoined observations may be significant. This is investigated in Abramsky and Vickers [90].

The idea that spectra can be constructed via quantales of ideals is not new (although as far as I know, the application to Cohn's field spectrum is). Indeed, the term *quantale* was introduced by Mulvey [86] in relation to work on spectra of C*-algebras. Niefield and Rosenthal [88] give a useful account of some of these ideas. In general, the work of Mulvey and his school uses a slightly different concept, with no 1 assumed and homomorphisms required to preserve the top element. They also tend to need additional properties, in particular in their work on defining the idea of "sheaf over a quantale". Note that Mulvey's "&" is our "·".

Quantales also arise in formal language theory. Given an alphabet X, one typically works with $\wp(X^*)$, the set of *languages* over X, each language being a set of words (sequences of letters, hence elements of the free monoid X^*). This is the free quantale over the set X. Various operations used here, such as left and right residuation \ and / (Lambek [58]; see Exercise 1), and the * operator of Kleene's regular algebra, can be defined in general quantales. In recognition of this, Conway [71] defines the notion of "standard Kleene algebra", which is essentially the same as a quantale.

Joyal and Tierney [84] study commutative quantales as "rings". They emphasize the fact that it is very fruitful to see quantales as rings in which the Abelian group structure has been replaced by that of complete [join semi-]lattices. In fact, large parts of the theory of rings, such as modules, tensor products and matrices, transfer to quantales.

A recent application in computer science is in Hoare and He Jifeng [87]. This uses the fact that if a complete lattice A is given, then there is a quantale Q whose elements are the functions from A to A that preserve all joins. In their case, A is a power set $\wp X$, and then Q is the set of relations from X to X. They call the right and left residuations respectively "weakest pre- and post-specifications". (Their notation is different from that of Exercise 1, where we follow Lambek. They write Q\R for R/Q and vice versa.)

Finally, just as frames provide algebraic models for intuitionistic logic, quantales do the same for the linear logic of Girard [e.g., 87] in its intuitionistic form, with the connectives &, $\oplus$, $\otimes$, $\multimap$ and !. The first four are represented in a quantale by $\wedge$, $\vee$, $\cdot$ and the residuation / (the linear connective $\otimes$ is commutative, so it is appropriate to use commutative quantales, in which the two residuations coincide). The "of course" connective "!" can be represented by $!a = \vee \{b: b^2 = b \leq 1\}$. In his *classical* linear logic, Girard introduces an involutary negation $(-)^\perp$. His *phase semantics* for this can be seen as using quantales that are universal over monoids, but can be made to work in arbitrary quantales.

Exercises

1. Let A be a quantale. For x and y in A, define the *left* and *right residuations*

$$x\backslash y = \vee \{z \in A: xz \leq y\}, \qquad y/x = \vee \{z \in A: zx \leq y\}$$

$z \leq x\backslash y$ iff $xz \leq y$ and $z \leq y/x$ iff $zx \leq y$, so these are analogous to division. Categorically, left multiplication by x preserves all joins, so it has a right adjoint $y \mapsto x\backslash y$; similarly for right multiplication. If A is a frame, then $x\backslash y = y/x = x{\rightarrow}y$. Hence residuation generalizes implication (in two ways).

2. Extend as many as possible of the results of Section 6.2 to describe surjective quantale homomorphisms from a quantale Q.

   In particular, *(quantic) nuclei* (Niefield and Rosenthal [88]) are characterized as the functions v from Q to Q satisfying

   - $a \leq va = v^2a$
   - if $a \leq b$ then $va \leq vb$
   - $va \cdot vb \leq v(a \cdot b)$

The quantic analogue of a sublocale is a subset S of Q that is closed under all meets, and for which if $x \in S$ and $a \in Q$, then the residuations $a\backslash x$ and x/a are both in S. Show how this can be used in Theorem 12.3.4 by taking the monoid M of all square matrices under $\oplus$, letting Q be $\wp M$ (the universal quantale over M) and letting S be the set of matrix ideals.

3. Let A be a coherent quantale in which 1 is the greatest element. Show that the universal frame congruence $\equiv_{Fr}$ has nucleus $\sqrt{}$ defined by

$$\sqrt{a} \quad = \vee \{b \in A: \exists r. \, r \geq 0 \text{ and } b^r \leq a \}$$
$$= \vee \{b \in KA: \exists r. \, r \geq 0 \text{ and } b^r \leq a \}$$

In ring theoretic terms, $\sqrt{a}$ is the radical of a. Show also that

$\sqrt{a} = \bigwedge \{ p \in A: p \text{ is prime and } a \leq p \}$

Define a to be *semiprime* iff

$b^r \leq a \Rightarrow b \leq a$

Show that a is semiprime iff $a = \sqrt{a}$ iff a is a meet of primes.

4. (Theorem 4.4.2 for quantales.) Let M be a monoid. Define a *coverage* on M to be a set C of *cover relations* $U \dashv x$ ($U \subseteq M$, $x \in M$) such that if $U \dashv x$ is in C, then so is $\{yuz: u \in U\} \dashv yxz$ for all y, z in M. Define a *C-ideal* of M to be a subset $I \subseteq M$ such that if $U \dashv x$ is in C and $U \subseteq I$, then $x \in I$. Show that the C-ideals form a quantale, C-Idl(M), ordered by inclusion, with I·J the C-ideal generated by $\{xy: x \in I, y \in J\}$. (Hint – use both residuations / and \ to show the two distributive laws.)

Define a function f: M $\rightarrow$ C-Idl(M) for which f(x) is the C-ideal generated by $\{x\}$. f is a monoid homomorphism, and if $U \dashv x$ is in C then $\bigvee \{f(u): u \in U\} \geq f(x)$; show also that f and C-Idl(M) are universal with respect to these properties for functions from M to quantales.

Use this result to show that quantales can be presented by generators and relations (as in Theorem 4.4.3).

Given a ring R, show how to construct its quantale of matrix ideals by a coverage on the monoid of square matrices under $\oplus$.

BIBLIOGRAPHY

S. ABRAMSKY

[87]   *Domain Theory and the Logic of Observable Properties*, PhD Thesis, Queen Mary
College, University of London, 1987.

[88]   "Domain theory in logical form", *Annals of Pure and Applied Logic*, 1990.

[90]   "A domain equation for bisimulation", *Information and Computation*, 1990.

[90']   "The lazy λ-calculus", in D. Turner (ed.) *Research Topics in Functional
Programming*, Addison-Wesley, 1990.

S. ABRAMSKY and S.J. VICKERS

[90]   *Quantales, Observational Logic and Process Semantics*, Report DOC 90/1,
Department of Computing, Imperial College, London, 1990.

H.P. BARENDREGT

[84]   *The Lambda Calculus: Its Syntax and Semantics* (revised edition), North-Holland,
Amsterdam, 1984.

G. BIRKHOFF

[67]   *Lattice Theory*, rev. ed., AMS Colloquium Publications vol. 25, Providence, 1967.

P.M. COHN

[71]   *Free Rings and their Relations*, London Mathematical Society Monographs 2,
Academic Press, London, 1971.

J.H. CONWAY

[71]   *Regular Algebra and Finite Machines*, Chapman and Hall, London, 1971.

MICHAEL DUMMETT

[77]   *Elements of Intuitionism*, Oxford University Press, 1977.

MICHAEL P. FOURMAN and STEVEN VICKERS

[85]   "Theories as categories", pp. 434-448 in David Pitt, Samson Abramsky, Axel Poigné
and David Rydeheard (eds) *Category Theory and Computer Programming*, Lecture
Notes in Computer Science **240**, Springer-Verlag, Berlin, 1986.

MARTIN GARDNER
[63]   *More Mathematical Puzzles and Diversions*, Bell [in Great Britain] 1963.
[86]   *Knotted Doughnuts and Other Mathematical Entertainments*, Freeman, New York, 1986.

G. GIERZ, K.H. HOFMANN, K. KEIMEL, J.D. LAWSON, M. MISLOVE and
    D.S. SCOTT
[80]   *A Compendium of Continuous Lattices*, Springer-Verlag, Berlin, 1980.

J.-Y. GIRARD
[87]   "Linear logic", pp. 1-102 in *Theoretical Computer Science* **50**, 1987.
[89]   *Proofs and Types*, translated and with appendices by Yves Lafont and Paul Taylor, Cambridge Tracts in Theoretical Computer Science, Cambridge University Press, 1989.

R. GOLDBLATT
[79]   *Topoi – The Categorial Analysis of Logic*, Studies in Logic and the Foundations of Mathematics **98**, North Holland, Amsterdam, 1979.

MICHAEL J.C. GORDON
[79]   *The Denotational Description of Programming Languages*, Springer-Verlag, New York, 1979.

CARL GUNTER
[85]   *Profinite Solutions for Recursive Domain Equations*, Technical Report CMU-CS-85-107, Carnegie-Mellon University, 1985.
[87]   "Universal profinite domains", pp. 1-30 in *Information and Computation* **72**(1), 1987.

PAUL R. HALMOS
[60]   *Naive Set Theory*, van Nostrand Reinhold, New York, 1960.

J. ROGER HINDLEY and JONATHAN P. SELDIN
[86]   *Introduction to Combinators and λ-Calculus*, London Mathematical Society Student Texts **1**, Cambridge University Press, Cambridge, 1986.

C.A.R. HOARE and HE JIFENG
[87]   "The weakest prespecification", pp. 127-132 in *Information Processing Letters* **24**, 1987.

M. HOCHSTER
[69]   "Prime ideal structure in commutative rings", pp. 43-60 in *Transactions of the American Mathematical Society* **142**, 1969.

KARL H. HOFMANN and JIMMIE D. LAWSON
[82]   "On the order theoretical foundation of a theory of quasicompactly generated spaces without separation axiom", pp. 143-160 in R.-E. Hoffmann (ed.) *Continuous Lattices and Related Topics*, Mathematik-Arbeitspapiere **27**, University of Bremen.

KARL H. HOFMANN and MICHAEL W. MISLOVE

[81]   "Local compactness and continuous lattices", pp. 209-248 in B. Banaschewski and
       R.-E. Hoffmann (eds) *Continuous Lattices: Proceedings, Bremen 1979*, Lecture Notes in
       Mathematics **871**, Springer-Verlag, Berlin, 1981.

H. HUWIG and AXEL POIGNÉ

[87]   *A note on inconsistencies caused by fixpoints in a cartesian closed category*,
       Forschungsbericht Nr. 216 des Fachbereichs Informatik der Universität Dortmund,
       1986; to appear in Theoretical Computer Science.

J.M.E. HYLAND

[81]   "Function spaces in the category of locales", pp. 264-281 in *Continuous Lattices*,
       Lecture Notes in Mathematics **871**, Springer-Verlag, Berlin, 1981.

P.T. JOHNSTONE

[81]   "Scott is not always sober", pp. 282-3 in B. Banaschewski and R.-E. Hoffmann (eds)
       Continuous Lattices: Procedings, Bremen 1979, Lecture Notes in Mathematics **871**,
       Springer-Verlag, Berlin, 1981.
[82]   *Stone Spaces*, Cambridge University Press, Cambridge, 1982.
[82'] "The Vietoris monad on the category of locales", pp. 162-179 in R.-E. Hoffmann
       (ed.) *Continuous Lattices and Related Topics*, Mathematik-Arbeitspapiere **27**,
       University of Bremen.

CLIFF B. JONES

[80]   *Software Development: a Rigorous Approach*, Prentice-Hall, 1980.

ANDRÉ JOYAL and MYLES TIERNEY

[84]   *An Extension of the Galois Theory of Grothendieck*, Memoirs of the American
       Mathematical Society **309**, 1984.

J.L. KELLEY

[55]   *General Topology*, Van Nostrand, Princeton, 1955; reprinted Graduate Texts in
       Mathematics **27**, Springer-Verlag, 1975.

JOACHIM LAMBEK

[58]   "The mathematics of sentence structure", pp. 154-170 in *American Mathematical
       Monthly* **65**(3), 1958.

SAUNDERS MACLANE

[71]   *Categories for the Working Mathematician*, Graduate Texts in Mathematics **5**,
       Springer-Verlag, 1971.

E.G. MANES

[76]   *Algebraic Theories*, Graduate Texts in Mathematics **26**, Springer-Verlag, 1976.

ERNEST G. MANES and MICHAEL A. ARBIB

[86]   *Algebraic Approaches to Program Semantics*, Springer-Verlag, New York, 1986.

C.J. MULVEY
[86]   "&", pp. 99-104 in *Supplemento ai Rendiconti del Circolo Matematico di Palermo*,
        Serie II no. 12,1986.

SUSAN B. NIEFIELD and KIMMO I. ROSENTHAL
[88]   "Constructing locales from quantales", pp 215-234 in *Mathematical Proceedings of
        the Cambridge Philosophical Society* **104** (1988).

C-H. L. ONG
[88]   *The Lazy λ-Calculus: An Investigation into the Foundations of Functional
        Programming*, PhD Thesis, Imperial College, University of London, 1988.

DAVID PITT, SAMSON ABRAMSKY, AXEL POIGNÉ and DAVID RYDEHEARD
[85]   (eds) *Category Theory and Computer Programming*, Lecture Notes in Computer
        Science **240**, Springer-Verlag, Berlin, 1986.

GORDON PLOTKIN
[76]   "A powerdomain construction", pp. 452-488 in *SIAM Journal on Computing* 5,1976.
[81]   *Post-Graduate Lecture Notes in Advanced Domain Theory* (incorporating the "Pisa
        Notes"), Dept of Computing Science, University of Edinburgh, 1981.

K.R. POPPER
[63]   *Conjectures and Refutations*, Routledge and Kegan Paul, London, 1963.

HELENA RASIOWA and ROMAN SIKORSKI
[63]   *The Mathematics of Metamathematics*, Panstwowe Wydawnictwo Naukowe, Warsaw,
        1963.

E. ROBINSON
[86]   *Power-domains, Modalities, and the Vietoris Monad*, Cambridge University
        Computer Laboratory Technical Report **98**, 1986.
[87]   "Logical aspects of denotational semantics", pp. 238-253 in D.H.Pitt, A.Poigné and
        D.E.Rydeheard (eds) *Category theory and Computer Science*, Lecture Notes in
        Computer Science **283**, Springer-Verlag, Berlin, 1987.

KIMMO I. ROSENTHAL
[90]   *Quantales and their Applications*, Research Notes in Mathematics, Pitman, London,
        1990.

D.S. SCOTT
[70]   "Outline of a mathematical theory of computation", pp. 169-176 in *Proceedings of the
        Fourth Annual Princeton Conference on Information Sciences and Systems*, Princeton
        University, 1970; and *Technical Monograph PRG-2*, Programming Research Group,
        University of Oxford, 1970.
[71]   "Continuous lattices", pp. 97-136 in *Toposes, algebraic geometry and logic*, F.W.
        Lawvere (ed.), Lecture Notes in Mathematics **274**,Springer-Verlag, Berlin, 1972; and
        Technical Monograph PRG-7, Programming Research Group, University of Oxford,
        1971.

[72] "Lattice theory, datatypes and semantics", pp. 64-106 in R. Rustin (ed.) *NYU Symposium on Formal Semantics*, Prentice-Hall, New York, 1972.

D.S. SCOTT and C. STRACHEY

[71] "Toward a mathematical semantics for computer languages", pp. 19-46 in J. Fox (ed.) *Proceedings of the Symposium on Computers and Automata,* Polytechnic Institute of Brooklyn Press, New York, 1971; and *Technical Monograph PRG-6*, Programming Research Group, University of Oxford, 1971.

M. SMYTH

[78] "Power domains", in JCSS **16**, 1978.

[83] "Powerdomains and predicate transformers: a topological view", pp. 662-675 in J.Diaz (ed.) *Automata, Languages and Programming*, Lecture Notes in Computer Science **154**, Springer-Verlag, Berlin, 1983.

[83'] "The largest cartesian closed category of domains", pp. 109-119 in *Theoretical Computer Science* **27** (1983), North Holland.

[87] "Quasi uniformities: reconciling domains with metric spaces", pp.236-253 in M.Main et al. (eds.) *Mathematical Foundations of Programming Language Semantics,* Lecture Notes in Computer Science **298**, Springer-Verlag, Berlin, 1988.

M.B. SMYTH and G.D. PLOTKIN

[82] "The category-theoretic solution of recursive domain equations", pp 761-783 in *SIAM Journal of Computing* **11**, 1982.

JOSEPH E. STOY

[77] *Denotational semantics: the Scott-Strachey approach to programming language theory*, MIT Press, Cambridge, Massachusetts, 1977.

PAUL TAYLOR

[86] *Recursive Domains, Indexed Category Theory and Polymorphism*, PhD Dissertation, University of Cambridge, 1986.

STEVEN VICKERS

[87] "An algorithmic approach to the p-adic integers", pp. 599-615 in M.Main, A.Melton, M.Mislove and D.Schmidt (eds.) *Mathematical Foundations of Programming Language Semantics,* Lecture Notes in Computer Science **298**, Springer-Verlag, Berlin, 1988.

[88] "A fixpoint construction of the p-adic domain", pp. 270-289 in D.H.Pitt, A.Poigné and D.E.Rydeheard (eds.) *Category theory and Computer Science,* Lecture Notes in Computer Science **283**, Springer-Verlag, Berlin, 1987.

G. WINSKEL

[83] "A note on powerdomains and modality", pp. 505-514 in M. Karpinski (ed.) *Foundations of Computation Theory*, Lecture Notes in Computer Science **158**, Springer-Verlag, Berlin, 1983.

INDEX

Printed in the United States
By Bookmasters